CHANGING PERCEPTIONS

Writings on Gender and Development

Edited by
Tina Wallace with Candida March

OXFAM

A catalogue record for this book is available from
the British Library

ISBN 085598 136 9
ISBN 085598 137 7 pbk

Published by Oxfam, 274 Banbury Road, Oxford OX2 7DZ
Designed by Jeffrey Meaton   OX 673 JM 91
Printed by Oxfam Print Unit
Typeset in 9.5pt Palatino

CONTENTS

DEDICATION

JOAN WRIGHT

For weeks after the death of Joan Wright on 13 October 1990, in a car accident in Namibia, messages of tribute, sorrow and great affection poured in to Oxfam from all over the world. Hundreds came from friends and development partners in South Africa alone, the focus of Joan's work since 1986. To many of us, friends of Joan for many years, the extraordinarily widespread response to her death had the quality of revelation — it was a window into the extent to which she had shared her exceptional qualities of integrity, compassion, humility and commitment to social justice with so many people. And she shared laughter too — Joan was a woman who enjoyed life to the full, with the same energy and great sense of humour which she applied to her work.

Joan joined Oxfam in 1974, and when the Gender and Development Unit (GADU) was founded in 1984 she was working in Oxfam's Education Department. Her concern with race and gender led her into active involvement in the development of equal opportunities policies and practices within Oxfam — working on early proposals for a workplace nursery and for improving maternity leave provisions.

Joan was involved in GADU from the beginning. The Unit began its life as a steering group with representatives from a wide range of Oxfam departments. Joan worked closely with me to get GADU off the ground. We were all full-time workers, and stole time when we could to meet and exchange ideas and discuss plans to make gender awareness central to Oxfam's work. For the first year, we had no budget and no office. We squatted in temporarily vacated offices, to be evicted when the residents returned. Joan's bubbly sense of humour — and strong arms! — were invaluable in those days, as together we humped boxes of books and papers and a discarded old typewriter around the building looking for a home.

Joan continued to support GADU once it was established. When she began work in South Africa, it was with a firm commitment to support work with women and women's organisations. In her trip to South Africa in the summer of 1990, Joan brought together members of several women's groups in a meeting to share information and experiences and help Oxfam place greater emphasis on gender in its development programme. She was excited and enthusiastic about the possibilities opening up in South Africa for women — an excitement shared by GADU — and looking forward to taking up the issues again when she returned in September 1990, to making new contacts and encouraging the networking and coordination she herself was so good at.

Now, she will never return to continue that work and share in its progress. But — as so many of her friends and colleagues have said — the work will carry on, encouraged and inspired by her warmth and dedication. And Joan will always be remembered with special affection in GADU, as one of its greatest supporters. This book is dedicated to Joan for her special contributions to the cause of women in Oxfam and its work.

Suzanne Williams

PREFACE

Tina Wallace

Oxfam's Gender and Development Unit (GADU) was started in 1985 as a result of lobbying from a number of women employed both in the field and in Oxford. They were concerned about the way that women had been left out of, or actually disadvantaged by, the aid and development process. They stressed the need to focus on the roles of both men and women in society in order to understand women's subordinate positions; and to understand that any changes to improve the lives of women would have to involve changes to the whole society. So the focus of the Unit was gender rather than only women's issues, though much of the work is concerned with redressing the balance for women in development.

GADU has a very wide remit within the Overseas Division of Oxfam, but the primary purpose is 'to promote the integration of a gender perspective into all areas of Oxfam's work and to ensure that women as well as men benefit from Oxfam's programmes'. This involves GADU in working to support Oxfam staff as they seek out and listen to women to find new ways of working with women and men, and in developing new tools and concepts for understanding and improving the gender relations and the situation of women in diverse cultural settings. GADU is involved in project advice, staff training, the development of research and evaluation, sharing information through seminars and a Newspack, and developing written and audio-visual resources for use by staff and project partners.

The purpose of the Newspacks is to share material written by academics for field staff on gender issues; to share the experience of staff in the field; and to learn from the ideas of project partners. Over a four year period the packs have developed into a forum where both theoretical and practical ideas are shared across a wide range of countries, staff and interested academics. The range of writers and material covered is of interest to a wider audience than the packs can reach, so the decision was made to select a number of key articles and publish them in this book.

The book covers a wide spectrum of issues all relating to gender as a development issue. It is divided into sections for easy use. The first section explores how some of the global issues of the 1980s and early '90s such as debt, structural adjustment, war and environmental degradation directly affect women and the relations between women and men. Many of the articles in this section have been written by academics in a way that is accessible to a wide range of people. Section Two looks at the specifics of women's experiences in different cultures, and how their subordination directly affects their day to day lives. The focus is especially on women's health and the range of factors that limit women's access to health care, and to all other critical resources, in the society. This section has largely drawn on the work of Oxfam staff or project partners.

The third section again primarily uses the work of academics to explore different ways of working with women. What tools and methods can be used to increase understanding of women's needs, responsibilities and rights, and to understand how existing gender relations affect these? Section Four is essentially a practical section, presenting a wide range of case studies which explore different ways of working with women — either in separate groups or in the wider community — to improve their lives. The range of direct experience is exciting and stimulating, and comes from staff and project partners.

The fifth section provides an opportunity for Oxfam staff to express their responses and views on the whole issue of working with women, and looking at gender relations. Gender is an intensely complex area of work which people have conflicting views on and feel very strongly about, and some of the reasons for this are explored here.

The book closes with a call for a wider and more radical vision of the future, where women are enabled to play their proper part. This call comes out of a Third World women's networking group called DAWN, an organisation growing in power and importance.

This is a book which is of interest to a wide range of readers: academics (who rarely have the chance to hear the views and experiences of practitioners); students of development, and development workers. It is a rare attempt to combine theory and practice in a way which illuminates the complexity and diversity of issues involved in working with gender in development.

I would like to thank all those who made this book possible, especially those who found it so difficult to write, and to those who had the vision to lobby for the Unit in the beginning. This book is dedicated to one of these women, Joan Wright, who was killed so tragically in a car accident in Namibia in October 1990.

I would like to thank those who gave their support to this book especially Candy March, who worked on this project with me for several months, Helen O'Connell, Anne Penny and other colleagues past and present.

In closing it is important to stress that the views presented here are those of the authors, and not necessarily of GADU or Oxfam. This book is intended to provide a forum for open debate, and for exploring a wide range of complex issues.

INTRODUCTION

WHY GENDER IS A DEVELOPMENT ISSUE

APRIL BRETT

The issues concerning women and their part (or not) in the development process have been increasingly examined over the years. However, the ways of addressing these issues have varied as understanding of women's position in development, and of gender roles themselves, has grown. Although the principle of equality of men and women was recognised in both the UN Charter in 1945 and the UN Declaration of Human Rights in 1948, the majority of development planners and workers did not fully address women's position in the development process. Several researchers have shown that development planners worked on the assumption that what would benefit one section of society (men) would trickle down to the other (women) (Boserup 1970, Rogers 1980, Mazza 1987).

The ways of defining women's position in development has changed through the years:

In the **1950s** and **1960s**, women's issues in development were subsumed under the question of human rights, and women were viewed as objects to protect or make recommendations for but not necessarily to consult. UN Conventions of particular concern to women included:

1949 Convention for the Suppression of Traffic in Persons and the Exploitation of the Prostitution of Others

1951 Equal Remuneration for Men and Women Workers for Work of Equal Value

1952 Convention on the Political Rights of Women

In the **1970s**, although women were still not necessarily consulted, their key position in the development process became more widely recognised. This was especially so in connection with population and food issues. Women were viewed as useful resources to be integrated into the development process, thus rendering the particular projects more efficient and more successful:

> 'These are the women (the more than 500 million women illiterates) upon whom the success of our population policies, our food programmes and our total development efforts ultimately rely. The success of these policies depends, in other words, on those who are least equipped to carry them out.' (Helvi Sipila, *The Times*, 23.4.75)

In 1972 it was decided to declare 1975 'International Women's Year', which led into the UN Decade for Women.

In the **1980s** there has been a growing trend towards seeing women as agents and beneficiaries in all sectors and at all levels of the development process. It is partly through an understanding of gender roles that this trend has emerged (Pietla, 1985).

In 1985 the UN decade culminated in a conference in Nairobi which, after a period of intensive discussions involving women from all over the world, resulted in the adoption of the 'Forward-Looking Strategies' (*Forward-Looking Strategies*, 1985).

The Forward-Looking Strategies took the main themes of the Decade for Women (equality, development and peace, with the sub-themes health, education and employment), and set out the obstacles facing women in each of these areas; proposed general strategies for overcoming them, and made recommendations to governments and other bodies for creating greater opportunities for equality for women at all levels.

What is gender?

The conceptual distinction between sex and gender developed by Anne Oakley (Oakley 1972) is a useful analytical tool to clarify ideas and has now been almost universally taken up. According to this distinction sex is connected with biology, whereas the gender identity of men and women in any given society is socially and psychologically (and that means also historically and culturally) determined.

Biological, and certain physical conditions (chromosomes, external and internal genitalia, hormonal states and secondary sex characteristics), lead to the determination of male or female sex. To determine gender, however, social and cultural perceptions of masculine and feminine traits and roles must be taken into account. There is considerable, but not total, correlation between female sex and feminine gender, and male sex and masculine gender.

Gender is learnt through a process of socialisation and through the culture of the particular society concerned. In many cultures boys are encouraged in the acts considered to display male traits (and girls vice versa) through the toys given to children (guns for boys, dolls for girls), the kind of discipline meted out, the jobs or careers to which they might aspire and the portrayal of men and women in the media. Children learn their gender from birth. They learn how they should behave in order to be perceived by others, and themselves, as either masculine or feminine. Throughout their life this is reinforced by parents, teachers, peers, their culture and society.

Every society uses biological sex as one criterion for describing gender but, beyond that simple starting point, no two cultures would completely agree on what distinguishes one gender from another. Therefore there is considerable variation in gender roles between cultures.

Division of labour in society

The division of labour between the sexes is best explained by gender but because reproduction is based on a universal biological difference between the male and female sex, societies use this as a basis for allotting other tasks. These tasks are allotted according to convenience and precedents in the particular culture, and determine masculine and feminine roles:

'Professor George Murdock has surveyed the data for 224 societies (mostly preliterate) and shows that the tendency to segregate economic activities in one way or another according to sex is strong. Taking a list of 46 different activities, he suggests that some are more often masculine than feminine, and vice versa. For example, lumbering is an exclusively masculine activity in 104 of his societies and exclusively feminine in 6: cooking is exclusively feminine in 158 and exclusively masculine in 5. Hunting, fishing, weapon making, boat building and mining tend to be masculine, while grinding grain and carrying water tend to be feminine. Activities that are less consistently allotted to one sex include preparing the soil, planting, tending and harvesting the crops, 'burden bearing' and body mutilation.' (Oakley 1972, p.128.)

Even in child-rearing men play a substantial role in some societies:

'The Arapesh, for example, consider that the business of bearing and rearing a child belongs to father and mother equally, and equally disqualifies them for other roles. Men as well as women 'make' and 'have' babies, and the verb 'to bear a child' is used indiscriminately of either a man or a woman. Child-bearing is believed to be as debilitating for the man as it is for the woman. The father goes to bed and is described as 'having a baby' when the child is born.... The Trobriand Islanders are renowned for their ignorance of the father's biological role in reproduction, but they stress the need for the father to share with the mother all tasks involved in bringing up children.' (Oakley 1972, p.134-135.)

We see, then, that tasks and the division of labour do not relate to the sex of the individuals concerned, and so are not common to one sex from one culture to another, but are culture specific. Thus gender is culture specific.

Gender not only varies from one culture to another but it also varies within cultures over time; culture is not static but evolves. As societies become more complex, the roles played by men and women are not only determined by culture but by socio-political and economic factors.

Why is gender a development issue?

The roles that women play are different in any given society, and their situation is determined by the legislation, religious norms, economic status or class, cultural values, ethnicity and types of productive activity of their country, community and household. Women are usually responsible for domestic work; the care of children, family health, cooking and providing food and other household services. In most societies they also play a major role in the productive activities of the family; in farming, paid domestic labour, services, industries and income-generating activities. In some societies they also have clear community roles.

In each of these areas — reproduction, production and the community — women have often been adversely affected by the development process. There is a wide gap between women's high, yet unrecognised, economic participation and their low political and social power, and development strategies have usually taken the needs of the most vocal and politically active as their starting point. To understand gender the activities of men and women need to be addressed separately. The reproductive, productive and social or community roles women are playing must be looked at as well as the roles played economically and socially by men. By examining men's and women's roles a greater understanding of their needs and involvement in power and decision-making around specific tasks and issues will be reached.

Historically, development workers have used notions of gender imported from the North. The majority of projects were — and still are — based on the false assumption that the nuclear household supported by a non-productive wife dependent upon a male head, is universal. This is not the pattern for many cultures. In *The Family Among the Australian Aborigines*, Malinowski wrote:

'A very important point is that the woman's share in labour was of much more vital importance to the maintenance of the house-hold than the man's work ... even the food supply contributed by the women was far more important than the man's share ... food collected by women was the staple food of the natives ... eco-nomically [the family] is entirely dependent upon women's work.' (Malinowski 1963 as cited in Oakley 1972, p 139.)

Studies of women's roles in agriculture from a sample of African peoples living in Senegal, Gambia, Uganda and Kenya show that women contribute between 60 per cent and 80 per cent of the total agricultural work done.

How to approach gender in development

It is of vital importance in development work not to use imported notions of gender, nor regard 'the community' and 'the household' as the basic units. One must go beyond the household and break it down into its component parts. By assessing and understanding the gender roles in a given society the specific needs of women (and men) can be ascertained and addressed within projects (Moser and Levy 1986).

The primary practical requirement for incorporating a gender analysis into development is to consult with and listen to women so that their roles and resulting needs are better understood. How the issues of gender are actually addressed depends upon the policy direction envisaged. (This is discussed more fully in Caroline Moser's and Sarah Longwe's articles later in this book.) One approach is to design projects and programmes to make life 'easier' for women and help them in their given gender tasks. For example, an agricultural project could include provision of support for female agricultural tasks, as well as those carried out by men. Women's needs for better equipment, improved seeds, and advice would be taken into consideration. In health projects the particular concerns of the women would be elicited from them and their priorities addressed in the project. On the domestic front, projects could aim to alleviate the drudgery and heavy physical demands of women's work by providing more efficient grinders or stoves, or improving women's access to water. Whether working with women alone or within the community as a whole the primary objective would be to enable women to perform their existing roles better.

An alternative but complementary approach is to challenge the status quo or address the perceived inequalities between men and women. This could involve, for example, working for change in laws that discriminated against women; increasing women's access to land; giving women decision-making power within projects, etc. The aim is social change and the empowerment of women. For agencies such as Oxfam, which espouse social change, justice and empowerment in their rhetoric, meeting women's needs for more radical change should be within the adopted policy approach to gender.

Why is it that addressing gender inequalities is taboo and yet tackling inequalities in terms of wealth and class is not? It is often argued that by addressing gender the traditions or culture of a society are being tampered with. This is not necessarily the case and the attitudes to gender may be no more 'traditional' than attitudes to class or power. When the traditions and cultural attitudes to gender are clarified, then the actual gender relations can be assessed and addressed within a programme or project. Development is a process that should involve all members of a society to the same extent, according to their individual needs.

References

Boserup, E. (1970) *Women's Role in Economic Development*, London: George Allen and Unwin; new edition (1989), London: Earthscan Publications..

Malinowski, B. (1963), *The Family Among the Australian Aborigines*, Schocken Books.

Mazza, J. (1987), *The British Aid Programme and Development for Women*, London: War on Want.

Mies, M. (1986), *Patriarchy and Accumulation on a World Scale: Women in the International Division of Labour*, London: Zed Books.

Moser, C. and Levy, C. (1986), *A Theory and Methodology of Gender Planning: Meeting women' practical and strategic needs*, Development Policy Unit Gender and Planning Working Paper 11.

The Nairobi Forward-Looking Strategies for the Advancement of Women, Nairobi 1985.

Oakley, A.(1987),*Sex, Gender and Society*, Aldershot, UK: Gower Publishing Company.

Pietla, H.(1985),*What does the United Nations mean to women? An NGO view.*

Rogers, B.(1980),*The Domestication of Women: Discrimination in Developing Societies*, London: Kogan Page.

April Brett has worked in nutrition and health care development in Papua New Guinea and Ethiopia. In 1987 she joined the Gender and Development Unit in Oxfam. She is now working in health promotion and education in the UK.

THE FORWARD-LOOKING STRATEGIES

ANNE PENNY

Did you know that all member governments of the UN have agreed to the forward-looking strategies passed in Nairobi 1985?

The World Conference on the Advancement of Women was held by the UN in 1985 to review the achievements of the UN Decade for Women (1975-85) and to put forward proposals for the future. These proposals are detailed in *'The Nairobi Forward-Looking Strategies for the Advancement of Women'* (FLS, 1985). FLS is a critical document since, for the first time, all the member states of the UN have approved strategies to improve the lot of women everywhere. For the first time, women's groups will be able to put pressure on their governments to implement the policies agreed.

FLS was published with a great deal of hope, but few women believe that governments will instrument changes which are often detrimental to them, without pressure. Such far-reaching and radical strategies as those outlined in FLS will only be implemented if non-governmental organisations (NGOs), women's groups and individual women work to keep governments true to their word. To do this, we must all be aware of the principles agreed to by governments.

FLS includes sections on each of the major objectives of the Decade for Women: equality, development and peace. It also stresses the inter-relationship of these objectives with employment, health and education. The latter is seen as being especially important for the achievement of the Decade's aims. We will look, in this summary, at what FLS says about development. It should be remembered, however, that this is only one part of the extensive set of recommendations.

Obstacles to development

The FLS identifies many reasons for the lack of development (it is interesting to note that the USA did not agree with the consensus over several of these points). Briefly, we can see that most Third World nations are forced into dependence on 'developed' nations through terms of trade, high interest rates, embargoes and the export of inflation; these all cause inequalities. Development has also been hindered by the channelling of funds into the purchase of arms, and by racial and inter-tribal discrimination. The world recession — as with all phases of economic stringency — hits the poorest and the weakest, both in terms of nations and of individuals. Thus unemployment affects women more than men. The high level of indebtedness experienced by Third World countries has further retarded the process of integrating women in development. It is indisputable that the issue of women in development has received a low priority. What, then, is to be done?

Basic strategies

Everyone should participate in formulating development policy. Generally, women are excluded from this process, in part because their status and earning power is low. FLS stresses again and again that women must be included in decision making at every level. This means that special measures must be taken on behalf of women. Initial emphasis should be placed on employment, health and education and this should be done at a grassroots level.

Employment

In the field of employment, governments are encouraged to legislate to improve women's opportunities. Laws should be passed to enforce women's right to paid employment and economic independence; to enable women to choose their work, providing training where necessary; to protect part-time workers; to encourage flexitime; to change tax laws so that married women are not discouraged from working and to enforce equal pay and conditions for equal work.

In addition, facilities at work should be provided to encourage women workers, as should proper occupational health care, and parental leave and supplementary services for women with children. FLS stresses that equal employment opportunities should lead to women attaining economic self-reliance. Supporting this aim, there should be structures giving women access to land, capital and credit.

Attention is drawn to the major roles of women in the informal employment sector and in rural development. Governments are urged, therefore, to give support to women's organisations and, in particular, to women's co-operatives in these areas.

Health

Women are vital providers of health care, free of charge to society and often at the expense of their own health. This should be taken into account by governments, who should promote primary health care for women. Women need better ante- and post-natal care in pregnancy. They also need to be able to control their own fertility. Women should be given a key role in the planning of sanitation and water projects.

Furthermore, health education should be designed to change attitudes towards women and women's health. Through such education and training more women should be involved in the health professions.

Education

Education has a dual role for women. In the first place women need education themselves in order that they may have access to better jobs, particularly in the areas of science and technology; raised standards of women's education benefit the whole community. Therefore, women must have access to education and training at all levels, and this education must be practical and well adapted to women's needs. Particular importance should be given to education in the fields of health, nutrition and legal rights, while training should especially equip women in the field of science and technology.

The second function of education, which is mentioned in all areas discussed by FLS, is to eradicate the stereotyped views of women so prevalent in both developed and developing nations.

The above summarises only a fraction of the far-reaching recommendations contained in FLS. It is clear that such aims are only to be achieved by a major change in the status of women. It is high time for such a change and it is up to women everywhere to put pressure on their governments to fulfil the commitments made to FLS.

We should all keep in mind the spirit in which FLS was written, which is clearly demonstrated by the following excerpt:

'By the year 2000 illiteracy should have been eliminated, life expectancy for all women increased to at least 65 years of good quality life and opportunities for self-supporting employment made available. Above all, laws guaranteeing equality for women in all spheres of life must by then be fully and comprehensively implemented to ensure a truly equitable socio-economic framework within which real development can take place.' (FLS Para 35, 1985.)

References

The Nairobi Forward-Looking Strategies for the Advancement of Women, Nairobi 1985.

Anne Penny has been the Administration and Resources Officer for Oxfam's Gender and Development Unit since 1987 and is also a freelance writer.

1

THE IMPACT OF GLOBAL CRISES ON WOMEN

Introduction

Tina Wallace

There are many global issues that have an impact on Third World economies and deeply affect the quality of life for their populations. The impact of the growing debt crisis in many countries, of structural adjustment packages, of the declining terms of trade for Third World products, of national and international conflict and war have been devastating, especially for poor people. Their conditions have deteriorated in recent years. Declining standards of health care and education, growing hunger and even famine, and lack of employment opportunities are common experiences in many countries. Many find themselves trying to eke out a precarious living under severe economic conditions and where environmental degradation is widespread.

The readings in this section focus on some of these international issues and explore the ways in which they specifically affect women, and women's relationships with men. The primary reason for analysing the impact on women and on gender relations is to redress the balance: most data and theories about, for example, the impact of debt or famine, have focused on men, and ignored the changes imposed on women's lives and the ways in which relations between women and men are changing under these external pressures. This lack of understanding of the situation of women has led to inappropriate and even damaging development or aid programmes. The analyses and descriptions presented here focus predominantly on women living in poverty; in the classes that are most vulnerable to war, to cuts in social services, to falling commodity prices, or to exploitation as cheap labour within the international division of labour. How are these women adjusting to changing circumstances and how does this affect their relationships with the state, with the community and with men — both in and outside the household?

These macro-issues affect in a very real way the daily lives of men and women, in both rural and urban areas. For those who work at the grassroots it is important to understand the global pressures and constraints under which people live, and the analyses and descriptions presented here relate directly to the realities at the micro-level of the community, organisations, projects, and households. Peggy Antrobus, in the article which closes this book, states the importance of understanding these connections:

'The analysis should be one which attempts to relate experience at the micro-level of the sector, community, project, or household, to that of macro-economic analysis. A gender analysis of the structural adjustment policies (for example) illustrate the ways in which macro-economic policies affect women's experience at the level of the poorest household. Unless this experience is used to inform macro-economic policies and vice versa no meaningful change can be effected.'

The environment

There is a growing awareness now of some of the appalling ecological consequences of both production and development policies that have been pursued in many parts of the Third World. These issues — like all the other topics discussed in this section — deserve a book to themselves, and indeed Joan Davidson and Irene Dankelman have written a very useful book covering many environmental issues affecting women in the Third World. However, even though the subject can only be touched on briefly here, it is essential to put it firmly on the agenda. The article we have chosen comes from an International Environment meeting for women, organised by the Women's Environmental Network and War on Want, attended by NGO's, activists and academics from all over the world. Chee Yoke Ling highlights the damage caused to the environment by the activities of transnational companies through deforestation, plantations, and the dumping of waste. She describes how women in particular are affected by these factors. Pollution can cause infertility or birth deformities; women as producers are exploited as cheap labour; and women as community managers have to carry on campaigns to oppose the mistreatment of their environment when the men are away or have been arrested.

However many of the micro-issues relating to the environment are not covered in this article. Women, because of their responsibilities to provide food, to gather fuel and water, and to care for the sick and elderly, often do have valuable knowledge and experience about their environments. This knowledge is often overlooked or ignored by development agencies as well as governments and international agencies because women are so rarely consulted about any of their expertise. These aspects of women's potentially key role in ecological management and conservation are touched on elsewhere in the book — in this section in Ann Whitehead's article where she describes women's crucial role in small-holding agriculture. In Brian Mathew's article on water in Section Four he clearly shows the critical role women have to play in managing and maintaining essential water resources. Other articles in Section Four describe women's role as harvesters of wild crops (Pugansoa), and as herders and waterers of small livestock in arid lands (Watson).

Of course populations under pressure are also users and abusers of the environment, and as people are pushed onto more marginal land, or herded into refugee camps, or forced to farm deteriorating soils they may increasingly use up precious scarce and often non-renewable resources. This aspect of women's potentially negative relationship to the environment has not been covered in this book, but this does not detract from its critical importance and the need to explore this area further.

Transnational Corporations

The increasingly global patterns of production, particularly in the fields of, for example, agribusiness, textiles, electronics, and information technology, have created within these industries an international division of labour. The high-technology, capital intensive work tends to be done in the North, with the low technology, labour intensive work carried out in the South. This work can be moved quickly from one country to another to maximise profits and critically depends on the use of cheap labour. Many countries in the South 'woo' Transnational Companies to come to their country with offers of tax benefits and other incentives partly because of their urgent needs to produce for export and to provide local employment.

The development, design, engineering and testing is usually done in Europe or USA while the assembly, labouring jobs and clerical work are done in the South: these relationships are especially seen in the Free Trade Zones (FTZs) and plantations of Asia, South East Asia and the Caribbean, although they are also found in Africa and the Middle East. Within these FTZ's and plantations women are usually the target for the cheap labour. Social and cultural stereotypes, traditions and expectations about the role and status of women are used to justify employing young women on low wages, refusing them access to Unions and denying them security of employment. Health and safety standards are minimal or almost non-existent, and way below those demanded for workers in the North.

> 'Thus the payment of low wages to an off-shore assembly workforce and the employment of a low-wage female workforce in the [electronics] industry generally has been a major strategy that has enabled the industry to grow and profit at a phenomenal rate.' (Hancock p.136.)

This sexual division of labour is not only confined to women in the Third World; women in Europe and the US are also largely confined within the lowest paid and labour intensive sectors of these industries:

> 'Thus transnational production in the electronics industry has developed a global division of labour which is made up of a high-technology, predominantly male professional and technical workforce in the US, supported by a labour-intensive, semi-skilled, assembly production workforce almost completely comprised of women workers from the US and to a greater extent women workers from off-shore sites in South East Asia.' (Hancock p.135.)

Some of the issues surrounding the growing international and sexual division of labour, and the mobility of international capital and its implications for women in the South (in this case the Caribbean) are looked at in the article from the Dominican Republic.

Structural adjustment

Most Third World countries have experienced economic deterioration in the past decade. The causes are many and complex, including particularly the falling prices of primary products produced in the South and purchased by the Northern countries and the rising prices of essential imports; the growing interest that is demanded on the money so freely lent by International Banks during the 1970s; and the increasing expenditure on arms and defence in several countries. However, this book is not the place to explore these causes in any detail; some of the critical issues will be covered in a forthcoming Oxfam publication on trade by Belinda Coote. We focus here on the impact of IMF stabilisation packages and World Bank structural adjustment packages,imposed because of growing debts, on poor people, especially women.

It is now well recognised that these adjustment strategies weigh most heavily on the poor; Diane Elson in her article argues that it is particularly women who are adversely affected in low income households, as employees in the public sector, and as farmers. Women are affected both as producers and as reproducers; and as carers for the children, the sick and the elderly.

Adjustment packages, while opening up markets, often do not enable women to compete effectively, because no assistance is given to alleviate their domestic workloads. Indeed, cuts in public expenditure and welfare spending are often made in the expectation that women will increase their work as providers of health and social services. Thus the increased domestic work imposed by these cuts actually prevents women from taking advantage of any new economic opportunities.

Diane Elson emphasises the acute shortage of disaggregated data showing the differential impact adjustment has on men and women, although research is now under way which shows that different classes and economic groups are affected very differently. This lack of gender specific data is a major obstacle to understanding fully and in detail how women are affected by structural adjustment in different countries; this lack of statistical data on women also limits our knowledge of their situation in relation to many other areas such as agriculture, pastoralism, health needs, etc. Aggregated statistics are the common tools of economic analysis and effectively hide gender inequalities and differences, so Diane Elson (and many others in this book — Watson, Ara Khan, Wallace) argues strongly for new and gender sensitive ways of measuring women's involvement, and in this case measuring the impact of structural adjustment on women and men separately. The existing evidence suggests that within the most vulnerable groups it is women who are being the hardest hit, in terms of experiencing both greater poverty and increasingly heavy work loads.

Diane Elson discusses a number of critical issues in relation to women and structural adjustment, which are of relevance to those living and working in the countries most heavily affected by these measures. However, this is a vast area, and those interested in studying the issue in more detail can refer to the report from the Women's Alternative Economic Summit on Structural Adjustment held in 1990 (forthcoming); and a recent report from the Commonwealth Secretariat, 'Engendering Adjustment'.

Conflict and war

The lives of many people in many nations are torn apart by wars; people are killed, communities fragmented or destroyed, there is forced migration, and societies undergo temporary or even long-term changes. Women are affected in different ways from men, because of the different gender responsibilities they have. It is usually men who are the fighters and suffer disablement and death through combat, and the women stay behind to feed and maintain the family and community; although, in some liberation struggles, women have also joined the fight and taken on new, military roles during the conflict. In some cases war can open up new areas to women, where they are allowed to take over the work, responsibilities and in some cases the decision making of the absent men. However, while in some cases these changes are accepted and become integrated into the working of the society (as, for example, in the Eritrean and Tigrayan situations), it is more often the case that women's position in relation to men is maintained unchanged (see Marie-Aimée Hélie-Lucas on Algeria). Once the men return home, women have to struggle very hard to hold on to their new found skills, responsibilities and wider roles within the community. This is well described in the interview with Myrna Cunningham of Nicaragua. Men usually succeed in taking back social and economic control from the women.

There are other ways in which women are affected by war. When the men leave, it is the women who have to feed and care for the elderly and children, at a time when the disruption and lack of labour has probably seriously undermined their ability to produce food. Famines and violence often force women to flee their homes and many move to refugee camps. The majority of the world's ·refugees and displaced people are women and children, and the implications of this are explored in Tina Wallace's paper. In these situations, while women often have to act as household heads, they continue to be viewed by aid agencies as dependents and are not given the support and status they need to carry out all these new duties and responsibilities.

During emergencies, international agencies and governments are often so caught up in the complex and demanding logistics and politics of the immediate situation that they are insensitive to changing gender roles, and the newly emerging needs of women are neglected. While women may be recognised as the main beneficiaries of aid, their right to be involved in planning and decision making is not; with serious consequences for the treatment of refugees.

The refugee women described in Tina Wallace's article stress the ways in which women themselves work to overcome their disadvantage and their subordinate position. There is a vital need for information about what happens to women in war and as refugees — what are their survival strategies; how are their gender relations changed and how can any positive changes be retained; what are their needs in terms of health, nutrition, education, skills training, and employment; and what support do they require to meet those needs? Women are finding ways to articulate what is happening to them, and to link their experiences and demands to those of other women and disadvantaged groups in order to make their voice heard. In this they want support from the international agencies.

The decline in the productive base, growing hunger and impoverishment

Government and international development policies, the focus on cash crops to the detriment of food crops, and the rural-urban migration of labour are all contributory factors to the decline in food production in many parts of the world, especially sub-Saharan Africa. In her article, Ann Whitehead looks at the changing nature of agricultural production. Men and women have often played very separate roles in agricultural production and have been responsible for meeting different needs within the household. In the past, women and men in Africa, for example, have both farmed for subsistence, and for income, which is usually controlled by them separately. However, as the economic situation has deteriorated, with worsening terms of trade and increasing scarcity of land, new pressures have been placed on farming relations; and these have been exacerbated by aid and government policies. The emphasis on commercial agriculture has meant that women have found it increasingly difficult to secure access to the scarce resources of land, labour and agricultural inputs they need to maintain their role as independent farmers growing food crops. In addition, their labour has become very important for their husband's cash crop production. This labour is seldom rewarded and so women find they have less income. Ann Whitehead argues that this can and does lead to increasing conflict between men and women, and that development projects which assume that women's labour is freely available to men exacerbate this conflict and further erode women's control over key resources.

Women's growing loss of control over independent farming makes them particularly vulnerable in times of crisis, such as war or famine. Ann Whitehead argues that the number of female-headed households increases during times of stress such as food crisis or famine, and that when recovery comes, these women and children do not regain reasonable levels of income and welfare. Famines and food insecurity are contributing to the development of an extremely poor female stratum in Africa. What this article demonstrates is the need to understand women's roles and responsibilities in the production of food and income (see also the articles by Clare Oxby and Cathy Watson in Section Four); how these are changing with the transformation of rural economies; and how so many past and present policies actually make the situation worse for women.

Concluding comments

In this section, we bring together the work of academics, NGO staff and partners to focus attention on some of the different macro-economic, social and political factors that are affecting — and impoverishing — Third World countries. Many of these factors are inter-related, and have significant and distinct implications in each country for the lives of women, especially poor women. These complex factors need to be recognised, researched using methods which separate out women and men, and understood by those involved in development work, in whatever capacity.

> 'We must recognise the links not only between the fate of Third World women, and the politics pursued by the developed countries... there is after all a connection between poverty and injustice and debt, drugs, militarism, food insufficiency, population pressure, and environmental degradation.'
> (Antrobus, postcript to this book.)

References

Antrobus, P.(1990), *'Women in Development'*. Postscript to this book.

Commonwealth Secretariat (1989), *Engendering Adjustment for the 1990s*, London: HMSO.

Dankelman, I. and Davidson, J. (1988), *Women and environment in the Third World: alliance for the future*, London: Earthscan.

Hancock, M. (1983), 'Transnational production and women workers', in Phizacklea, A. (ed) *One way ticket: migration and female labour*, London:Routledge and Kegan Paul.

WOMEN, ENVIRONMENT AND DEVELOPMENT: THE MALAYSIAN EXPERIENCE

CHEE YOKE LING

As a country rich in natural resources with a population of 16.5 million people, Malaysia is often regarded as having an impressive record in terms of development. The country was drawn into the international market place when it was a British colony, producing the greatest quantity of natural rubber in the world.

Since independence in 1957 economic growth has intensified, leading to the exploitation of timber, petroleum and tin. Large tracts of forest have been cleared and much arable land turned to the mono-cultivation of palm oil and rubber. Industrialisation has been embarked on enthusiastically, geared towards the export market.

In the process, environmental protection and resource conservation have been largely made subservient to material growth. In the agricultural sector the introduction of high-yielding varieties of rice, oil palm and rubber has increased the use of chemical fertilisers, pesticides and herbicides. Land control and ownership has shifted from small farmers to large land holders, be they local individuals, corporations (local and foreign) or government agencies.

Cash crop production rapidly excluded women's usufructuary rights to cultivate and control land for food production. The cash economy and new technologies placed men at the centre, marginalising the role of women in the traditional rural economy, reducing women to a role of dependence.

Encouraged by government policies to provide cheap labour for factories, many women have drifted to the industrial sector. Most of them end up in low-paid jobs and are exposed to hazardous and stressful conditions, damaging to health.

In the cash crop sector, thousands of Indians were brought from India to work in British Malayan plantations at the turn of the century. They came from the lowest and most oppressed castes in the Indian society and the oppressive social and economic situation of women was carried over to the plantations, where it still persists.

The majority of the plantation workers exposed to hazardous conditions, particularly with respect to the use of toxic pesticides and herbicides, are women.

The following are three case studies showing the impact of economic growth on the environment and women.

Poisoning of women workers in the plantations

The agricultural sector is a major revenue earner in the Malaysian economy. Malaysia is presently a leading world exporter of palm oil and rubber. The implementation of large-scale cash crop plantation was started in British colonial days and extensively expanded in the past 25 years. This has resulted in the wide and rampant use of chemical pesticides and herbicides for weed control to increase yield, which has created an adverse impact on the environment and workers' safety. Up to 80 per cent of herbicide sprayers in the plantations are women. They have to spray paraquat, a highly toxic chemical which has been responsible for more poisonings than any other weed killer. Many of the cases result in death. Less than a teaspoonful of concentrated paraquat is likely to be lethal if swallowed.

Exposure to paraquat over a period of time can cause damage to the lungs, heart, kidneys, adrenal glands, central nervous system, liver, skeletal muscle and spleen. Paraquat can be absorbed by the skin in amounts leading to toxic effects. There is no known antidote to counter the poison once it enters the body.

Paraquat has been banned or heavily restricted in its use in many countries, but is still actively encouraged by the government in Malaysia. Almost all plantations use paraquat. Each day for eight hours women ranging from their teens to their fifties are exposed to this highly toxic chemical. The women are normally not provided with proper equipment to handle the chemical when they dilute it, nor are they provided with protective clothing.

Women who dilute the chemical are then required to shoulder it in containers strung on a pole to be distributed to the sprayers at different points on the plantation. Very often water from the streams and monsoon drains are used for dilution and the washing of containers, which has resulted in contamination of the streams.

The women themselves are often splashed with the paraquat solution as they carry the half-exposed containers to and fro about 20 times a day. The sprayers who receive the paraquat solution then pour it into pumps which weigh as much as 25kg each. They are seldom provided with protective clothing. Pregnant women are sometimes also required to carry a pump on their back to spray paraquat. Cases of miscarriage are therefore on the increase.

Female plantation workers are largely uninformed of the dangers inherent in the chemical which they use so regularly. They therefore do not understand the toxicity of paraquat. Even where warnings and instructions are printed on the label, these are inadequate or useless since most of the women are illiterate.

For these women their long and hazardous work as income earners is further burdened by household work and caring for the family. Since the plantation workers are one of the most exploited and neglected groups in the country, poverty and frustration have driven the male workers to alcoholism, wife and child battering. Thus the women suffer immense stress, hardships and rapidly deteriorating health.

The rapid expansion of the cash crop economy which is hailed as a 'development success story' has plunged thousands of women into a poisonous trap. The few who are aware and feel confident enough to protest by refusing to carry out such hazardous jobs are intimidated. In one case, a young woman who asserted her right not to be forced to perform a dangerous task (i.e.spray toxic paraquat) was transferred to an even more remote part of the plantation. For wages of less than £2 a day, the women sprayers in the plantation sector are exposed to poisoning and exploitation.

In 1985 the 'Campaign to Ban Paraquat' was launched by Sahabat Alam Malaysia (Friends of the Earth Malaysia). Hundreds of women demonstrated peacefully before the Deputy Minister of Health, but many thousands are still unaware of their rights. Education to build awareness and confidence is thus of primary importance. Workshops and discussions are being conducted all over the country and plantation owners, including transnational companies and government agencies, are being pressurised to meet the demands of the workers. Ongoing research on the impact of pesticides on water and soil is being carried out to strengthen the case for the phasing out of toxic chemicals, particularly paraquat.

Women against radioactivity

In 1982, in a little town called Bukit Merah, a Japanese-Malaysian joint venture, Asian Rare Earth (ARE) began its operations of processing monazite to produce yttrium, a rare earth used in the electronics industry. The process produces thorium hydroxide, a radioactive waste which can remain hazardous for ten billion years.

Thousands of tonnes of thorium were dumped in plastic bags and old drums in the open and in ponds which flowed into a river. Some were even used as fertiliser by people unaware of the danger. A court order was obtained in October 1985, stopping ARE from operating until adequate safety measures were taken to prevent radioactivity escaping from the factory. Unfortunately in 1987 the factory resumed its operations after obtaining a licence from the newly-established Atomic Energy Licensing Board.

Thousands of residents affected by the indiscriminate dumping of radioactive waste walked six miles every day to the Court when the hearing started in 1987. One of the women, a 70-year-old grandmother, said:

'I'm walking here twelve miles every day to and from the court to show how serious and concerned we are. It's my grand-children's lives I am fighting for.'

Although cancer is the worst risk, radiation can also damage the skin, cause rashes, and damage the bone marrow, while children can become mentally handicapped and deformed. The factory also emitted radon gas which can cause lung cancer.

Medical evidence that came to light during the first part of the court case revealed horrifying facts. Women under 30 years old and in good health in Bukit Merah were found to have suffered an abnormally high rate of miscarriages, neonatal and perinatal deaths between 1982 and 1986. The rate of problems associated with pregnancy and childbirth was 7.5 per cent in Bukit Merah compared to the national average of 1.8 per cent.

Blood tests were also carried out on children to identify the level of lead. The wastes produced by ARE comprised lead and radioactive thorium hydroxide in almost equal proportions. Since it was difficult and expensive to test for the presence of thorium hydroxide, the presence of lead was used as an indicator. Tests conducted by Dr Rosalie Bertell, a renowned scientist in the field of low-level radiation and public health, revealed that 100 per cent of the 60 children tested had higher than normal lead levels. A year later levels were still on the increase.

A general health survey of 260 children revealed that they were more affected by common ailments (running nose, cough, swelling in the neck region and rashes) than children on a less nutritious diet. Evidence was strong that the radiation was affecting the immune and reproductive systems in the affected population.

The women and men who stand vigil during each part of the court case (which is still unfinished) are strong in their struggle to close down the ARE factory. The women have taken a leadership role since late 1987 when some of the male leaders were arrested under the Internal Security Act, which permits detention without trial for an indefinite period. The violation of their bodies and their children's health in the name of development is unacceptable to these women.

Industrial projects which fail to take into account the impact on human health and the environment cannot be justified. Mitsubishi Corporation (the Japanese partner) were forced to close down a similar plant in Japan when they failed to comply with environmental standards in their own country. Yet they have no compunction in dumping such hazardous industries on developing countries in the pursuit of profit.

The setting up of hazardous industries in the midst of long-established low-income residential areas is common. The decisions to locate these operations do not involve public consultation. The environmental and health impact is grossly neglected.

Deforestation for timber wealth

In March 1987, thousands of indigenous people in Sarawak, Malaysia, formed human barricades across logging roads in the deep interior of the tropical rainforest. For more than 20 years, their forest has been ripped apart for logs which are predominantly exported to Japan. Soil erosion is widespread and farmlands being damaged, resulting in dwindling food resources; water supplies are becoming polluted and unfit for drinking, and diseases are on the increase. In a desperate attempt to stop the destruction of their ancestral lands and forests, after years of unsuccessful appeals and petitions to the government, the people of the area organised simultaneous blockades.

The Penan community are the worst affected because they are nomadic hunters and gatherers, and therefore rely solely on the forest. Their struggle is crucial because 2.8 million hectares had been logged between 1963 and 1985, and at the end of 1984 another 5.8 million hectares were licensed out for logging. Most of the timber license-holders are politicians, their friends and families.

For thousands of years the Penan have lived in harmony with their environment, harvesting and not destroying the forest which sustains their survival. This is a society where women and men participate equally in maintaining the communal life in the forest. They collect food, herbs and materials to make their shelters and baskets. The destruction of their forest to feed the greed of timber tycoons, businesses and consumers leaves them no choice but to physically stop the logging. According to one Penan woman: 'We'll stay here until they listen to us. We want them to leave our land. That forest is our source of survival. Without the forest we are all dead.'

Entire villages walked for days across the mountains to the logging roads which traverse their lands. While the men set up wooden fences and built rest shelters, the women wove leaves for roof thatch and organised food supplies. Breastfeeding mothers, old women, young children and men stood in vigil, stopping logging operations for almost seven months. The police and army forcibly dismantled the blockades and arrested some of the men. Blockades were set up again at the end of 1988, and in early January 1989, more than 100 Penan men were arrested under a newly-created offence designed to criminalise the Penans' battle for their legitimate land rights. The women take over the responsibilities of seeking food and water supplies. Many have to stand by helplessly while their children have less and less to eat and polluted water causes diseases to increase.

The profiteers are local timber tycoons and Japanese timber traders. The beneficiaries are urban consumers who utilise tropical hardwoods and paper products, often wastefully, with no thought that each paper bag or crate or piece of furniture which is used and thrown away is the product of a violation of both human rights and the environment. Official Japanese aid is given for the construction of access roads and bridges to facilitate logging in the interior areas.

The struggle of the Penan to maintain their culture and way of life is dismissed as 'primitive'. They are urged to join the mainstream and be 'developed'. But the reality is that no alternative is offered for the deprivation of their forest resources. Where resettlement has taken place in other native communities, the effects have been negative, leading to a breakdown in the community itself and a dependency on the cash economy.

Meanwhile arrests and intimidations continue but the Penan refuse to give up. Blockades are planned again for March/April 1989. As the forest dwindles, the Penan have to walk for days to seek food and clean water. The land is their life. 'If we don't do something now to protect the little that is left, there will be nothing for our children. Until we die we will block this road.'

Conclusion

Exploitation of natural resources for development has led to depletion and further environmental damage, as seen in the case of the Sarawak rainforest. This has led to human suffering and loss. The aid needed by communities such as the Penan is a restoration of their rights to the forest, the attainment of their right to be consulted in any plan which is supposed to benefit them, and the right to determine how their cultures and values should be maintained. The wealth of their knowledge on how to live in harmony with nature is a gift yet to be appreciated by modern society. The Penan have 'aid' for the rest of us.

For the women of Bukit Merah who, like many thousands of others, find their health and safety (and that of their families) jeopardised by industries beyond their control, the aid they need is the abolishing of double standards when hazardous industries and technologies are dumped on developing countries with (often) the collusion of local governments. The reorientation of development from pure economic growth to one of ecological advancement is urgently needed. Be it a grant, a loan or an investment, aid must pass the environmental and social audit too, and not merely the economic consideration.

Modern agriculture which is market and cash oriented has also become a lucrative profit source for pesticide and fertiliser industries. While agribusiness, plantation owners and the traders and manufacturers of final products record annual profits, thousands of women pay with their health and their very lives. The aid they want is assistance to create awareness and strengthen their power to resist and reject a working environment which slowly poisons them.

References

Hong, E. (1984), *Women, Consumers and Development*.

Sahabat Alam Malaysia (1989), *The Battle for Sarawak's Forests*.

Sahabat Alam Malaysia (1984), *Pesticide Dilemma in the Third World — a Case Study of Malaysia*.

Chee Yoke Ling is a lawyer by profession, and Honorary Secretary of Sahabat Alam Malaysia (SAM). She has been working full time on environmental and development issues since 1989, and volunteering for SAM since 1980. She is also active in the Asia-Pacific Peoples' Environmental Network.

FREE TRADE ZONES AND WOMEN WORKERS

MARIVI ARREGUI AND CLARA BAEZ

Free Trade Zones (FTZs) are, as their name suggests, opportunities for transnational companies to take advantage of a tax-free situation afforded by the host government, along with subsidised utilities. All international studies on FTZs report that most of the manual labour they use is carried out by women. This tendency is so strong that it is seen even in countries whose ideology is opposed to women working outside the home. The real motive for the predominance of women in these industries has nothing to do with the greater manual dexterity of women, supposed to make them more suitable for the clothing and electronic industries which predominate in FTZs. The great attraction of female labour is that, in all areas of the world and throughout history, it is usually cheaper than that of men.

The role of women in the clothing industry

The exploitation of women workers is not a contemporary phenomenon. Even in the first stages of the development of industrial capitalism, the accumulation of capital was made possible in part by the exploitation of the most vulnerable section of the workforce: women and children, who made up about 60 per cent of the total workforce at the time.

The history of the clothing industry in the United States falls into three phases. In the first phase, at the beginning of the nineteenth century, the textile industry of New England employed largely native labour; mostly young white women recruited in the country from rural families, who generally gave up work on marriage. Their working conditions were relatively good, so that their labour was expensive for the textile factory owners.

In the second phase, the local labour force was replaced by immigrants from Europe. Immigrant women arriving in the United States had great need of work and were prepared to accept poor working conditions. They did not object to working after marriage and were even willing to do piece-work at home for very low wages in order to combine paid work with their family responsibilities. As these women became americanised, and the reform movements of the early twentieth century attempted to improve working conditions for women, their labour became more expensive. However, further immigrants, this time from the Third World, provided the clothing industry with cheap labour. These women could not easily obtain other types of work because of language difficulties and poor education.

In the third phase, the clothing industry moved to the countries of the Third World, especially Asia and the Caribbean, where there is high unemployment and rapid population growth, and set up factories in the FTZs, producing for export. This third phase in the development of the industry has intensified the dependence of Third World countries on powerful capitalist countries such as the United States, because foreign companies, generally multinationals, control the markets.

The range of work in the clothing industry covers monotonous and repetitive tasks as well as work requiring great skill. The internationalisation of the production process has led to work which requires more skilled labour, such as the cutting of material (traditionally performed by men), being carried out exclusively in the United States, while less skilled work, such as sewing, has been transferred to the Third World. Now, low skilled tasks are performed by a new proletariat created by the new international division of labour: workers in the FTZs.

Sexual differentiation in the labour market

Studies of employment in the manufacturing industry show that sexual discrimination is the true cause of the lower rates of pay for women. A study on Brazilian business examines why one group of workers, who had been carefully selected and tried out in the job over several months, were paid less than others who had been unconditionally recruited, without having any qualifications or previous experience. The latter were men, the former were women. Another study shows how, in a large organisation, women all remained in jobs at a lower level than their qualifications and experience would merit. A third study, carried out in Taiwan, showed that being married had a positive effect on the salaries of men while it had a negative effect on those of women. The reason seemed to be that married women were expected to take more time off work after marriage but men were thought to be more likely to turn up regularly and be effective workers. However, the few studies there are comparing absenteeism among men and women show there is little difference, and often female absenteeism is lower.

The strategies used by employers to benefit from women's lower pay include the following:

whole aspects of production are confined to one sex or the other, with different salary levels, which are always lower in the areas where women are employed;

women and men work on the same aspect of production, but men always have jobs further up the hierarchy and so are paid more;

women and men perform the same tasks, but the women are paid less because their salary is considered as supplementary to that of a man, the latter being seen as the main family support.

Another aspect of sexual differentiation in the labour market reviewed by Joekes (1985) is that women tend to have a lower level of education than men. However, this position needs to be qualified, since the educational gulf between the sexes is diminishing and the educational advances won by women in the last three decades are considerable. It would be better to refer to an inadequate 'supply' of qualifications for women, generally limited to a sexually stereotyped range of subjects, which often puts them at a disadvantage in competing against men for jobs in industry. It is ultimately the gender of the worker which explains the differences in salary, which in turn determine the pattern of a segmented labour market, supported by the discriminatory gender relations of women in all social spheres (Beneria, 1985).

Involvement of women in Free Trade Zones in the Dominican Republic

In the Dominican Republic, women have been traditionally less involved in industrial work, which was largely carried out by men. Women's labour was concentrated in services, especially domestic labour. Those women who did obtain industrial work were employed mostly in food and clothing factories, where work was most poorly paid.

The creation and growth of the FTZs has seen a change take place, to the point where, currently, this sector has become the main employer of women's labour in the cities after domestic service (Duarte et al, 1989). According to a study carried out by Joekes in 1986, more than 70 per cent of the workforce employed in the FTZs are women. The percentage of women workers varies in different industries, with electronics the highest at 85 per cent, clothing and textiles 74 per cent, shoes 50 per cent and tobacco 30 per cent.

It is estimated that the number of men employed has increased recently (Aleman, 1989), possibly under pressure from growing male unemployment due to the decline of industries such as sugar refining. Even so, women remain in the majority.

Who are the women employed in the Dominican FTZs and what are their working conditions like? There is little up to date information to answer this question. The investigations which gathered primary data on these workers date from 1981, when the only FTZs existing in the Dominican Republic were at La Romana, San Pedro and Santiago. However, we will attempt to present a picture of these workers from this basic information, supplemented by visits to the FTZs, informal interviews with workers (or ex-workers) and unionists carried out by CONSA.

Sociodemographic characteristics

The numerous studies which have been carried out on FTZs in the rest of the world report certain common findings: women who work in FTZs are young and single, they have a minimal level of education, they have no previous experience of paid work and they do not stay in the job for very long. The data obtained in the Dominican Republic agree generally with these trends, but they differ in certain respects.

Age

Dominican women working in FTZs are generally younger than the workers employed in national industry, but older than women workers in FTZs in other countries, especially in Asia. About 70 per cent of Dominican women working in the FTZs are between 20 and 35 years old, with an average age of 26.9. This contrasts with the situation in Asia, where 85 per cent of women FTZ workers are less than 25 years old.

Marital status

Women workers in the FTZs in the Dominican Republic differ from those of other countries in that they are less likely to be single. Studies carried out throughout national industry, as well as FTZs, show that nearly half of female workers are married or cohabiting. Approximately 25 per cent are separated or widows and the rest are single. Some employers may prefer married workers because they have family responsibilities, need more money and are therefore likely to be reliable workers and to accept less favourable working conditions; but this is not universal, and some women conceal their marital status when seeking employment. Another explanation for the predominance of married women in industry in the Dominican Republic is that women marry very early, the average age at first marriage being 17. Most of the available female workforce in the country is married; so employers' preferences are of less significance.

Level of education

Studies on FTZ workers in other parts of the world show that their level of education is generally lower than in national industry. In the Dominican Republic, women working in FTZs have a higher level of education than most women in the country, although it is lower than the average in national industry. Level of education is one of the criteria used by employers. However, workers perform tasks, learnt in two or three months of employment, which do not bear any relation to their qualifications. Not using their previous training causes these women to be, in effect, dequalified; what Duarte and Corten call 'educational proletarianisation'.

Children

The majority of workers in the FTZs have children (84 per cent in Duarte and Corten's survey and 63 per cent according to *Centro de Investigacion y Accion femenina* (CIPAF)). A significant percentage of these women are family heads (31.5 per cent in Duarte and Corten's survey and 38 per cent in the CIPAF survey). Some of the working mothers have to leave their children with their parents' family. Childcare, given the absence of creche facilities, is a problem or a constant worry for most women working in the FTZs.

Working conditions

Studies carried out in FTZs in other countries all confirm that in general the work done is monotonous and repetitive, and is characterised by the intense pace of production, with strong work discipline. It does not qualify women for other better paid jobs or lead on to them. The data for the Dominican Republic confirm these findings.

Training

Workers usually spend from one to three months in training, although this training period can sometimes be extended to as much as six months. In reality, the work is simple and does not take very much time to learn; what the women have to learn is the pace of work and its intensity. However, while a worker is in training she receives half the normal salary, so some employers prolong this period unnecessarily.

Salaries

When the FTZs first set up in the Dominican Republic, companies paid 80 per cent of the official minimum salary. They lost this concession in 1979 and since then, have had to pay the minimum salary. The only ways in which the majority of workers can increase their pay is to meet production quotas, for which an additional amount of money is usually (but not always) paid, and to take on overtime. This effort to increase their salary is made at the cost of damaging their health and shortening the period of their active life. However, salaries in FTZs are higher than those paid in domestic service, agriculture or informal sector work. While the legal minimum salary is paid in the FTZs, this requirement is frequently not met in other labour sectors.

Labour rotation

Studies carried out in the Dominican Republic, as in other parts of the world, report a high rate of labour rotation in the FTZs; almost half of FTZ workers interviewed by CIPAF had been working in the firm for less than two years. Various factors have been put forward as causes of this phenomenon. One reason may be the difficulty of fitting in the reproductive role with the exigencies of work. Another factor is that the work discipline and the intensity of labour often wear women out to such an extent that they often leave work or are dismissed.

A study in the electronics industry shows that women who have worked with a microscope for several years develop eyesight problems which lead to their dismissal. Sometimes workers are dismissed without any definite reason. In La Romana, according to our information, many workers have been dismissed on the grounds that they have 'already worked five years for the company'. But women themselves sometimes move companies, seeking those in which work conditions are less oppressive.

Labour rotation is fairly characteristic of FTZs. It is the means used by these industries to renew the workforce when their physical deterioration begins to affect the volume of production.

Working environment

The majority of FTZ firms establish rules and discipline which enable them to obtain the greatest productivity from the workforce. This discipline takes the form of the establishment of individual and collective production quotas, denying time off for health reasons, often limiting the frequency with which women may go to the lavatory, making overtime obligatory, and asking for pregnancy tests when new workers are being recruited. The pettiness of some managers is such that in several factories in San Pedro, women had to go on strike to demand clean toilets. It was beyond the efforts of the workers to get fans installed to relieve the unbearable heat of certain sections of the factory. Music played at high volume is another characteristic of the work environment in many of these factories.

Social perspectives

The growth of FTZs has been so rapid that the social and economic impact on the lives of the workers is hard to measure. But there are certain obvious consequences which create problems, particularly for women, and raise many questions for the future.

The tendency for FTZs to employ women rather than men has implications for the gender pattern of industrial employment and, as industries which have traditionally employed men contract, there has been a rise in male unemployment. Sugar refineries and plantations in the Dominican Republic have closed down and been replaced by FTZs, leaving many men without work. Although there has been a tendency, under social and government pressure, for FTZs to increase the number of male workers, the high degree of industrial competitiveness means that women will be preferred because of their lower rates of pay.

It is likely that sooner or later an organisation for FTZ workers will be created in the Dominican Republic. The possible integration of a significant number of women into the union movement could bring about profound changes in the nature of workers' organisations and political parties. It remains to be seen whether existing unions will join the struggle for general and specific improvements in the lot of women working in FTZs.

If the tendency for women rather than men to be in paid employment continues, this could bring about far-reaching changes in family relationships. Will men assume more responsibility for domestic tasks and the care and education of children? The alternative is for women to become even more overburdened. Another possibility is that the economic independence of women workers in FTZs may result in a large increase in the number of female heads of households.

Children could also be affected by their mothers' working in FTZs. The stressful and exhausting working conditions in FTZs could have serious long-term effects on the physical and mental health of women, and so on their pregnancies and their ability to care for their children. The lack of adequate alternative childcare provision for working mothers could result in increases in levels of child malnutrition and the number of accidental injuries to children.

Female patterns of employment are likely to change, and already there are signs of a reduction in the number of women entering domestic service, and an increase in salaries. This trend could in turn affect the lives of middle class women, making it more difficult for them to work outside the home.

The consequences of the development of FTZs may be profound, not only for the women who work in them but for social relations in society as a whole.

(This is taken from a report prepared for Oxfam by Consultoras Asociadas S.A.(CONSA))

References

Aleman, J. L., 'Zonafranquismo santiaguero', *Periodico Listin Diario*, 26 November 1987.

Beneria, L. (1984), *Reproduccion, Produccion y Division Sexual del Trabajo*, Santo Domingo: Populares Feministas, Coleccion Teoria.

Duarte, I.(with Corten, A. and Pou, F.) (1986), *Trabajadores Urbanos. ensayos Sobre Fuerza Laboral en republica Dominicana,* Santo Domingo: UASD.

Duarte I. et al (1989), *Poblacion y condicion de la Mujer,* Estudio 6, Santo Domingo: Instituto de estudios de Poblacion y Desarrollo.

Joekes, S. P. (1985), 'Industrialisation, trade and female employment in developing countries. Experiences of the 1970s and after', (mimeo), Santo Dominigo: Instraw.

STRUCTURAL ADJUSTMENT:
ITS EFFECT ON WOMEN

DIANE ELSON

The last decade has been marked by a contrast between rising awareness of the importance of women's contribution to the economy and continued deterioration of the world economy. Women's Bureaux and women's groups across the world have campaigned for proper recognition of women's work both as producers of goods and services, and as reproducers of human resources; and for women to have better access to the resources they require to improve their productivity. There has been some success in opening up new activities to women and increasing their incomes through special training programmes, through projects with women's components, or projects specifically directed to women. Much of the energy in developing countries has been directed towards women's projects, often in partnership with aid agency officials who have special responsibility for women and development. In market economy developed countries, much of the emphasis has been on introducing new equal opportunities legislation and enabling women to fight their cases through the courts.

But more important for women than either projects or legislation is the general condition of the economy. Low rates of growth of output, exports and employment undermine all these efforts. The 1980s have seen not just low rates of growth, but absolute declines in economic well-being in many areas.

It is therefore very important that policy makers concerned with the well-being of women should develop the capacity to analyse the implications of global economic deterioration for women, and to assist in the formulation of policies to cope with that deterioration.

Conceptual tools: gender bias in economic analysis

Macro-economic trends and policies are usually presented in a language which appears to be gender neutral: no specific mention is made of gender or of the sexual division of labour. The focus of attention is on the gross national product; on imports, exports and the balance of payments; on efficiency and productivity.

However, this apparent gender-neutrality hides a deep gender bias in the analysis and policy formulation. The economy is defined principally in terms of marketed goods and services, with some allowance made for subsistence crop production in developing countries. The work of caring for children, of gathering fuel and water, processing food, preparing meals, keeping the house clean, nursing the sick, managing the household, is excluded from the economy. It is, of course, this work which largely falls on the shoulders of women, even in the most developed countries. By not considering this work or the resources it requires, macro-economic analysis and policy have a built-in conceptual bias against women.

The economy and human resources

This conceptual bias has important practical consequences. Macro-economic policy assumes that the process of raising children and caring for members of the labour force carried out by women unpaid will continue regardless of the way in which resources are re-allocated. Women's unpaid labour is implicitly regarded as elastic — able to stretch to make up any shortfall in other resources.

Now it is true that the production of human resources is different from the production of any other kind of resource. It does not respond to economic signals in the same way: if the price of a crop falls far enough, it may be uprooted or left to rot; if there is insufficient demand for a manufactured good, the factory is closed and the machinery mothballed, sold off, or scrapped. But if the demand for labour falls, mothers do not 'scrap' their children or leave them to rot untended.

However, women's unpaid labour is not infinitely elastic — breaking point may be reached, and women's capacity to reproduce and maintain human resources may collapse. Even if breaking point is not reached, the success of the macro-economic policy in achieving its goals may be won at the cost of a longer and harder working day for many women. This cost will be invisible to the policy makers because it is unpaid time. But the cost will be revealed in statistics on the health and nutritional status of such women. What economists regard as 'increased efficiency' may instead be a shifting of the costs from the paid economy to the unpaid economy. For instance, a reduction in the time patients spend in hospital may seem to be an increase in the efficiency of the hospital; the money costs of the hospital per patient fall but the unpaid work of women in the household rises. This is not a genuine increase in efficiency; it is simply a transfer of costs from the hospital to the home.

In considering policy responses to global economic deterioration, we need to ask: does this policy work by increasing the amount of unpaid labour women have to do?

Adjustment and the 'magic of the market'

Though the International Monetary Fund (IMF) stabilisation programmes focus primarily on cutting demand, and World Bank structural adjustment programmes focus on boosting supply and increasing productivity, they do share an emphasis on reducing the role of the state, and increasing the role of the market in resource allocation. Both institutions hold the view that a major reason for poor economic performance is distortions in resource allocation. These distortions are caused, they say, by government policy e.g. by over-expansion of the public sector and by the use of direct controls and subsidies. A major element of both types of programme is the removal of direct controls and subsidies and a reduction in the role of the public sector.

IMF stabilisation programmes typically consist of deflation, devaluation and decontrol. Public expenditure is cut, including expenditure on social services and food subsidies. Controls over imports and foreign exchange are loosened. The exchange rate may even be determined by a weekly auction of foreign exchange rather than being fixed by the central bank.

World Bank structural adjustment programmes improve the incentives for private sector producers (particularly of exports) through changes in prices, tariffs and other taxes, subsidies and interest rates; and by reducing the resources allocated to the public sector to make more resources available to the private sector.

The thinking that underlies IMF and World Bank adjustment programmes is shared by governments of some important donor countries. President Reagan spoke of the 'magic of the market' and the UK government has made some aid conditional upon agreement of structural adjustment programmes with the World Bank.

Women, the market and the state

The relation between women, the market and the state is complex. The state does not always operate in the interests of women, and the market does not always operate against the interests of women.

The state frequently plays a major role in perpetuating social, economic and ideological processes that subordinate women. It frequently treats women as dependents of men in legal and administrative procedures, and upholds the patriarchal family in which women do not have the same access to resources as men. Examples of public sector projects and programmes which ignore the needs of women as producers, and direct resources towards men, abound.

The market appears to treat women as individuals in their own right. If women can sell their labour or their products and get a cash income of their own, this lessens their economic dependence upon men, increases their economic value, and may increase their bargaining power within the household. Access to an income of their own tends to be highly valued by women, not only for what it buys, but also for the greater dignity it brings.

However, while women have to carry the double burden of unpaid work in the home, as well as paid work producing goods and services, they are unable to compete with men on equal terms. Equal pay and equal opportunities legislation, and removing the 'traditional' barriers to women working outside the home, cannot by themselves free women from domestic burdens and expectations. Access to markets has benefits for women, but the benefits are always limited because raising children and caring for family members is structured by unequal gender relations, and cannot be directly and immediately responsive to market signals.

Women with high incomes can reduce their relative disadvantage in the market by buying substitutes for their unpaid work — employing cleaners, maids, nannies and cooks — but this still leaves them with the responsibility for household management.

If most women are to gain from access to markets, they also need access to public sector services, such as water supplies, electricity, waste disposal facilities, public transport, health care and education, to lighten the burden of their unpaid work and enable them to acquire the skills they need to enter the market.

This suggests that most women have an interest not so much in reducing the role of the state and increasing the role of the market, as in restructuring both the public sector and the private sector to make them more responsive to women's needs as producers and reproducers.

It is necessary to distinguish different activities within both the public sector and the private sector. In the public sector, we need to distinguish between social services; transport and energy; police, the legal system and armed forces; and state-owned factories, farms and marketing and distribution facilities — often called parastatals. Then within each category we need to examine exactly what is being supplied (primary health care or open heart surgery, for example) and to identify who is benefiting from these activities. We need to examine the relationship between the producers and the users of public sector goods and services. How responsive are producers to the needs of users? What mechanisms are there for users to influence the allocation of resources in the public sector? The structural adjustment required in the public sector may not be a reduction in expenditure, but a change in priorities. The mobilisation and organisation of women who use public sector services may be a way to achieve this.

The private sector needs separating into the formal and the informal sector; foreign and locally owned firms; large and small; those which employ wage labour and family labour; joint-stock companies and co-operatives; farming, trading and manufacturing; activities directed by women and activities directed by men. If greater reliance is to be placed on private enterprise — we need to ask whose enterprise? The enterprise of the woman farming or trading on her own account, or the enterprise of agribusiness and merchants with monopoly power? The enterprise of a women's co-operative or the enterprise of a multinational corporation? The mobilisation of women's enterprise to provide a decent income and a basis for sustained economic growth requires support from the state, particularly in the provision of credit and training, and in services that free women from domestic duties.

The impact of adjustment on women: a framework for analysis

The process of adjustment affects households in the following ways:

changes in incomes, through changes in wages and the level of employment for employees, and through changes in product

prices and product demand for the self-employed;
changes in prices of important purchases, especially food;

changes in the levels and composition of public expenditure,
particularly those in the social sector, including possible
introduction or increase of user charges for services;

changes in working conditions, through changes in hours of
work, intensity of work, job security, fringe benefits and legal
status; this applies to unpaid work as well as paid work.

These changes will not affect all households in the same way: some
will lose and some will gain. Neither will these changes affect all
members of households in the same way. Distribution of resources
within households, as well as between households, must be taken
into account. When households have to reduce food consumption
because of rising prices and falling incomes, available evidence
suggests it is very likely that the consumption of women and girls
will be reduced by more than that of men and boys. If charges are
introduced or increased for education and health services, there is a
strong possibility that the access of girls will be reduced. When
attempts are made to compensate for reductions in purchased
resources by increases in unpaid labour (e.g. buying cheaper food
that requires more preparation time), it is likely to be women who
bear the main burden.

Available research shows that neither joint decision making nor
equal sharing of resources within households is common. The
standard of living of wives can be lower than that of husbands; and
that of girls lower than boys. Nevertheless, it is generally women
who have the responsibility for seeing that members of the
household are fed, clothed and cared for, and their obligation to
meet children's needs is generally regarded as stronger than men's.
Men's obligation is limited to providing some of the cash or
productive assets required. Women, then, must meet their families'
needs by 'stretching' the husband's cash contribution with 'good
housekeeping', or by earning a wage income, or producing food or
clothing themselves, or engaging in barter and petty trade. It is
women who must devise survival strategies when household
incomes fall and prices rise.

Changes in income

Many adjustment programmes include limitations or complete

freezes on wage and salary rises in the public sector. Employment in the public sector may be frozen or reduced. Because urban formal sector employees are likely to face adverse changes in their incomes there will be a knock-on effect in the informal sector which supplies goods and services to formal sector employees.

Women public sector employees will be adversely affected. The public sector, rather than the private sector, has hitherto provided most of the professional and managerial urban jobs for women, often with a high degree of security. The best career opportunities for educated women in many countries have been in the public sector. This is often no longer the case: for example, in Jamaica, nurses and teachers are leaving the public sector because of the low levels of pay. Professional women remaining in the public service have been driven to doing extra jobs at night in the informal sector, such as running snack shops.

One category of employment that has expanded for women in some countries is work in export-oriented, labour intensive manufacturing. For example, Sri Lanka and Jamaica have set up Free Trade Zones (FTZs) as part of their adjustment strategy. These employ women in garment production. Wages for women in FTZs do tend to be higher than the average for comparable work outside the zones, so employers in the zones have no difficulty in recruiting women to work for them. But workers in FTZs tend to enjoy fewer rights than workers in the private formal sector factories outside the zones.

On the whole, the incomes and the quality of job opportunities available to women in urban areas have probably deteriorated, though more detailed information on this is required.

In the rural areas, some groups have enjoyed increases in incomes as a result of higher prices for producers of marketed crops. For instance, Ghana increased cocoa prices by more than seven times between 1982-3 and 1986-7 as part of a major World Bank supported programme to rehabilitate the cocoa industry. In most sub-Saharan countries, producer prices for food crops have risen substantially since 1980, mainly as a result of dismantling price controls. For instance, Zambia increased the official price of maize by 142 per cent between 1980-85. However, the impact of high prices for crops/livestock has been eroded by higher prices for consumer goods and production inputs that farmers buy. Many of these are imported and devaluation has raised their prices. Though the price of maize rose in Zambia by 142 per cent, the real price rise for farmers, taking into account the rising prices of what they buy, was only about 6 per cent. So the incentive effect is much less than the change in nominal producer prices would suggest. The impact that such price increases have on women depends crucially on whether the extra cash income is controlled by the men or the women; and if it goes to the men, how do they dispose of it? Do they increase their personal consumption, or make part of it available to their wives for family consumption?

The benefit from higher crop prices also depends on the producers' capacity to increase output. While there is evidence that rural producers do switch from one crop to another in response to changing relative prices, it is far less clear that they will be able to increase output of a wide range of crops in response to a general increase in crop prices. For this depends on their ability to mobilise more of the inputs required — in particular fertiliser, credit, and labour. Women's double burden of crop production and domestic work leaves little spare time. There are many time-budget studies showing the long working day of women farmers. Moreover, other elements of structural adjustment programmes may also make increasing demands on women's time; cutbacks in the public provision of rural health services, education and water supplies, for instance. There is a limit to the extent that women can switch time from human resource production and maintenance to crop production. Thus the provision of public services which reduce the time women must spend in domestic duties is essential in affecting their ability to respond to higher crop prices with higher output.

Even if they do have some 'spare capacity', women may be reluctant to increase their workload because they are unlikely to enjoy the proceeds of extra work. Production of cash crops is frequently under the management of men who then control the resulting proceeds. In such cases, women may refuse to spend extra time weeding and harvesting in their husbands' fields.

The constraints on women's time can also be lifted by making each hour more productive, but that, too, requires public provision, particularly of extension services and credit.

Agricultural labourers will not benefit directly from increased crop prices, though they may benefit if there is an expansion of output which may create more employment. For them, as for urban workers, increased food crop prices will increase their cost of living.

It must also be remembered that many poor farmers are forced to sell their food crops just after harvest to repay debts, and they, too, have to purchase food for the rest of the year.

Changes in prices of consumer goods

Increased food prices for consumers are major features of adjustment programmes. Where food imports are high, devaluation, which increases the price of imports, will have a substantial impact on food prices. Removal of food subsidies is also a major feature of adjustment programmes. It is advocated as a major contribution to reducing public expenditure. In Sri Lanka, following the removal of food subsidies, prices rose by 158 per cent for rice, 386 per cent for wheat flour, 331 per cent for bread and 345 per cent for milk powder in the period 1977-84. In Zambia, the price of maize meal, the main consumer staple, was raised in one step by 50 per cent in 1985, as the first stage in removing the subsidy.

If wages are frozen while food prices (and prices of other essential items, such as kerosene) are rising, then real incomes will fall. Urban wage earners in Tanzania faced a 50 per cent fall in real income between 1980 and 1984, while in Ghana over the same period, the fall was 40 per cent.

UNICEF studies reveal a widespread deterioration in the nutritional status of children and pregnant and lactating mothers in both rural and urban areas in countries with IMF stabilisation and World Bank structural adjustment programmes. Mothers are unable to buy enough food of the right type to feed the whole family, and in many cases priority is given to adult males.

Changes in levels and composition of public expenditure

Public expenditure on social services has fallen in many developing countries. For instance, in Jamaica, social services expenditure fell by 44 per cent in real terms between 1981-83 and 1985-86. Some schools have been closed and services offered by some hospitals and health centres downgraded. Charges have been introduced for health services, even for the low paid and unemployed. In Nigeria, state governments have imposed fees on both primary and secondary education, and the enrolment rate among poor children has fallen drastically.

Expenditure cuts have often hit recurrent expenditure harder than capital expenditure, leaving schools short of books, paper and pens and hospitals short of bandages and drugs, even while new hospitals and school buildings have gone ahead. Expenditure cuts have also often hit rural services harder than urban services.

In Sri Lanka, a serious deterioration in the delivery of health care has been noted. Large investments in new and more sophisticated hospitals and equipment have gone ahead while rural services and preventive medicine have remained short of resources. Private practice by doctors employed in the Health Service has been introduced, and studies have found that private patients get preferential access to health service facilities. Privatisation of social services has probably gone furthest in Chile. For example, educational coupons have replaced state-sponsored education, but at a time of recession poorer households have endeavoured to survive by cashing in their coupons, rather than spending them on schooling. Literacy levels have fallen.

One item of public expenditure has been growing, however, and has reached very high levels in many parts of Latin America, the Caribbean and sub-Saharan Africa. This is the payment of interest and servicing of foreign debt. In Jamaica, this accounted for no less than 42 per cent of total budgeted recurrent expenditure in 1985-86.

Changes in working conditions

It is very likely that for many women, adjustment programmes mean longer hours of work, both paid work and unpaid. Maintaining a household on reduced resources takes more time — hunting for bargains, setting up informal exchange networks with neighbours and kin, making and mending at home rather than buying, etc. Increasing agricultural output takes more time. Making a living in the informal sector in conditions of falling demand takes more time, yet the involvement of urban women in this sector is likely to grow.

However, there is a difference between survival strategies and activities that can form the basis for sustained growth and development both on a personal and a national level. There is a trend towards the casualisation of the work of urban women, not just in the informal sectors of cities in developing countries, but also in developed market economies, where outworking at home is growing. The distinction between the formal sector and the informal sector is being eroded. Women's jobs in the formal sector are being made more 'flexible' — which frequently means loss of security, loss of fringe benefits such as sick pay, pensions and maternity leave, and increasing intensity of work. Free Trade Zones are one example of this trend. The contracting out of some public sector activities in some countries is another. Increased 'efficiency' in the public sector may be bought at the cost of deteriorating working conditions for women.

The overall impact on women: information priorities

Given the present availability of information, it is not possible to present a definitive picture. In many cases, adjustment seems to have led to a redistribution of real income away from urban areas and towards rural areas. It is estimated that in Tanzania, between 1980 and 1984, there was a 5 per cent increase in real farm incomes, while urban wage earners suffered a 50 per cent fall in real incomes. In Ghana, over the same period, farm incomes stagnated, while urban real incomes fell by 40 per cent. Rural incomes have increased relative to urban incomes in Brazil, Chile and Mexico. However, there are still large numbers of rural people living in abject poverty. None of these general estimates looks at the effects within households.

It should be a priority to monitor the impact of adjustment on the following groups of women:

women in low-income urban and rural households;
women employed in the public sector;
women farmers.

Some work is under way on the impact of adjustment on the poor (notably that by UNICEF on the impact on children). It is necessary to supplement this with specific monitoring of intra-household resource allocation processes. The resources of local research institutes and universities could be called upon to conduct sample surveys of how exactly, within the household, women get access to the inputs they require for their work of raising children and caring for other family members.

Statistics should be compiled from information supplied by the public sector on the employment of women in the public sector; levels of pay; working conditions; turnover, etc. Co-operation with public sector trade unions may be fruitful in helping to monitor the extent to which conditions have deteriorated. This group of women is undoubtedly still likely to be much better off than women in low-income households, but deterioration in the major source of modern careers for women is still a matter of concern.

The position of women farmers needs monitoring to see to what extent their incentives have improved, and to what extent they are in a position to respond to better incentives. These women are the group who seem to have some chance of benefiting from adjustment, and it is vital to identify any barriers to those benefits being realised.

Modifying the adjustment process: policy objectives

Considerable criticisms have already been voiced about the costs of adjustment strategies. It is argued that they bear most heavily on the poor and erode the human resource base of the economy. UNICEF has called for 'Adjustment with a Human Face'; the Overseas Development Institute in London has called for 'Adjustment with Equity'. The World Bank has indicated that structural adjustment must include policies for 'strengthening the human resource base'.

There is scope for Women's Bureaux to participate in this dialogue about modifying the adjustment process. One way would be to join their voices to those of organisations like UNICEF who are arguing for protecting the vulnerable during the adjustment process. There is, however, the disadvantage that this would focus attention mainly on women as victims and runs the danger of deteriorating into paternalism. It also tends to focus only on women in low-income households. It focuses mainly on the detrimental impact of adjustment on women, and not on the contribution that women can make to effective adjustment.

An emphasis on women as producers of goods and services and as reproducers and maintainers of human resources may prove more effective. A dialogue with the World Bank could be opened which emphasises that a prime need for strengthening the human resource base is more time for women, and more control over resources for women. Policy reform and structural changes need to encompass not just relations between public sector and private sector control of resources, but between women's control and men's control of resources.

An overarching objective would be to give the 'Adjustment with Equity' objective a 'gender' content. The objective would then be that poor women should not become worse off than other sections of the population in absolute terms; and that better off women (including farmers and public sector employees) should not become worse off than men in comparable social groups. The indicators of well-being should include not just income, but also total hours of work (paid and unpaid) and health and nutritional status. This might be called an 'Adjustment with Gender Equity' objective.

Modifying the adjustment process: areas of intervention

The achievement of Adjustment with Gender Equity requires greater selectivity in public expenditure cuts, a restructuring of public sector activities, and a greater emphasis on self-reliant food production.

It also requires more finance from donors, to permit a slower pace of adjustment; and provision of appropriate technical assistance and training.

While reductions in public expenditure may be unavoidable, there is scope for much greater selectivity in the cuts. Before reducing food subsidies, other subsidies could be cut (for example, subsidies to national airlines). Food subsidies could be redesigned to increase the benefits to poorer women by removing subsidies on foods consumed mainly by middle and higher income families, and concentrating them on food consumed mainly by poorer families. Or poor families could be cushioned by a food stamp scheme in which they are issued special stamps (or vouchers) which can be exchanged in the shops for food (as has happened in Jamaica and Sri Lanka) though food stamps are not without problems. Direct feeding programmes for children and mothers in poor districts may be the most appropriate measure. Such a programme, supported by food aid, now exists in Jamaica.

Social expenditure on education, health and sanitation, can be given higher priority than prestige urban projects, or the building of new factories that will be unable to operate anywhere near full capacity because of lack of imports. Within social expenditure, there needs to be restructuring to direct services to the poor. UNICEF proposes an emphasis on primary health care, based on rural and urban community clinics, in preference to expensive urban hospitals. It recommends training of more para-medics and traditional midwives in preference to specialised doctors. Such restructuring could also preserve, or even expand, women's employment opportunities in the public sector, since while specialised doctors are more likely to be men, para-medics may well be women. Restructuring could be linked to incentives for public sector employers to work in rural areas or poor urban districts: jobs in difficult or unattractive environments could be exempted from wage freezes or given special allowances.

If user changes are introduced for social services, these could be differentiated. Fees for university students could be introduced rather than fees for primary schools; or greater increases in charges for electricity, water and sanitation services introduced for those living in wealthier urban areas than for those in low-income areas.

The danger is that public expenditure cuts are determined by administrative ease and the power of organised interest groups. But an expenditure cutting exercise is an opportunity to re-order the priorities of the public sector. A Women's Bureau can intervene in this by requesting statements of impact of the proposed cuts on women, and by suggesting a different pattern of cuts, if appropriate, and a restructuring of the public sector to meet women's needs more effectively.

Adjustment is not just about public expenditure cuts and re-organising the public sector. It is also about increasing productivity and promoting growth. World Bank structural adjustment programmes emphasise increasing export crop production, especially through reducing the gap between the price farmers get and the world market price.

Though increasing export crop production may increase foreign exchange earnings when undertaken by one country facing given world market prices, it is questionable whether such a policy is valid when applied uniformly across a large number of developing countries. Since demand for most export crops is growing only very slowly, increased export volume by several countries is likely to depress world market prices and reduce the benefits of increased production. World market prices for primary products, relative to manufactures, are now at their lowest level in real terms since the 1930s.

Expansion of export crop production has not historically benefited women very much, and has often made their position worse. Typically, such crops have been grown under the control of men. Women have been required to work in the fields planting, weeding and harvesting them, but the income accruing from the sale of such crops has been under the control of their husbands. Women have frequently lost access to better land when it was diverted from subsistence crop production under their control to export crop production under men's control. Export crops have always been allocated better seeds, fertilisers, credit and extension services — and that has meant discrimination against women.

Many governments have been sceptical of World Bank arguments, and have argued that local food production for the local market is a less risky growth strategy. However, many of them are attracted to strategies of large scale irrigated and mechanised food production, highly dependent on agribusiness and imported inputs. The results of many of these schemes have been disappointing and the costs substantially underestimated. One of the reasons for the disappointment has been a lack of recognition of the crucial role of women farmers in food production. What is needed is not simply an emphasis on food production, but an emphasis on self-reliant food production. This means increasing the productivity of small-scale women farmers who do not rely so much on imports, and who grow foods which are staples for poorer groups, such as cassava, as well as food grains such as maize and rice. There are a whole host of critical policy reforms required here to increase the productivity of women farmers. Increasing real crop prices is a necessary condition but it is by no means a sufficient condition. It is essential that more inputs and support services are directed to women farmers, and that strategies are devised for restructuring gender relations to end discrimination against women farmers. This is necessary not only to enable women to reap some gains from the adjustment process, but also to assure an effective adjustment process with some real prospects of sustained growth.

This article draws on a paper originally written for the Commonwealth Secretariat, a revised version of which was published under the title 'The Impact of Structural Adjustment on Women: Concepts and Issues', *in Bade Onimode, B. (ed.) (1989),* The IMF, The World Bank and the African Debt, Vol.2, The Social and Political Impact, *London: Zed Books.*

Diane Elson teaches in the Economics Department, University of Manchester. Her books include Male Bias in the Development Process, *Manchester University Press, forthcoming and (with Ruth Pearson) (1989),* Women's Employment and Multi-nationals in Europe, *London: Macmillan. She is active in developing links between women workers in First World and Third World countries through Women Working Worldwide.*

NICARAGUAN WOMEN IN THE WAR:
AN INTERVIEW WITH MYRNA CUNNINGHAM
FROM THE NORTH ATLANTIC COAST

EUGENIA PIZA LOPEZ

The isolation of the Atlantic Coast region of Nicaragua has economic, ethnic, linguistic, religious and historical dimensions and the people have differing development needs from the rest of the country. At first the Sandinistas did not respond effectively to these needs. Consequently the Contras exploited the area for physical and political support in their US-backed fight to overthrow the Sandinista Government. The Nicaraguan National Assembly then proposed regional autonomy.

The following extracts are from an interview with Dr Myrna Cunningham, Minister for North Atlantic Coast Region to the Nicaraguan General Assembly. This took place late in 1988, during the Sandinista period.

Interview

Does the war mean a change in women's lives?

Women have to play new roles now that men have gone to the war. Women do the productive work in our co-operatives, in the mining areas, in the fields, etc. This has not been very easy for women. In the mining area, for example, women have tried to take on the role that has been traditionally male; they are working as miners. At first they were totally rejected by men who did not agree that women should be allowed in the mines. We had a three-year struggle trying to guarantee mining jobs for women and to break down prejudices. I think we have advanced. Now we are working on a child day-care unit in one of the mines.

In the past those who made the decisions were men, and those who did the work were women. We have been trying to change this. In the Atlantic Coast region, most of the people armed and fighting against the revolution were men. The women worked and, as happens very often, were the victims of what was happening.

During the Contra war, women stayed in the community or were taken to the refugee camps in Honduras. They took care of the children while their husbands or their sons were armed by the Contras.

This is why the first people to begin the struggle for peace in the Atlantic Coast were a group of women from the villages. They said 'O.K., we are all victims, but women and children are suffering the most so we should fight for peace'. The members of the first 'Peace and Autonomy Commission' were all women. And this movement which began three years ago has increased. In February we elected a Committee in which the four different ethnic groups all participate.

A serious problem occurs as a result of repatriation. Men are leaving their weapons behind, leaving the Contras and coming back home. This is good and shows that women's efforts for peace really work; but the men want to become the leaders and the decision makers, to take back their jobs, displacing the women who remained holding the community together for years. So we have tried to train these women to continue to hold power. We have to train them because women are accustomed to say 'O.K. if they are going to do it, let them do it and I'll go back home'. With the women's training programmes we are trying to provide assertiveness courses and support women's self-confidence.

What kind of participation do women have in defence?
In the same way that the government calls men to 'reserves', we also have a group of women who are army reservists: they are militia members and in the police. We encourage the participation of women in all sectors. Women have been killed as members of defence units.

Another consequence of the war is death and destruction, and women have also been victims of this. We have over 800 orphans in the region and over 300 mothers whose children have been killed. They don't have any kind of support, so one project is looking into what we can do for women whose close relatives died for the revolution. We have to give these women an opportunity to advance and overcome their pain.

What happened when a Contra armed group arrived in a village?
You have people who are killed and others who are kidnapped by

the Contras. They usually kidnap women, and make them cook and work for them. They rape women in the villages and sometimes take them as their 'partners'. Later they will just throw them away after only a few days. In other areas we have encountered Honduran troops who cross the river and the border, and rape the women. This is the single most serious aggression against women. It is an orchestrated effort to undermine and terrorise a community through violence against women.

And of course, any disruption means that women will have more problems in guaranteeing assistance for their children, the disabled and the elderly.

There were more than 60 per cent of women who were heads of households. How do they survive?
It is very difficult. Women have a lower level of education than men and it is very hard to get a job. We have a high incidence of prostitution. We also have a high incidence of women begging because they can't find work. The family structure has become broken. You can find women who would live with someone; he would then beat her up and treat her badly so she would take another partner.

Is domestic violence more of a problem as a result of the war?
No, domestic violence was there before the war. Maybe we did not mention it before because we had so many other problems and maybe women themselves saw domestic violence as something natural. Well, 'if you love me you beat me'. That's one of the ways in which women experience and justify domestic violence. There is now a national campaign against it.

Eugenia Piza Lopez is the Gender and Development Unit adviser for Asia and Latin America. Her previous experience includes research on images of the Third World in the UK, work on popular education with Central American women and participatory research in Costa Rica.

WOMEN IN THE ALGERIAN LIBERATION STRUGGLE

MARIE-AIMÉE HÉLIE-LUCAS

'Even in the hardest times of the struggle, women were kept in their place, and confined to the kind of tasks which would not disturb social order in the future. Nurturing and maintenance were the tasks of Algerian women freedom fighters, and occasional medical service. We now know for sure where the liberated women were: in the kitchen, sewing clothes (or flags?), carrying parcels, typing...

'The overall task of women during the liberation struggle was symbolic. Confronted by colonisation, the people had to build a national identity, based on the values of their own tradition, religion, language and culture. Women bore the heavy role of being the keepers of this threatened identity and they paid the heaviest price for agreeing — but were there choices? — to play this role.

'One of the early slogans of nationalism in Algeria was promoted by the Ulemas, the religious leaders. It said: "Arabic is our language, Islam is our religion, Algeria is our country". Women especially were in charge of raising their sons within the religious faith, reviving traditions, keeping moral standards and teaching the language of the forefathers. (We will not discuss here the legitimacy of Arab language in a country where the dominant ethnics are Berber and speak the Berber language.) Women had to behave according to tradition, while men could have some access to modernity; only traditions which suit the purposes of those who are in power are kept as truly traditional...

'Nevertheless, since there is no humble task in the revolution, we have not argued about the roles we had. It would have seemed so mean to question the priority of the liberation of the country, and raise issues which would not be issues any more after the liberation: we believed that all the remnants of women's oppression would disappear with independence.

'What makes me angry, in retrospect, is not the mere fact of confining women in their place, but the brainwashing which did not allow us, young women, to even think in terms of questioning the women's place. And what makes me even more angry is to witness the replication of this situation in various places in the world where national liberation struggles are still taking place. We still witness women covering the misbehaviour of their fellow men and hiding, in the name of national solidarity and identity, crimes which will continue after the official liberation.

'This is the real harm which comes with liberation struggles. People mobilise against such a strong, powerful, and destructive enemy that there is no room for practical action in mobilising women at the same time. But worse, liberation struggles erase from our mind the very idea of doing so, which is seen as anti-revolutionary, and anti-nationalist. This vision remains after independence and alienates generations of young women...

'At no point did we see that a power structure was being built on our mental confusion: a power structure which used the control of private life and the control of women as a means to get access to and maintain itself in power. It is in this context that I would like to look again at the activities to which women were confined within the liberation movement. During this crucial period, women had been assigned a place in society which could not be challenged without questioning both the past and the future; the roots for a tightly controlled society were set.

'We are made to feel that protesting in the name of women's interests and rights is not to be done NOW: it is never and has never been the right moment: not during the liberation struggle against colonialism, because all forces had to be mobilised against the principal enemy; not after independence, because all forces had to be mobilised to build up the devastated country; not now that racist, imperialist Western governments are attacking Islam and the Third World, etc. Defending women's rights "now" — this now being ANY historical moment — is always a "betrayal": of the people, of the nation, of the revolution, of Islam, of national identity, of cultural roots...

'It is very hard to persist, in total isolation, in denouncing the stepping back from the women's question of so many once "revolutionary" countries, and to go on organising the struggle. My deepest admiration and regard goes to those of us who stubbornly trace their way through this ideological jungle to promote the cause of women.'

(We have selected these extracts from an article published in IFDA dossier, July/August 1989. This was based on a longer article, originally published by Women Living Under Muslim Laws, Working Papers, 1988, *and also published in that year in a book,* Women and the Military System, *London: Harvester-Wheatsheaf.)*

Marie-Aimée Hélie-Lucas is a sociologist, who taught and carried out research for some years at Algiers University. She is the founder and present coordinator of Women Living Under Muslim Laws Solidarity Network.

'TAKING THE LION BY THE WHISKERS': BUILDING ON THE STRENGTHS OF REFUGEE WOMEN

TINA WALLACE

Conflict and refugees

War, and the often associated scourges of famine and impoverishment, cause disruption to very many nations, communities and households across the Third World. Conflict and armed struggle cut across the cycles of production and reproduction leading often to displacement and forced migration, as well as death for many. These upheavals lead to temporary, and often permanent, changes in social and economic relations in the society and within the households of that society; war, and resulting hunger, suffering and migration, change gender relations. As men are usually the ones who leave to fight, or when famine strikes move to search for food or work in towns, women are increasingly forced to take on new social and economic roles. They often become effectively the heads of households and take on the responsibilities for providing for the family; yet they rarely acquire the status and rights that accrue to male heads of households. So they are forced to meet new demands, without adequate access to resources such as land, credit, or training. For many women the option of staying at home ceases to be viable and they start the long and painful process of migration across international borders or to safer-but-alien parts of their own countries. The ever-growing numbers of refugees and displaced people worldwide are evidence of the widespread conflict now characterising many parts of the world; the majority of them are women and children who are forced into taking on new responsibilities, shouldering new burdens and surviving under often hostile conditions.

'Refugee women and girls represent the majority of refugee populations in many countries hosting sizeable refugee caseloads today. They, like most refugees, are confronted with the inherent dangers characterising their flight to safety, together with insecurity and often interminable waiting periods in camps pending identification of durable solutions on their behalf. Yet, it is evident that refugee women are doubly disadvantaged for, confronted with the trauma of uprooting, deprived of normal family and community ties, property and personal belongings, they have been forced to assume abrupt changes in role and status. Faced with loss, due to death or frequent absences of husbands and young male family members, women headed households are a common phenomenon in many refugee populations today.' (UNHCR Commissioner, quoted in Kelly, 1989, p.85.)

Until recently, the specific problems encountered by refugee women, and the multiplicity of roles they have to play while balancing the competing demands on their time and energy, in situations where they often have no status or support, were largely invisible. Even now, while there is some recognition of the particular needs of refugee women, there is very little basic information and data about them; about their health needs, the productive work they undertake, their experiences of stress, and their subjection to many kinds of violence. But at least there is a growing awareness that women make up the bulk of the refugee (and displaced) populations and that they have definable needs which arise from their roles and responsibilities as refugee women. The UNHCR now has official guidelines stressing the need to take account of women's social and productive roles in order to meet their needs and improve their situation. The objectives of this policy are based on the Nairobi Forward-Looking Strategies.

An earlier set of guidelines was drawn up in 1988 at an Assembly in Geneva. The preparation for this meeting, the work done during the meeting, and subsequent work, have been crucial in bringing to the attention of agencies and officials both the special problems of women refugees, and also their strengths and resources.

The Geneva Assembly

This assembly, which took place in November 1988 in Geneva, was not the usual meeting of international refugee experts, familiar with each other and with the issues under discussion. Rather, it was a vibrant meeting of women from all over the world, many of them refugees themselves — some settled in the West, many directly from camps or refuges to which they returned after the Assembly — who came together to focus on refugee women. Many new issues were raised as the refugee voice became dominant; the other, non-refugee women from Non-Governmental Organisations (NGOs), Universities, and the United Nations High Commission for Refugees (UNHCR), spent much time listening to them, as well as contributing from their own experiences drawn from working closely with refugees in different countries.

The universal roles that women play in almost every refugee situation came through clearly during the week. Refugee women are the ones caring for the sick and elderly, for the children and the daily needs of the household. They are often alone in being responsible for the maintenance of the family — and the community — for providing food, water, fuel, health care, education and cultural cohesion. They are often the sole breadwinners, being newly widowed or separated.

At the same time, the dramatic differences between the refugee women from different parts of the world were highlighted, and the need for NGOs and UNHCR to understand the history and culture and specific needs of women and children in very varied refugee situations was stressed. The women in Somali refugee camps have very different problems from those in camps in Southern Africa or the Middle East; there are major differences between refugee women in Central America and South East India. The political, economic and social conditions of their past and their present experience impose different problems and possibilities on women refugees, and these need to be understood by those trying to work with them. It was obvious that information on refugee women is very sparse and the conference played a major role in revealing the glaring need for proper data. Material provided during the meeting began the long process of building up knowledge and understanding about particular groups of refugee women, and about some of the universal issues they face.

Moving personal testimonies were presented in the plenary sessions, workshops and over mealtimes. The enormity of the struggle that refugees are involved in, and the specific burdens and suffering carried by women were graphically communicated. So, too, was their determination and impressive ability to carry on; and the repeated hope for a future time when they will be able to return and rebuild.

Protection

Protection was felt by all to be a central issue, and one that is usually ignored by NGOs and even by UNHCR. Yet the pain of being a female refugee was especially evident during the discussions around protection; the harassment of women often starts from the day they leave their homes and begin dangerous journeys through hostile territory. There is a lack of physical protection against hunger for themselves and their children, and a constant danger of being captured, bombed or shot. The very real danger of rape and sexual harassment mark their journeys from Namibia, South Africa, Ethiopia, Eritrea, from Sudan, Vietnam, Afghanistan, Central and Latin American countries. The threat of piracy for the boat people and sexual traumas experienced on the high seas are all too real; women can also suffer from the brutality or insensitivity to their suffering of their own men, who are themselves suffering stress and breakdown.

Protection issues affect every aspect of life for a female refugee. For example, without papers (which are often denied to women refugees and only given to men) women are unable to establish businesses or income generating projects legally and so fear harassment by the police; without papers they cannot travel for health, work or education. Fear of physical and sexual harassment within and outside refugee camps can keep women confined to their homes, yet the mental and physical suffering experienced by those women who have been or fear being molested or raped is largely ignored by officials.

Women often need protection also from those organising the distribution of food, blankets and other scarce resources. Women are expected to provide sexual favours in exchange for essential items or safe passage. The refugee women at the assembly said that many organisations feel this to be outside their competence or mandate and so choose to ignore it. The Deputy High Commissioner of UNHCR, however, does take these issues very seriously indeed and in his address to the meeting stressed that these violations must be seen by the world as human rights violations. He urged NGOs and other agencies to return home to advocate that those states who have influence should take up their responsibility and stand behind UNHCR on this issue.

The protection issue was seen to carry over into other areas of health, education, employment and cultural adjustment. Refugee women usually have very unequal access to goods and services, which puts them in highly vulnerable situations. In addition, their specific needs are often ignored or little understood, even in the spheres of nutrition and health.

Health

Compelling presentations about the official lack of understanding of the food and health needs of women in refugee camps were made by Angela Berry and Roxanne Murphy. Women are still seen primarily as mothers and reproducers, and their health needs relating to their role as producers are often forgotten. Men are usually chosen — for reasons of speed, or because they speak the language of the UN or NGO, or because they are better educated — to provide health training and services. The voices and needs of women are simply not heard, and their special health problems remain unaddressed. These can include, for example, food taboos harmfully restricting their diets; circumcision; sexually transmitted diseases; childhood marriage; or their special energy needs because of their roles as collectors of water and firewood, and as pounders of grain. Their mental health problems, caused by disruption, abuse or rape, are totally ignored in most refugee situations. Yet women are frequently suffering from chronic stress, and are alone as household heads for the first time: many are pregnant or have small children.

Angela Berry focused on the politics of power in food aid. Food is now increasingly being used as a weapon, and control over food resources is one of the root causes of famine and forced migration in conflict situations. She explored some of the macro-political factors affecting the control of food and food aid between countries, and then went on to look at the politics of food aid at the camp level. In the camps, the distribution of food is a central source of power. Although there are 7 million refugees in camps, and most of them are women and children, men control the food supply. Inevitably, food distribution as a form of power is open to exploitation and consequently the most vulnerable (women and women-headed households) are often mistreated.

Within households, women are usually last in the pecking order, so in times of food scarcity they get very little. Angela Berry spoke of the suffering of women she has seen in over twenty different refugee situations throughout the world. In Africa, in addition to issues of the quantity of food aid and its distribution, the lack of minerals and vitamins in the rations provided have had a very serious effect on refugee populations — especially on women because of their reproductive role. Deficiency diseases lead to many unnecessary deaths, and yet there is still no plan to fortify basic rations for refugees in Africa. She reminded the audience that every loaf of bread in Europe is fortified, yet this is not done for the hungry. Scurvy, particularly among pregnant and lactating women, is now endemic among refugees in the Horn of Africa.

Many common issues emerged from the geographical and cultural diversity. These included the absence of women at decision-making levels within the institutions dealing with refugees. The concerns and perspectives of women refugees are not usually discussed at the highest levels, indeed little is known about them and there is almost no research on them. In UNHCR there are two women out of fifteen staff in the technical services, and similar or worse figures would hold true for NGOs and host government agencies. At the grassroots level there is little attempt to involve the refugee women themselves in food distribution, health training, decision making about employment, education and training, and there were strong statements that refugee women want a voice. They want to take more control over their own lives and make their needs understood, so that outsiders can start to address their real problems, assist them better in their main roles, and build on their abilities.

Employment

In discussing employment, these themes were reiterated. Many projects designed by agencies for women do not meet women's real needs and only add to their workload. This is true of many income generating projects. Women wanted access to more training and education so that they themselves could increase their potential; at present, many projects keep women at a minimal skills and income level. These discussions were enlivened particularly by the exchange of extremely diverse experiences across continents. For some Central American refugees the key issues were first, access to formal employment, and second, that for those in informal employment the primary focus should not be on competitive marketing but rather on building co-operatives and teaching new forms of community co-operation. For many in Africa the priority was to eke out a meagre existence under harsh economic conditions. Some excellent examples of good practice came out of Central and Latin America where, in some countries, employment for women refugees is accorded a proper status. Conversely, it emerged that, in other countries, refugee women are ultra-exploited by transnational companies and have no rights at all. They are extremely vulnerable members of the labour force.

In many refugee situations it was said that women may not need income generating projects, but rather adequate protection or childcare facilities, training or better access to food and water so that, where it is possible, they can find time to earn money from activities they know how to do, in their own way. The lack of appropriate employment opportunities for women refugees in so many situations, especially for those who head households, were seen as a major factor pushing many refugee women into prostitution, in and outside the camps.

Education

Education emerged as a priority area for women refugees, as it is for all refugees. Living in a hostile environment with little immediate hope of a return home, education is seen as an essential tool for survival for themselves and their children. In long-term refugee situations, education is seen as the only way to create a better future for the next generation. The women wanted education for their children to be set up immediately during the emergency phase; it was seen as essential as food, shelter and health care. The women voiced a deep need for literacy classes, basic training courses and language training for themselves because they need new skills in refugee situations. The priority placed on education by all groups of refugee women at the Assembly has not, as yet, been taken up by most NGOs or international agencies.

For the future

Underlying all the discussions, speeches, and resolutions was a primary concern that the international agencies must address themselves to root causes. They must find ways to work towards reducing the relentlessly growing number of refugees around the world, caused by wars, civil strife, human rights' violations and oppression. The level of political and economic analysis and understanding shown by many of the participants around major issues such as debt, trans-national expansion, the arms trade, militarisation, and superpower rivalry, was sophisticated and deeply felt. They saw little future in only treating the symptoms — refugees — while ignoring the political and economic causes.

The Assembly, which was organised by the Coordinating Group of Women Refugees based in Geneva, produced a detailed set of recommendations on each of the main areas: protection, health, cultural adjustment, education and employment. These, along with guidelines for working with refugee women, have been published and are being distributed as widely as possible to agencies, governments and NGOs working with refugees all over the world. Working with refugee women provides one of the first steps in looking at and understanding the realities and needs of refugee women in different countries throughout the world. Only when these are known can UNHCR, NGOs and others work with refugee women to improve their situation.

The challenge is there, now it is time to meet it; or, as one delegate from South Africa so graphically put it, 'to take the lion by the whiskers'.

References

Kelly, N. (1989), *Working with Refugee Women: a practical guide*, Geneva: International NGO Working Group on Refugee Women.

FOOD PRODUCTION AND THE FOOD CRISIS IN AFRICA

ANN WHITEHEAD

There is a long-term crisis in agricultural production in many countries in Sub-Saharan Africa. Drought and famine years aside, and notwithstanding the effects of political and military disturbances, the farming base is increasingly incapable of supporting, in income or food terms, many of the rural populations on whom national governments and urban populations depend. This effect of the world economic recession within African economies requires a redirection — and successful redirection — of resources to agricultural development in the context of protecting overall economic development. This article examines the role of women in this agricultural crisis, and suggests how aid policies can deal with the interlinkage between the sexual division of labour and the food crisis, especially in the smallholder sector.

Concern over Africa's food crises has focused attention in the last decade on the sexual division of labour in African agriculture. One stereotyped view is that food crises have arisen because the economic changes of the twentieth century have relegated rural women to food production within an under-resourced 'subsistence sector' of small-scale agriculture. This article contests this simplification, arguing for a more complex understanding of the links between the changing structure of gender relations in African farming households and the crises in food production and availability. Women farmers' relation to imperialism is different from that of male farmers, and these differences must be the focus of economic and political analysis. It is also argued here that increasing gender conflict is a response to economic stress and poverty among many strata of peasants and is a symptom of the deep economic crisis in Africa.

The early and mid-1980s in sub-Saharan Africa were marked by full-scale famine in some countries and precarious rainfall in others; also by international awareness of a deepening crisis in food security in the continent as a whole. Debate about the possible causes of, and remedies for, this food crisis coincided with the rise of a vociferous 'Women in Development' lobby which pointed out the very substantial role that women play in food production in sub-Saharan Africa. As a result, discussion focused on the link between the food crisis and women's role in African food production. A dominant view developed that socio-economic change had resulted in rural women being 'relegated to the subsistence sector'.

This model pictures African agriculture as sharply divided between a low-productivity 'subsistence' sector with unimproved techniques and a cash-cropping sector of modern high-productivity techniques. In Women's Role in Economic Development, Ester Boserup used this model to popularise the idea that sub-Saharan Africa had initially been a female farming area, and that modernisation had captured men but had left women behind. Some of these men migrated to urban employment, yet others became heavily engaged in the production of agricultural exports. Boserup's work, which has been very influential, was exceedingly important for bringing to the attention of policy makers and academics the productive roles of rural women. It also contributed to the idea that African agriculture exhibited a dualism based on gender: a cash crop sector in which men grow high-income-earning export crops, and a food crop sector in which women use traditional methods to produce food for their families to consume. For some commentators the diversion of resources to export cash crop production was closely bound up with the development of food shortages.

It is still not widely realised that research has shown that this model is far too crude, for a number of reasons, not least of which is the enormous variety in the nature of contemporary African agricultural systems. African men have long grown and continue to grow food crops for self-consumption and women also work on cash crops and are engaged in market production. Cash crops are sometimes food crops, for example maize, groundnuts and rice. Both cash and food crops are grown using a wide variety of techniques; and not all cash crops are grown with modern inputs by any means, for example, groundnuts and cocoa in West Africa. Research on the sexual division of labour has shown that Boserup overstated the extent of female labour in African farming systems and underestimated their involvement in the 'modern' sector of the economy.

Nevertheless it is true that men and women do have a different relationship to the agricultural sector as a whole and that African farming families need to grow food both for consumption and for cash income. The main problem is not that cash cropping produces rural starvation, nor that food production is in the hands of under-resourced women, but that there is a competition over which crops should be allocated the scarce resources of land, labour, fertiliser and other inputs. Men and women, because of their different economic roles within the family, experience this competition differently.

In famine and food crises women suffer most

Although we do not have the kind of statistical information for rural Africa that we can blaze across the headlines, the information that is available suggests that in food crises and possibly in famines, it is the women who suffer most. This is not because they are physically more vulnerable, because they have babies and rear children (although this must be a factor). Firstly, it is because women are less mobile; when a food crisis hits, men tend to leave to look for work or income to buy food in towns. Women usually have to stay in the rural areas and sit it out. Secondly, food crises hit the poor first and hardest.

The poorest group in rural Africa are women and children living in female-headed households. Large numbers of women-headed households are increasingly the reality in tropical Africa. Indeed, the process of retrenchment into poverty, of women and children, as a result of the world recession, is one of the most important things to emerge as a result of the recent UNICEF studies on poverty. Recovery from food crisis and famine as the good years arrive, does not appear to bring these women and children back up to reasonable levels of income and welfare. The food crisis contributes to the development of this predominantly female pauperised stratum.

Women's economic roles in the farm family

To understand women's roles in agriculture requires a careful examination of the nature of the African farm household and women's economic position within it. In addition to that domestic work, and work transforming raw agricultural products into food supplies, for which women are almost universally responsible, most

African women have always done, and still do, independent productive work. Economically they are not expected to rely completely on their husbands or families but to have separate work of their own. Earlier this century, there were places where, in addition to other economic activities, women grew the bulk of the food crops, most of which were consumed by their immediate and extended families. Elsewhere they did a great deal of trading and marketing, while food farming was the men's responsibility.

These different areas of men's and women's work were organised within many kinds of sexual division of labour which were an essential part of rural kinship and households. Although there were numerous aspects to the various family, kinship and household relations of rural African societies, an important dimension was the way in which they organised the exchange of labour between people. This social exchange of labour was not confined to households and could range widely between them, especially where households were small, and/or matrifocal and/or changed frequently in composition. Nevertheless, for many women (and often for younger men too), membership of the rural household meant that they were regarded as lower in status than its senior men or its male head. These men could call upon their social inferiors to work for them, and a wife's most significant obligations could be to work for her husband and his senior close kinsmen.

The effect was that many women combined farming independently for themselves with work done as unpaid labourers on the farms of others. This provided two very different kinds of social environment for their economic effort. For their independent work women required effective access to resources, including land to farm. Many African feminists have pointed out the importance of these guaranteed rights to resources for rural women in the precolonial economies. Complex conventions surrounded a woman's rights to dispose of the crops she produced and her obligations to share them with her children, husband and others but in this independent work she did have direct access to the agricultural produce from her land. The work she did for a husband and other senior men was also surrounded by complex claims and obligations. Here the return for her labour was not direct, and if thought of as a return at all, was seen in the context of her general rights to welfare and maintenance as a household member or wife. Occasionally some work took the form of a contract between husband and wife, the terms of which could be negotiated.

All these arrangements were in the context of a domestic economy in which there was no assumption of an automatic sharing of resources in marriage. Land, cattle, hoes, money, clothes, domestic utensils and much else tended to be owned separately by the husband and the wife. So, too, it was rare for there to be a joint family budget or a single common purse out of which family needs were met. Rather, the separate resources of husbands and wives, which were the basis for their independent economic activities, also involved ways of keeping their incomes separate. These often included divided responsibilities for different aspects of household spending and consumption, for example for the clothes or medical and other needs of children, and a complex division of responsibilities for providing different items of food. (Whitehead, 1981.)

The important contribution made by rural women to African agriculture was realised within this dual work role in a household setting characterised by separate budgets and negotiated responsibilities. These aspects of women's work need to be understood in order to see what has happened to women within the changed economies of contemporary Africa.

Economic transformation and women's work

During the last century, the African smallholder sector has seen a historical process, largely under the impact of colonial policies, in which rural work burdens have been increased. Male labour has seeped away to urban employment or into agricultural employment with the development of commercial agriculture. Women's agricultural work burdens have increased, with relatively little increase in productivity. It is true to say that as a result many rural African women's work burdens are now intolerably high, and this contributes to rural hunger. Some reports link malnutrition in children to women not having enough time left in the day to cook when they get back from the fields. Also because their work burdens are high, some analysts argue that the food crisis arises because there is no possibility of getting women to produce more food without substantially changing the levels of productivity in farming.

I think the picture is even more complicated than this. While it is true that women work too hard, and improved productivity in

African farming is an important factor, many structural and institutional features effect the utilisation of the resources of land, labour and inputs that are already available. The development of more commercial agriculture has created considerable economic pressure which in the case of women is of two main kinds.

Firstly, in their work as independent farmers mainly growing food crops, women are finding it very difficult to get the resources they need; they lose out against men in the competition for land, for labour and for improved agricultural inputs. As more land is taken into production and as it becomes scarce, so women have had difficulty in protecting their land rights on the basis of either local or state codified procedures and laws. The resource base for their independent farming is therefore undermined.

At the same time an increasing proportion of the woman's labour time has been spent in production for her husband, and wives' labour has become relatively more important within the total family labour supply. Most development projects write a woman's labour in as family labour, without checking whether it will be available and what the costs are of her foregoing her work in other areas. When African households' cash requirements were increased by colonial rule either directly (by tax demands) or indirectly (by new consumption goods), the main immediate avenues for earning such income were men's cash cropping or migrant labour. Women members of the household were able to make their contribution to increased cash needs by their work as family labour in cash cropping, or by increased trading. In the initial phases of these processes, insofar as women's welfare was bound up with that of their households, there were simple incentives for them to do this work.

The second pressure arises because, over time, these decisions to undertake more work as 'family labourers' have taken on new economic meanings. As the terms of trade declined for peasants, as land became scarce, and as rural differentiation proceeded, there was increasing evidence of acute stresses and strains. There is no guarantee that the increase in labour time now required for peasant domestic and productive activities affects men and women equally. Among the poorer peasantry, female-headed households emerge as one response to this economic stress. Additionally, as Pepe Roberts explains, the wives' situation as 'unfree labour became increasingly important to the household as commodity relations destroyed other bonds securing non-free labour (e.g. that of sons) to the peasant household' (Roberts, 1983). This increasing demand for women's labour is reflected in several reports of increased rates of polygamy as well as of conjugal conflict as commodity production increased. The potential for coercion within the customary obligations of a married woman to her husband may become an important element in her increased workload.

In general, women obviously have much greater control over how they spend their income and who benefits from their own independent farm work. It is very much harder for them to determine the spending patterns of the 'household' income from their work as family labour. Different spending preferences between husbands and wives, including different assessments of the importance of children's welfare, reduce the incentive for women to do this family labour. There is widespread evidence that some wives are resisting increased work on their husband's fields because of the welfare effects on themselves and their children. In this case the problem is not the heaviness of the work burdens but whether women perceive any benefit to themselves or their children from working much harder.

Yet all the members of the family need both food production and cash cropping to take place within it. Many items of household consumption must necessarily be bought (e.g. clothes) and withdrawal from the market would imply a deplorable level of unmet basic needs. It is in this light that we should reconsider the struggle over household income. Rural women complain at the selfish way men spend and men complain reciprocally at the constant financial demands from wives. In reality husband and wife have conventionally been allotted different responsibilities for spending, which come into conflict in conditions of economic stress. Women may be particularly responsible for short-term spending — for example, for food — while men are responsible for long-term spending, especially the purchase of farming inputs. Both are essential to survival but where there is not enough income to meet both, impoverishment is experienced as sharp domestic conflict.

Similar considerations apply for the growing number of female-headed households. Abandoned by their husbands and sons, women blame modern men's low standards of personal responsibility, while men argue that women drive them away with unacceptable sexual or domestic conduct and their new desires for

personal freedom. The mutually expressed anger and disappointment obscure poverty as a source of crisis. The main problem here is
not the selfishness of rural African men. It is the poverty of many
peasant farming households and the way development projects
plan for family production.

Extension services, agricultural innovation and planning intervention

Let me now turn from African farmers, men and women, to the
form of intervention that national and international development
planning involves and the role of African states and international
agencies.

Whether or not they are successful in their own terms, many
rural development projects funded by a combination of overseas
and national agencies appear to make women worse off. Small
wonder then that there are often reports of women resisting these
changes; in some cases projects have failed because of women's
resistance to their role within them.

This cruel paradox — development making women poorer — is
what underlies some of the food crisis, so sorting out the reasons for
it are important for the wellbeing of all. Examining these projects,
we find they have a depressingly similar format. One problem is
that many projects ignore the scale and significance of women's
independent farming; leave it unmodernised, and recruit women
primarily to work as family labour in their husbands' fields. This
kind of project leads to poor utilisation of limited resources and
exacerbates the conflict between men and women within the family.

African women farmers may be placed in difficult and
contradictory situations in which an unenviable choice may have to
be made. They may, for example, have to choose between loss of
autonomy and poverty. As a 'family labourer', a woman will lose
the autonomy of independent farming. However, she may produce
more crops and more income: as an unpaid labourer for her
husband she may become better off if she helps him become
successful. More important, she may also feel that her children's
welfare is more secure. However, in addition to a lack of control
over spending and welfare decisions, as unpaid workers women do
not build up their long-term resources. The decision to do more
unpaid family work may hook a woman into a dependence which
leaves her very insecure at times of crisis.

But there are other problems. Firstly, historically speaking, the direction and objectives of much agricultural planning and research has definitely not involved a two-pronged strategy of increasing both local food crop production, and cash crop production. Rather, it has neglected food crops, such as millet and yams, in favour of cash crops, such as rice, coffee or cattle farming.

The database is a second problem. Women's role in farming is partly ignored or misunderstood because their work was, and remains, largely invisible in national statistics. This results partly from international conventions about what constitutes work (mainly production for the market, or paid work); from data collection methods; and from stereotypes that both African and European men hold about women's contribution to the economy.

A third problem is much less widely recognised, but emerges very strongly from recent research. It is that there is widespread, systematic and simple sexual discrimination against women in agricultural delivery systems.

I say 'simple' sexual discrimination because not only are there few women in agricultural extension work, and not only are women's crops not targeted for improvement, but innovative, efficient and resourced women farmers are ignored in favour of less endowed and less efficient male farmers (Standt, 1985). A major source of these attitudes is in Western development and agricultural extension training.

Misogyny in development and planning agencies combines with women's disadvantage in access to resources to produce considerable divisions between rural men and women. The reluctance to address this social conflict arises partly because of ideologies which protect family and domestic behaviour from public scrutiny, but it also looks uncannily like a male alliance between 'patriarchal' male farmers and sexist male bureaucrats.

It is a major failing of development projects that they are based on a conceptual model of the African family farm which does not reflect the complex and particular forms of their social relations described above. The planners' model centres on the idea of the conjugally based household as an economic enterprise in which the members work together. The husband/father is regarded as managing the resources on behalf of other members, and those others, conceptualised as his dependents, as providing labour under his direction. Hence the projects require a family labour input from household members (especially wives) other than the supposed male head. Sub-Saharan African domestic organisation, as shown, is emphatically not of this kind.

The difference between the planners' model and rural reality has important consequences. These are illustrated in a well-known example — that of largely unsuccessful attempts to introduce irrigated rice production in the Gambia (Dey, 1982). The lack of success stemmed in part from just this male-dominant, domestic sharing model of the household which shaped the project. An initial assumption was that the men were rice growers with full control over the necessary resources. Incentive packages including cheap credits, inputs and assured markets were offered to the male farmers. But it was the women who traditionally grew rice for household consumption and exchange, within the kind of complex of rights and obligations between husbands and wives discussed above. The scheme proposed to develop irrigated rice production on common lands to which women had secured use rights. Backed by project officials, men established exclusive rights to these common lands, pushing the women out to inferior scattered plots to continue cultivating traditional rice varieties. All access to inputs, labour and finance was mediated through husbands, and women became notably reluctant to participate in their planned role as family labour. Husbands had to pay their wives for what work the women did do on the irrigated rice fields. Dey and others have argued that the disappointingly low levels of improved rice production arose in part from these misunderstandings.

In other words, forms of stereotyping and discrimination which are rife in Europe and in the international agencies are being reproduced in African national agricultural ministries and extension bureaux.

Implications for policy

It is important to highlight the role of agricultural extension services, agricultural innovation and the conventions of development planning because this is an area in which the public voice in the First World has greater relevance.

Agricultural development requires a two-pronged strategy increasing the amount of food produced for self-consumption, at the same time as increasing the amount of marketed crops to provide income.

In order to do this, development intervention must recognise female farmers as part of the human resources in that agricultural strategy; and that they are farmers who face a specific set of constraints and opportunities.

Support must be given to efforts at national level which combat straightforward sexual discrimination in agricultural planning and delivery. This, together with much else of what I have said, implies projects which first listen to, then empower women to farm, within the farm household, in ways in which they can benefit from changed forms of income. This implies channelling resources directly to female-headed households and to wives. If they are written into projects as family labour, this must not been done in such a way that their husbands control all the cash income.

This paper has been adapted from the article (1990), 'Food Crisis and Gender Conflict in the African Countryside', in The Food Question: Profits versus People?, *London: Earthscan Publications.*

References

Boserup, E. (1970), *Woman's Role in Economic Development*, London: George Allen and Unwin; new edition, (1989), London: Earthscan Publications.

Whitehead, A. (1981), 'I'm hungry mum: the politics of domestic budgeting', in Young, K., McCullagh, R. and Wolkowitz, C. (eds), *Of Marriage and the Market*, London: CSE Books.

Dey, J. (1982),'Development planning in The Gambia: the gap between planners' and farmers' perceptions, expectations and objectives', *World Development*, 10: 5; see also Carney, J. (1988), 'Struggles over crop rights and labour within contract farming households in a Gambian irrigated rice project', *Journal of Peasant Studies*, 15: 3.

Roberts, P. (1983), 'Feminism in Africa; feminism and Africa', *Review of African Political Economy*, 27/28.

Staudt, K. (1985), 'Agricultural policy implementation: a case study from Western Kenya', in *Women's Roles and Gender Differences in Development, Case Studies for Planners*, prepared by the Population Council, West Hartford: Kumarian Press.

Ann Whitehead teaches at the University of Sussex, in the School of Social Sciences, and has written and researched for a number of years on issues to do with women in rural production in sub-Saharan Africa.

2

BARRIERS TO WOMEN'S DEVELOPMENT

Introduction
Tina Wallace

In this section, the issue of gender is approached from a different perspective: that of the specific experiences of women in different countries. We look at some of the barriers they face when trying to overcome discrimination and related poverty, or to change the relations between women and men. While the particular problems and opportunities facing women vary greatly according to the culture they live in and their individual circumstances (their class, race, economic situation and whether or not they are married), there are a number of themes that are common to many (poor) Third World women. The themes we focus on here are the lack of access to formal education, to adequate health care, to secure, reasonably paid employment; and the cultural, religious or state attitudes which inhibit change and keep women in socially inferior roles.

Heavy demands are placed on women to maintain the domestic economy and contribute to production; increasing numbers of women are now household heads and solely responsible for family maintenance. Yet at the same time they often cannot get access to key resources or support, and have to continue to try to meet their responsibilities under adverse conditions.

A number of the articles focus on women's poor health: their particular health problems and some of the causes of these, their lack of access to appropriate health care, and negative attitudes towards their health needs. This does not mean that issues such as women's access to education, employment, land or animals, or law are less important: each of these merits a book in their own right! Rather, we are using health issues as an example to illustrate how attitudes and behaviour towards women seriously limit their access to the critical resources necessary to improve their daily lives, and are thus development issues.

In the first article in this section, Julia Cleves Mosse clearly shows how attitudes to women in India are rooted in the culture of that society; the custom of paying a dowry profoundly affects the position of women there. It means that girls are seen as a financial liability to their families from birth; dowry can be a very heavy burden, especially for poor families. Recently, this has led to an increasing incidence of female foeticide (the aborting of babies if they are found by tests to be female), which is now possible with modern medical technology. The negative attitude to daughters means that, if and when girls are born, they often receive less food, health care, and education than their brothers. Early marriage, and pregnancy while they are still young, compound the health problems they experience — health problems which are usually left untreated.

The discrimination discussed by Julia Cleves Mosse in India is also seen in the summary by Hosne Ara Khan of the health problems of women in Bangladesh. She stresses that the ill-health experienced by poor women is caused by their low income, their lack of education, and the bad environmental conditions they are expected to endure because of their low status. Yet women's health needs often remain unrecognised. While the specific cultural practices vary, the outcome in many countries is the same: that many of women's real health needs remain unrecognised and untreated.

Claudia Garcia Moreno takes up this theme of active discrimination against women within the health sector, focusing on AIDS. Her article shows how negative attitudes towards women, especially prostitutes, have until very recently meant that women in the Third World have primarily been seen as transmitters of AIDS, i.e. the cause of the problem, not as sufferers from AIDS. While AIDS in the Third World is primarily spread through heterosexual relationships, AIDS control programmes have totally failed to consider women's needs as both sufferers from AIDS and as the main carers for AIDS patients. She graphically describes the implications of this approach for women, both for prostitutes and the wives of male carriers of HIV. This prejudiced approach to the problems of women and AIDS is echoed in the interview with the prostitute in Brazil, where it is clear that women's lack of rights in the eyes of the Church and the State mean that prostitutes are open to abuse, including violence from individuals and the police. Yet most women are pushed into prostitution for economic reasons and come from the poverty-stricken areas of the country; lacking education, their only options for employment are extremely low paid jobs as servants, or prostitution. The majority of prostitutes suffer triple discrimination because of their class, race and gender. The issue of dowry appears again in the case of Brazil: because of the need for the payment of a dowry, families may push one daughter into prostitution to pay for the dowry of another daughter.

These issues of women's lack of status and rights in the field of reproduction and sexuality are vividly brought to life by a poem, written by a Somalian woman who writes of the triple sorrows of women — in this case, female circumcision which causes many women to suffer pain during intercourse and childbirth. The poem speaks powerfully of the subservient position of women in the society and the woman's need to obey and accept her suffering silently.

Women have few rights to education, employment, health care, land and productive resources in many societies. In addition, women have heavy workloads both within the home and in their productive activities. Very little new technology has been developed for use by women in domestic or agricultural work; and yet women's heavy workload undermines their health, and limits their ability to become involved in organising, meeting together, decision making and other aspects of social development. Even when technology is introduced, for example mills or water pumps, it is usually taken over by men, thus removing the processes from women's control (see Brian Mathew in Section Four on water technology). Women are seldom able to benefit in terms of increased time for rest or income earning activity.

Heavy workloads, their domestic responsibilities, their restriction to low paid and insecure seasonal work, their lack of land/animal rights combined with 'macho' attitudes upheld through education, religion and the mass media, are all major barriers to women becoming involved in organisations or development programmes at the decision-making level. Their participation is confined all too often to providing the labour and support, and so they lack an effective voice in community organisations, unions and political parties; and as a result, their interests are ignored. Eugenia Piza Lopez describes the way these factors intertwine to undermine women's confidence and keep them marginalised. Suzanne Williams looks at the changing roles of women and women's organisations in the long struggle against apartheid in South Africa.

However, the situation of women is not static; attitudes, economic conditions, and social behaviour change over time. In many countries in the Third World, the economic and other crises discussed in Section One have accelerated all kinds of changes, some of which have profound implications for women. Doris Burgess (in Section Four) shows how war has brought about dramatic changes in gender roles and relations. As conditions change, and with painstaking education, it is possible to counteract women's lack of confidence and men's anxieties, and genuinely involve women in pioneering development work. Rhoda Ibrahim closes this section with another example, from Somalia, of how social and economic changes are affecting the roles and status of women. The traditions of Somali culture are that women are very subservient to men, with little or no economic or social independence. Changes brought about by the liberation struggle, urbanisation, increasing education, and the rise in the number of female headed households, are altering the lives of both men and women, especially in towns. She describes how many men are trying to resist these changes and keep women in their more traditional roles, finding it hard to accept the new position of women in urban Somalia. She argues that development agencies need to understand and relate to these changes and give support to both women and men in their new roles and relations.

THE RISKS OF BEING FEMALE

JULIA CLEVES MOSSE

'Better 500 now than 5 lakhs later'

'Pay 60 plus 60 and get a desired child'

So run the hoardings in Bombay, blatantly advertising the availability of amniocentesis and the selective termination of female foetuses who, if not quietly dealt with now, may cost Rs 500,000 in dowry payments later on. Amniocentesis is in the headlines in India at the moment. But so too are dowry and the ever increasing toll of dowry death (*sati*), the sex-ratio and the higher female mortality rate; if you read the right journals you can read about all sorts of practices that systematically discriminate against girls and women.

This article will chart some of the risks of being conceived — and born — female in India. There are inherent dangers in a white woman writing about discrimination in a country not her own, with the implication that somehow Indian citizens are more culpable, more sexist than people in the West. But by focusing on the blatant, institutionalised sexism experienced by women in India, as reflected in the mortality figures for example, the subtle but equally pervasive forms of sexism in the West come more clearly into focus. More specifically the stand of the Indian women's movement against female foeticide, dowry, early marriage and other discriminatory practices raises significant questions about abortion, property relations in marriage and teenage sexuality in the West.

Amniocentesis and the subsequent abortion of female foetuses is a sufficiently established activity for the Government of Maharashtra to have put a recent ban on the practice. Bombay has frequently been cited as the leading centre of sex-determination tests, with the service being offered by most leading gynaecologists, maternity homes and abortion clinics. It is difficult to get hold of reliable statistics to indicate the extent of the problem, for obvious reasons. One article in *The Times of India* cites statistics from a 1985 seminar in Delhi in which it was claimed that of 8,000 abortions following amniocentesis only one involved a male foetus. According to another survey 78,000 female foetuses were aborted between 1978 and 1982, while a survey carried out by the Government of Maharashtra put the annual number of tests carried out at 50,000 (*Social Welfare*, 1987). Following the ban in Maharashtra an interesting debate is developing in the press, exposing the limitations, and openness to abuse, of the concept of 'abortion: a woman's right to choose'.

The anti-sex-testing movement has articulate spokespersons; no one is deluding themselves as to the extent of the problem and how deeply this technology is rooted in the anti-female sentiments of Indian society. In an interview conducted by the journal *Social Welfare*, the director of a family welfare project described sex-testing as 'like alcohol, it knows neither class or caste barriers. All sections of the population, irrespective of their social standing are hypnotized by this magic wand to eliminate the female' (*Social Welfare*, 1987). The women's movement recognises that the demand for dowry lies at the heart of the problem. Only when social reform takes place in all levels of society, and the grip of the dowry system is loosened, will the negative attitude towards daughters be lessened.

The women's movement, however, confronts major opposition from those who see female foeticide as a logical solution to the problem of unwanted daughters. If 7,999 female foetuses are aborted for every male foetus, the argument goes, what would be their chance of survival through infancy and childhood, the pitfalls of adolescence and dowry marriage? The cynicism of this approach neatly twists feminist arguments as to the necessity of legal abortion for women to control their own bodies, back on itself. If a woman has a right to choose, why shouldn't she choose whom she adds to her family? In an article in *The Times of India*, J.B.D'Souza offered his support for amniocentesis and abortion, taking the notion of individual freedom to an uncomfortable conclusion: 'It is sad that in a matter so intimate, personal and private as the choice of an addition to your family you may lose the freedom to choose.' (*The Times of India*, 1988). It will be interesting to see what effect, if any, government measures to prohibit sex-testing will have.

But surviving gestation is not the end of discrimination. In a survey carried out by three doctors in the Punjab, in which they studied the progress of 1,500 infants born in the 32 months following August 1977, they came to some disturbing conclusions. Having already noted that 55.5 per cent of the children who died were 'females of the underprivileged communities' they wrote the following:

> 'We have found that the only female who is high priority is the first born, so long as she is the only living child. However, a subsequent pregnancy or a delivery of a male diminishes her priority status... This is particularly true of the underprivileged whose response to nutrition and health education for the third and fourth female is often: *Let her die...* the accuracy of this subjective assessment has been confirmed by field workers and medical staff in homes of nearly 1,000 infants over a four year period, and *team leaders and field workers are able to predict at birth and by continuous assessment which children will be neglected and are therefore high priority targets for extra efforts.'* (*Future*, 1982)

The low priority of girl children is borne out by infant mortality rates (India has one of the lowest sex ratios in the world with only 935 females to every 1,000 men, compared to 1,060 females per 1,000 men in the UK), nutritional surveys and hospital registers, which show that medical attention is sought much later for girls than boys. Education and literacy rates provide further evidence of the low priority parents give to furthering the life chances of their daughters. While in 1978, 61.73 per cent of boys were enrolled in primary schools, only 32.3 per cent of girls had the same advantage. And while by 1981 almost half of the adult male population of India were literate, less than a quarter of women could read and write. Girls are expected to participate in the domestic life of the household long before their brothers, and despite the hours they put into minding siblings, fetching water and firewood and helping with the cooking, they frequently get less to eat.

The move into adult status, marriage and childbirth represents a shift in the complex web of relationships in the extended family. Through the work of childbearing, women gain acceptance and status, but not without attendant physical risks. Of an estimated 4.5 million marriages in India each year nearly 2.5 million appear to be in the 15-19 age group; 55 per cent of girls under 19 are already married, with every other village girl and one in four urban girls having husbands. In some parts of India, especially in the north, the figures for marriage for girls under 19 are higher, rising to 65 per cent. The 1981 census revealed that 6.59 per cent of girls aged 10-14 are already married.

The significance of early marriage and consequent early childbearing is not simply that it cuts short childhood, educational opportunities and raises the birth rate rapidly by diminishing the gap between the generations. In personal physical terms rapid childbearing, especially if it begins around the age of 15, brings with it considerable risks both to the mother and the baby. The onset of puberty may mean that a girl is fertile; it does not necessarily mean that she has reached sexual maturity and can cope easily with pregnancy and birth. Pregnancy puts a halt to growth, and so a girl who is pregnant at 15 is denied the advantage of the better growth and better body build that would have occurred if she had been able to put off pregnancy for another four years. The WHO standard for considering high risk pregnancy puts a cut-off point on 145cm in height and 38kg body weight. A study in Kerala showed that as many as two-thirds of 15 year olds were below this point, but only 19-23 per cent of 19 year olds fell into this category. Kerala, with a mean marrying age of 22 for women, has an accordingly low maternal and infant mortality rate.

Early childbearing results in high maternal mortality. While statistics from developed countries show maternal mortality rates of around 10-20 per 100,000 live births, in India rates vary from 418-592. (Other sources put the figure even higher.) One in four deaths in adult women stem from pregnancy and childbirth, and for every death there is a far greater toll of sickness and malaise.

Maternal mortality tends to be age specific. A recent study in Bangladesh suggested that a woman under 20 is twice as likely to die as a woman between 21 and 25. Girls becoming pregnant between the ages of 10 and 14 face appalling risks, with a maternal mortality rate of 5 girls in every 300. Girls who married under 18 have everything stacked against them. Given that they may have three or more pregnancies by the time they are 20, they risk giving birth while physically immature, they face the risks that increase after three births, and the risks that accrue when babies are born too close to each other. The risks are severe anaemia, bleeding, complicated labour, toxaemia and premature, low-birth-weight babies, and of course, death. In addition to this there is the tragic toll of infant mortality to women who bear children when they themselves are not fully grown. A hospital-based survey in Delhi showed that mothers under 15 faced a perinatal rate of 166 per 1,000 babies while for mothers between 20 and 29 the rate dropped to 68. We have already noted that among deaths in the first year, it is the daughters who are more likely to die. (*Future*, 1987.)

What are we to make of these statistics? For behind each statistically 'significant' death lie the lives of thousands of women, their daughters and sons about whom we know nothing. On their own, statistics tell us nothing, except that statistically speaking the dice seem to be stacked against being a girl or a woman in India. They say nothing about the tug between economic forces and familial ties, the reasons why women may act against the interests of their daughters. And even while the statistics tell one story, most women will tell you another. There is a paradox at the heart of the attitude towards daughters in India. The anthropologist Margaret Egnor came to the conclusion that for South Indians at least, the most profound bond of all is that between mother and daughter, a 'bond which is felt to be part of all growth, of all continuance and creation. The bringing to birth of one like oneself, who in turn will bear another, is an image engraved everywhere in Tamil culture.' But Tamil Nadu is also the State where pockets of female infanticide can be found. That the relationship between mothers and daughters is fraught with conflict is clear from folk songs and stories. The daughter cries out to her mother to save her from the separation and pain marriage will certainly bring:

> ...O mother who bore me, O father,
> I am an uncrushed body, mother.
> They crush me and take me away.
> In this town without you, they make me suffer harm.
> I am red gram, mother;
> O father who bore me, O mother,
> I am gold with unbending body, mother.
> They bend me and take me away.
> In this town without you, they make me suffer pain.

(*Another Harmony: New Essays on the Folklore of India*, 1986)

But mothers inevitably let their daughters go and the circle repeats itself.

References

Anjali, (1987), 'Prejudice Against Girls; Abuse of Scientific Discovery', *Social Welfare*, December, p. 10.

Mohanty, P. (1987), 'On Female Foeticide', *Social Welfare*, December, p. 14.

D'Souza, J.B. (1988), *The Times of India*, 10 January, p. 3.

Das, D., Dhanoa, J. and Cowan, B. (1982),'Letting them live', *Future*, third quarter, p. 51.

Chhabra, R., Raleigh, V. and Jindal, A. (1987), 'Early Marriage, high fertility and poor health', *Future 21*, pp. 35-38.

'Internal Iconicity in Paraiyar 'Crying Songs'', in *Another Harmony: New Essays on the Folklore of India*, edited by Stuart H. Blackburn and A. K. Ramanujan, (Delhi: Oxford University Press, 1986), pages 307, 330. The reference to 'gram' is to a type of Indian pulse, which is crushed to make flour.

Julia Cleves Mosse is a freelance writer specialising in the area of women, health and development. Publications include (with Josephine Heaton) The Fertility and Contraception Book *(Faber 1990). She is currently living and working in India.*

WOMEN'S HEALTH IN BANGLADESH

HOSNE ARA KHAN

Health is determined not only by physical make up but also by socio-economic status. Patriarchal society limits women in many ways including their diet, the division of labour and the way that they relate to their family. These all have a direct impact on women's health.

A breakdown of the life expectancy statistics show that women do not live as long as men. Is this because of women's physiology, or because of the nature of women's lives, their work and discrimination?

Low levels of income and education, and bad environmental conditions all have detrimental effects on health. Poor women suffer both from diseases caused by poverty, for example malnourishment which may lead to chronic diseases such as anaemia, as well as diseases caused by a lack of knowledge of basic hygiene. Despite this, ailments that are considered serious for men are often unrecognised in women. In Bangladeshi society it is an unwritten rule that a woman is forbidden to become sick. She is used as machinery for domestic and social work as long as her body will support her and any illness is always neglected. She only sees a doctor or receives medicine at the eleventh hour and very often only when she is bed-ridden.

Many customs discriminate against women. It is customary for female members of both rich and poor families to take food only after the males have finished eating. Women are, therefore, left with the inferior and unwanted foods and rarely eat the more nutritious ones such as eggs, milk and meat. Thus women, and especially poor women, fall victims to malnutrition.

The impact of women's labour and their long work days is often ignored since the work, although it includes diverse and heavy tasks, is usually invisible, without any economic or social recognition. No-one considers the health hazards of working in smoke-filled rooms when cooking yet while cooking women inhale up to 40 times the volume of suspended particles considered safe by the World Health Organisation. When women venture outside the home in search of work, they are faced with a gender-biased division of labour created by their society's norms. Forms of employment open to women in Bangladesh are, for example, sewing in the garment industries, packaging in pharmaceutical industries and cleaning the waste from shrimps. These labour intensive jobs are often performed in poor conditions with low pay.

Little consideration is given to women's health needs outside those connected with their reproductive role. Existing mother and childcare centres are aimed primarily at the provision of birth control. Health workers tend to be male. Because of Bangladesh's Muslim culture this greatly restricts women's access to general health care; family planning workers are female. Since health policy is aimed at women as reproducers only, it effectively means that health 'care' is aimed at men.

Development of women's health is not possible in the present socio-economic climate of this patriarchal society. Discrimination is prevalent in the women's health sector as it is in other sectors. Discrimination cannot be eliminated until and unless structural changes take place in the society. Health is a gender issue.

Hosne Ara Khan is the executive director of Unity for Social and Human Action (USHA), an organisation working for gender equality in Bangladesh. She previously specialised in the area of health, working for Save the Children (USA) and Oxfam (UK), and as a consultant for other non-governmental agencies.

AIDS: WOMEN ARE NOT JUST TRANSMITTERS

CLAUDIA GARCIA-MORENO

Until recently, AIDS was perceived in the West as a problem affecting mainly homosexual men. The biggest impact of AIDS on women's lives there had been until recently as carers for people with HIV disease or AIDS. However, more women are now becoming infected and the number is likely to increase in the next few years — in New York AIDS is already the leading cause of death in women between 25 to 34.[1] In Africa and some parts of Latin America, mainly the Caribbean, HIV has always been transmitted predominantly through heterosexual sex, and in these areas AIDS has affected women and men equally.[2] Yet women have received, until recently, little attention in the AIDS literature and when they are referred to it is usually only in their role as transmitters of the infection. There has been little focus on women as sufferers from AIDS.

Prostitutes

Prostitutes especially have been singled out as a high risk group, and have even been portrayed as being responsible for the spread of the HIV and AIDS epidemic in some places. The word 'prostitute' means different things in different cultures. In some countries prostitutes are an easily identifiable group, whereas in others they are much less visible. Where prostitutes form a definable group they are accessible and easy to study and have become the focus of research in some cities of Africa.[3] They have been found to have a higher rate of HIV infection than the rest of the population and have therefore been designated a high risk group.

A common assumption in much of the AIDS literature is that prostitutes are always female. In some countries this is not the case and male prostitutes may be common. Yet women, particularly prostitutes, are frequently referred to as AIDS transmitters. While they may constitute a pool of infection, the role of their clients in transmission is rarely mentioned. Gabriella Leite, a prostitute in Brazil, put it bluntly:

'As for AIDS, official bodies, society, attempt to define it in terms of people: prostitutes, homosexuals, the promiscuous, drug users. The political question is, what about the people who frequent prostitutes? They are not regarded as a high risk group ... Sure AIDS kills, but so do many other things. Prostitutes have always been at risk of diseases and the government and health services have never lifted a finger before.'[4]

The concern with prostitutes is as transmitters of AIDS, not as sufferers. This is not new or limited to AIDS. An article from Brazil draws a comparison with what happened previously with syphilis and gonorrhoea.[5] In the 1930s and 40s a poster aimed at soldiers in World War II portrayed a young woman and underneath the caption reads:

'SHE MAY LOOK CLEAN — BUT ... pick ups, "good time" girls, prostitutes ... Spread syphilis and gonorrhoea. You can't beat the Axis if you get VD.'

This in spite of the fact that female to male transmission of gonorrhoea is documented to be around 20-25 per cent after a single exposure, and from male to female 50-80 per cent. The same article points out that although 95 per cent of the AIDS cases in Brazil are male, the official information on prevention portrays the face of a woman with the message, 'You can't see AIDS when you see the face', i.e. she may look beautiful, but ...

The possibility that a prostitute may catch HIV from an infected customer is rarely considered. For example, a study in *The Lancet* on the effectiveness of condom promotion and health education among prostitutes in Kenya concluded:[3]

'We believe that this programme has prevented the transmission of a large number of HIV infections in men ... In view of the sexual activity of these women and their high prevalence of HIV, every day approximately 3,750 men are sexually exposed to HIV through contact with them.'

The phrasing makes one wonder whether the researchers were equally concerned about the health of the women. In the Philippines 'hospitality girls' have identified this risk for themselves and together demanded testing for the men from the army who are frequent clients.

Men infecting women is never highlighted. However, in fact, the little information that is available on heterosexual transmission seems to suggest that male to female transmission is slightly higher than the other way around.[6] Also, in many African countries, men who have acquired the infection in the cities then return to their wives in rural areas and possibly start a new cycle of infection. There are anecdotal reports from some countries where HIV is prevalent in urban areas that some men are now looking for younger women in rural areas for the exchange of sexual favours, thinking that such women are less likely to be infected with HIV.

'Sex tours' for Western businessmen are well-known, particularly in some Asian countries, yet this group is not usually mentioned as a high risk group. A study of prostitutes in London showed that they were more likely to use condoms with their clients than with their own partners, even though these partners often engaged in high risk behaviour such as intravenous drug use.[7]

Harsh economic realities push women into prostitution, particularly in developing countries; for poor women on their own in urban areas there may be few choices other than becoming domestic servants or prostitutes. Often, they have been abandoned by a partner and have children to support. Women refugees also frequently end up resorting to prostitution, sometimes illegally, as their only survival strategy. With little education or access to other resources, their opportunities are non-existent, and it is unrealistic to blame prostitutes and single them out for education and other programmes without offering them some kind of economic alternative. While education may help them to protect themselves (though even as prostitutes women are not always in a position to enforce the use of condoms by their clients), for many of these women abandoning prostitution would mean destitution.

Projects which aim to support women in prostitution or women sex workers should not limit themselves to giving health education; condoms need to be made available at an affordable price. General health services, including access to birth control, are also important. It is also essential to explore alternative income generating activities with these women and to provide the relevant assistance, as well as to explore other social and economic needs they may have.

Women and AIDS in Africa

The number of women infected with HIV in some African countries is high, particularly in certain urban areas. The female to male ratio is approximately one to one i.e. at least 50 per cent, or sometimes slightly more, of those infected are women.[2] The peak incidence of infection for women in Africa is between 20 and 29 years while for men it is between 29 and 39, probably reflecting an earlier start of sexual activity for women. Yet few AIDS control programmes have considered women's particular needs; neither those of urban women nor of the wives of men returning to the rural areas bringing HIV with them.

AIDS cannot be separated from the extreme poverty, lack of resources and the heavy burden of work of women. For women the possibility of transmission to their babies is a cause for additional concern and when it occurs it adds to the guilt and worry.

Women traditionally have been the carers for children, the sick and the elderly and have already experienced the problem of caring for partners or others with AIDS. Who will take over this role for women when they themselves need to be cared for?

A research project in a capital city of an African country is following a sample of 1,500 women (selected from those attending antenatal care in the national hospital) for five years. The study, concerned with more than the research itself, has expanded to provide a valuable educational service, condoms and spermicides, and counselling for the women as well as offering counselling and testing for their partners. Discussions with the women have helped to identify areas where they would like to receive some help. Testing was carried out, with informed consent and appropriate counselling. Approximately 25 per cent of the women were found to be seropositive. Marital conflict arising after disclosure of a positive result and the role of counselling in helping to overcome this have been particularly relevant.

This study exemplifies many of the problems faced by women in relation to HIV infection and AIDS. Many of these women were single and had little in the way of social or economic support. It is a generalised assumption that in Africa the extended family provides support and care for the sick. However, among the group of HIV seropositive women interviewed, 60 per cent of them said they would not be able to rely on husband or family for support.[8] Support from self-help groups, particularly with an income generation component, was very relevant to these women.

The same study identified the needs of women with AIDS. The provision of childcare, food and funeral services were major areas of concern to them. For women who were seropositive but asymptomatic, housing and employment assistance were a higher priority, although another important consideration was concern about preparing for the future in the event of illness or death. It is important to identify priorities and needs with the women themselves and to support projects which allow them to have more control over their situation and improve their economic status whenever possible.

Many of the women experience feelings of terrible isolation after being told they are seropositive; stigmatisation is real and many have been abandoned by friends, relatives or lovers; nurses and health workers have been known to refuse care. Hopefully, this rejection will decrease with appropriate information and education. Meanwhile, in the words of 'Rosie' (a pseudonym), a sick woman in Zimbabwe:[9]

> 'That's the worst part, the loneliness...I have it (AIDS). I can't change that, but if only I could talk about it openly, and stop hiding it. People think I've got cancer, because that's what I tell them, I can't admit I have AIDS, I would be stoned.'

AIDS and children

The majority of women with HIV or AIDS are of childbearing age. HIV can be transmitted from an infected mother to her child, either during pregnancy or at birth.[10] There have been eight reported cases so far where transmission has been possibly related to breast-milk, all of them in special circumstances.[10] (Present evidence is that the benefits of breast-feeding far exceed the potential risks and breast-feeding should continue to be encouraged.)

The risk of a baby being infected is still not known with certainty. Results from different studies vary from less than 10 per cent to 30 per cent, and the risk of transmission appears to be associated with the stage of the disease.[10] The problem is bigger in those places in Africa and the Caribbean where a large number of women may be infected. In the West, women with HIV are advised to avoid pregnancy or to consider termination of pregnancy but for most women in developing countries these are not options. (And in some areas the risk of a baby dying of other diseases in the first year of life is probably higher than that of dying of AIDS.)

The debate on whether women should be offered testing for HIV as part of antenatal care is an ongoing one. In a survey in one African country about half the women said that knowing their HIV status would not affect their decision to become pregnant.[11] In a clinic in London when women were offered a confidential test, 99 per cent of them declined.[11] In some developing countries women have been tested without their knowledge. In the USA some reports suggest that women, mainly from deprived or minority groups, accept testing because they fear they will be denied access to health care if they decline.[11] It is imperative that confidentiality be maintained if one is to encourage those women most in need of counselling and support to come forward. Even though it is now well recognised that pre- and post-test counselling is an essential part of testing for HIV, in many places it is often lacking. Doctors often have not informed patients of their diagnosis because they lack counselling skills and feel unable to provide the necessary support.

Policy implications

The above discussion has relevance to health and health education policies. Women's needs are different from men's and policy makers have to take this into consideration.

Women should be offered appropriate information and education so that they can make informed choices. This should take into account their particular social and economic circumstances, as information is not enough if women are not in a position to have control over their own lives and bodies. The messages will be different depending on which women are being addressed. Sex workers, women in stable relationships or adolescent girls about to start sexual activities need to be approached with messages that are relevant to their particular situation. In the case of prostitutes it is important not to make them scapegoats. Health education should be aimed at their clients as well.

Education on prevention of HIV infection/AIDS and other sexually transmitted diseases (STDs) should ideally be in the context of education and information on sexuality. There is a need for sex education which empowers women and encourages them to feel more confident to express their own needs and to negotiate over condom usage with a partner. Education with men on these aspects is necessary as well. Participation of the male sexual partner in an education and testing programme in Rwanda positively affected change to lower risk sexual behaviour. Access to family planning services offering appropriate choice and to early treatment of other STDs are also important.

The experiences of women who are beginning to organise themselves and to come up with their own solutions for support, sharing of childcare and income generating activities need to be taken into account. In relation to income generating activities, particularly for prostitutes, it is important to ensure that activities are genuinely productive. 'Traditional' income generating projects like jam-making, knitting, weaving, etc., do not usually generate much money and large group activities are not profitable in most cases. It is difficult to find successful income generating projects but access to credit through revolving credit schemes could be explored. Access to childcare remains an important issue on which self-help groups could, with some external support, organise their own schemes.

Whatever the activity, it is essential to listen to what women and men identify as their needs and work out appropriate solutions in each particular situation.

Concluding comment

AIDS has been used to legitimise prejudices that already exist in societies. It is important therefore to consider carefully our attitudes and even the language that we use when dealing with the subject. The social, political and economic aspects of AIDS are as important as the medical and biological ones in improving the understanding of the disease and in decreasing transmission. Amongst these, gender is an important aspect and all of those involved in this field need to be aware of the existing biases.

Update on women and AIDS

This article was written in February 1989. Rather than update it, I have left it as it was (with only minor editorial changes) because it captures the issues as they were then. Also, because it exemplifies how in moments of crisis the specific problems of women are the last to be considered and taken into account.

Since it was written, much more attention has been paid to women in the AIDS literature. Women have been — and continue to be — the focus of various publications in the last year.[1,12,13] The fact that women are not just transmitters of AIDS or carers for people with AIDS, but also sufferers from HIV infection and AIDS has received attention. In fact, the theme for World AIDS Day in 1990 will be Women and AIDS. Dr Nakajima, the Director-General of the World Health Organisation has said this 'will reflect the increasing impact of AIDS on women, as well as the crucial role women play in preventing infection with the human immunodeficiency virus (HIV) and caring for HIV-infected people and people with AIDS.'[14]

It is encouraging to note that the issue of AIDS and its impact on women is being recognised. However, the general situation of women still remains in most places that of second class citizens and many of the issues raised previously remain valid. Health policies in general and health education in particular still need to take gender issues more seriously.

Discrimination

Fear and stigma are still present, and people with AIDS continue to die in silence. 'Rosie' the Zimbabwean woman who talked for the first time to a newspaper about her situation, and whom I quoted in the article, has since died at the age of 38. She was supported throughout her illness by Island Hospice who gave her loving care, but it was only in the last two weeks that she finally told a friend or two that she was not dying of cancer but of AIDS.[15]

Disturbing reports of discrimination in various forms (not just against women) continue.[16] An example which particularly affects women is the case of women prostitutes in India. They are detained under the Prevention of Immorality Act, and continue to be held past the expiry of their sentence if they are known to be HIV-positive. In March 1990, Shyamala Nataraj, an Indian journalist who had been researching the case, filed a writ in the Madras High Court seeking their release. The case is still pending.

In Thailand, although cheap sex and heroin are easily available, there had been very few reported cases of AIDS until 1988. Since then, the rates of seropositivity have increased at an alarming rate: from just over 100 in 1988 to 2,901 and then 13,600 by the end of 1989. At the beginning of February 1990 the number of people with HIV reached 14,116.[17] Among prostitutes the rates of seropositivity varied depending on whether they were 'low class' (72 per cent) or 'higher class' (16-30 per cent). For a long time the government refused to do anything on AIDS education as they were worried about the adverse effects it would have on tourism. It is only now that the government is starting its AIDS education programmes.

The blame continues to be laid on women, with little consideration of the economic and social realities faced by them. Health education continues to target the prostitutes rather than their clients, although presumably the latter are better educated, have more resources at their disposal and are more in control of the use of condoms.

Other disturbing occurrences have been reported. In Uganda 'some Kampala men have begun to search out schoolgirl lovers in the belief that they will be free of HIV; the government has had to enact a law against sugar daddies'.[18] In West Africa some men believe that sex with a virgin will cure AIDS.[19] In many countries women continue to be blamed for the transmission of AIDS even when it was their husband's behaviour that infected them in the first place. A married woman in Kenya wrote of her concern that in spite of being monogamous she could get AIDS through her husband's behaviour. In her words, married women remained 'faithful but fearful'.[20]

Women organising themselves

On the positive side, there are various groups which are attempting to deal with the problems of women in a different way. Some of these are particularly concerned with helping women sex workers. Empower is one such group in Thailand. It is an association of bar workers set up to help women working in Patpong (a sex centre in Thailand where about 4,000 women work). They have staged shows on safer sex aimed not just at sex workers but at their clients and bar and brothel owners. They also have a drop-in centre which gives information on AIDS and other STDs, nutrition, safe drug use and family planning, and they provide education for the women. The main problems they face are discriminatory attitudes towards sex workers who often get beaten up when they insist on the use of condoms. Yet women are still blamed for transmission (the local Thai expression for STDs is 'woman's disease').[12,21]

Another example of positive activities are those undertaken by Gabriela, a national coalition of Filipino women's groups. This group has been involved in demanding the dismantling of US military bases in the Philippines and the compensation by the US government for 'hospitality women' infected with HIV.[22] They have drop-in centres and provide information and education for sex workers. They also have formed a Task Force on AIDS to do advocacy work and attempt to educate people in the media and

general public about the problems of AIDS in particular and the
sexually prostituted in general.

In Zimbabwe a group of women have formed the Women's AIDS
Support Network. The Network aims to make AIDS a concern for
all organisations working with women in the country and to help
women gain confidence to fight AIDS in a society where they have
little control over the sexual behaviour of men.[12]

AIDS in children

As the number of women infected with HIV increases so will the
number of children being born with HIV. While abortion may be an
option for infected women in some developed countries, in many
countries in the developing world having children is an important
part of life for a woman. 'The HIV positive woman must balance the
chance she might infect her baby against the possibility that her
husband might leave her if she refuses to give him children.'[23]

Orphans

An added dimension to the problem is that of the social and
economic consequences of AIDS which are now becoming evident
in areas of high prevalence. One of them is the increase in the
number of orphans. Precise figures are difficult to come by and
there are problems of definition, but an increase in the number of
orphaned children has been reported from parts of Uganda and
Tanzania.[23]

Mission hospitals in the worst affected areas also report this and in
some places the number of orphans is so large that it is difficult to
envisage how to deal with the problem other than by creating
welfare institutions.

One of the many issues related to orphans is that it usually falls
on the extended family to care for these children. This burden of
care has tended to fall on elderly grandmothers. It is difficult for
elderly frail grandmothers to provide enough food and money for
schooling. This is another issue in relation to women as carers and it
is compounded by the loss of the main wage earners and its effects
on family structures.

Conclusions

Some progress has been made on issues related to women and
AIDS. Certainly, women's concerns have become an integral part of

the 'AIDS agenda'. In practice though, gender biases still permeate health policies in general and AIDS 'health messages' in particular. The links between AIDS and poverty are evident and poverty continues to affect women most severely. Prostitution continues to thrive, not usually from choice, but as a means of survival in an increasingly difficult economic situation.

At the same time women have organised themselves, and will continue to do so, in attempts to improve their (and their children's) situation. The solutions are not easy and daring thinking will be required of those involved in trying to find some. Let us hope we are up to the challenge.

References

1. Women and AIDS Resource Network (WARN) (June 1988), '*Women and AIDS: The Silent Epidemic*, New York: WARN.

2. Mann J. (1988), 'Global AIDS: Epidemiology, Impact, Projections and the Global Strategy', paper presented at the World Summit of Ministers of Health on Programmes for AIDS Prevention, WHO, London, 26-28 January 1988.

3. Ngugi E.N., Plummer R.A. *et al* (1988), 'Prevention of Transmission of HIV in Africa: Effectiveness of Condom Promotion and Health Education Among Prostitutes, *The Lancet*, October, pp.887-890.

4. McGrath J, 'No Human Rights - Brazil', Interview with Gabriella, a prostitute, in Rio de Janiero, May 1988. Next article in this collection.

5. Ramos S, 'Um Rostro de mulher', magazine article.

6. (Abstract) (1988/9), 'Heterosexual Transmission of HIV', *The AIDS Letter* No.10, Royal Society of Medicine, December/January, p. 4.

7. Day S., Ward H., Harris J.R. (1988), 'Prostitute Women and Public Health', *British Medical Journal*, 297: p.1585 .

8. Keogh P., Allen S., Calle Almedal R.N., 'Study of Needs of HIV - seropositive women in Rwanda'. Study completed in August 1988, report in progress.

9. Throncroft P.(1988), 'Dying in Silence', *Parade*, Zimbabwe, December.

10. (Editorial), (1989) 'Vertical Transmission of HIV', *The Lancet*, 2, pp.1057-8.

11. Mariam J. and Radlett M. (1989),'Women face new dilemmas', *AIDS Watch 5*, IPPF.

12. Women and AIDS Action Issue 9, 'Women, HIV and AIDS', AHRTAG, December 1989.

13. Campbell (1990), 'Women and AIDS', *Social Scientist and Medicine* 30(4): pp 407-15.

14. Press Release WHO/5, 22 January 1990.

15. Thornycroft P. (1990), 'AIDS Victim "Rosie" is dead', *Parade*, Zimbabwe, January.

16. Panos Dossier (1990), 'The Third Epidemic: Repercussions of the Fear of AIDS', Panos Institute in association with the Norwegian Red Cross, May.

17. Anderson J. (1990), 'AIDS in Thailand', *BMJ*, 17 February, pp.415-6.

18. 'The Terrible Trail of "Slim"', *The Guardian*, April 12, 1990.

19. McFadden P. (1989), 'AIDS - Who is the Culprit?', SAPEM, April.

20. Anon, 'AIDS and Married Women', *The Weekly Review*, Kenya, 12 September 1989.

21. (1989) 'Empowering Bar Workers in Bangkok', *Community Development Journal* 24 (30): 202.

22. Tan M., de Leon A., Stoltzfus B. and O'Donnel C.(1989), 'AIDS as a political issue: working with the Sexually Prostituted in the Philippines', *Community Development Journal* 24 (30): 202, pp.186-193.

23. Panos Mini-Dossier No.2, (1989), 'AIDS and Children: a family disease', Panos Institute in association with Save the Children.

Claudia Garcia-Moreno is a Health Adviser for Oxfam, covering Latin America and Southern Africa. She has particular responsibility for AIDS work and policies and is interested in women's issues. She has experience of primary health care (PHC) in Mexico and Africa.

NO HUMAN RIGHTS:
INTERVIEW WITH GABRIELLA, A PROSTITUTE,
IN RIO DE JANEIRO

JOHN MAGRATH

How do girls, here in Rio, become prostitutes?
Well, most are already prostitutes. As soon as the girl begins to grow breasts she is put out by the family as an aid to family income. There then comes a point when the young girl has had enough of handing over her money to her father, and she leaves the family and travels by hitching lifts, using prostitution as a means of paying her way.

Most prostitutes start at 12 or 13. I started when I was 25, so my reality was different. I'm white, urban and educated, but most prostitutes are uneducated, they are from the north east or they are black. Their options are prostitution, domestic service or unskilled factory work. In areas of high unemployment the last two options are only for a few.

If a family has got two daughters, one will be sacrificed to prostitution and one will be saved for marriage. The earnings of the one will pay the dowry of the other. The mother accepts this because the man says so: this is the basis of family life, especially in the north east. Attitudes have not changed much there, the father controls the income which comes in. Prostitution cannot be seen in isolation. For example, if there is no land reform, people have no other option for survival.

There are also the street children to consider, born in the streets and abandoned. The girls, when they reach adolescence, that is, 10 to 12, have no other option but to survive. They might well have been thrust out of the house because they were pregnant. People say now there are 10 million street children; in a few years, with this economic situation, there might well be 25 million.

Could you explain what your organisation is trying to do?
The National Collective of Prostitutes is the likely name for our new organisation. It will be independent of the church and have local

associations. There are three main questions we are looking at: first, how to work with young girls? You cannot say 'don't become a prostitute' unless you have other options. Children of 10, 11 and 12 are prostitutes and they have not the least idea about sex or biology. Girls get pregnant and they don't know how because they know nothing whatsoever about their bodies. When we go to the children's organisations and work with street children and say one of the most important things is to stop these children becoming pregnant, they give no support because they think we are supporting prostitution. Such institutions as UNICEF work with the boys but they don't know what to do about the girls. They ignore them. When the police pick up young girls they take them to Funabe, the state reform schools. To survive in there they become prostitutes of other girls, often without any conception of what sexuality is. When they are released most will return to prostitution and set up with another woman in a sexual relationship where the other woman is dominant. The most important thing is that these children need to have access to information. The most important thing is that they should learn to read and write. Then they are given information so they can control their lives more.

Second, what to do about old prostitutes? Prostitutes in the city can often work until they are about 50 because clients often feel that a more mature woman has more patience and experience and is less likely to pass on VD. After that their options are that either they manage to get a pimp and that the pimp won't work them as a prostitute, or they become domestic servants in the houses of prostitutes. Their other option is begging. They are not recognised as citizens therefore they have no rights to old age pensions. Maybe we will be able to create our own but to do so we have to have at least 10,000 paying members to make the scheme viable. Or maybe it will be possible to campaign for changes in the pensions legislation.

Third, drugs. This affects the mental capacity of the user and quite often a person is out of her mind by the age of 50. There is no work being done through the health system.

What is the legal status of your association?
The law in Brazil is based on the thesis that prostitutes have to exist, to protect the virginity of the daughters of the country. It seems to embody ideas from Greek philosophy that prostitutes are the drains

of society that allow men to purge what is bad! However, to live off prostitution by pimping is a crime. The association could be seen as living off the earnings of prostitutes and so be against the law. So the association is working with the Association of Brazilian Lawyers to research case law. Until we have the case law to defend the legality of the association, local associations will call themselves 'the association of Maria da Fe'. This comes from a Bahia book called Viva Polvo (the life of the people) and is one of the characters.

Legal status is vital so local associations can have autonomy and seek funds, and, on the other hand, because there is nothing in the new constitution about prostitution. Having legal status will allow us to call for reforms in the law.

How is prostitution organised in Rio?
There are three classes of prostitutes. First, in the massage parlours; second, in night clubs and striptease joints; third, on the streets. Although pimpage is illegal, it exists. Some of the pimps are 'cafitineas', they are women, ex-prostitutes who have saved money to buy a patch. The relationship between them and their prostitutes is not bad. Indeed, many participate in the prostitutes' movement. They provide us with food and sandwiches at meetings.

The most difficult case is the massage parlours where we have no access. We can only wait for these people to come to us. The prostitutes there get more money, a lot more sometimes, but their professional life is very short and they are forced to take drugs. Drugs are used to make the woman more active, they are stimulants. They use cocaine and appetite suppressors. The whole network is controlled by a Mafia-like group who fund it through an illegal but very popular lottery. The only way for a girl in one of these places is down, to the streets. In Sao Paulo prostitution is like gold and it is controlled by a Federal Deputy.

Outside the zones ('Red Light' districts) controlled by female pimps there are women who work on the streets and there are men who control the area and who will have four or five women under their control. He provides some protection and care to all the women — indeed, it is an exact parallel of many middle-class marriages where the man controls the woman and has her as a consumer durable.

How much do prostitutes earn, on average?

The amount of money paid relates to the client and the type of service. But if the prostitute is lower class and has one client she will gain 600 cruzados or 18,000 cr a month. But they will have more than one client. Of course that is vastly more than the minimum salary of 8,700 cr a month. Remember, most domestic workers get less than the national minimum wage per month, and domestic servants are treated like dirt. In the interior of Minas Gerais a servant gets just 100 cr a month.

The average number of clients for most prostitutes is five a day but it can be ten a day if she works hard. She will usually charge 650 cr and 50 cr will go to the pimp. If there are no clients she does not have to pay the pimp anything. At the night club level the price is 3000 cr per client. But, she has to pay for the drinks the client has, to keep the club turnover up. They would then go to some hotel. Some let them stay free, some charge. Prostitution isn't necessarily a full-time job. It depends on the person and the shifts they are working and their financial obligations.

As for the clients, it is very rare for them to marry a prostitute. A client wants a prostitute for very clear reasons. The saint of a woman at home, who is the mother of his children, is one thing but the prostitute acts out all his desires and fantasies.

Do you have problems with the police?

They extort protection money and beat up and arrest prostitutes. The main violence is from the police. In a recent case someone in Bahia was picked up, tortured and killed. Prostitution itself is not illegal. It is the police attitude that creates a feeling among prostitutes who don't know the law or know their rights, that they are acting outside the law. They believe that they are criminals and the police take advantage of that and feed that fear. The police do not extort money from pimps, who really are acting illegally. The going price for payment to the police is 200 cruzados a week. If you don't pay you get picked up, but as you can't be charged with a crime, except maybe not having a proper ID, you get taken down to the station, you are forced to have sex and you are released when they have finished with you.

I was doing a TV interview in Sao Paulo when the police had just doubled the rate to 400 cr a week and I denounced it. The prostitutes were very angry with me because they said the police would come down on them heavily, but I explained the payments were not necessary and now because of the publicity the police have stopped demanding this much.

What is the attitude of the church to prostitutes?

To the church a prostitute is a *minina*, a girl. The church does not see that the options for a poor woman are to be a domestic servant or a prostitute. It is much easier for the church to evade that utterly. The church has never complained against, for example, police violence against prostitutes. If the church accepted the rights of prostitutes it would be seen as promoting prostitution. Prostitutes, to the church, have no rights. They are victims, there to be helped.

What are the main problems prostitutes have with their health?

One is TB. Also, many take a type of penicillin as a preventative measure against VD. Regular use of this builds up a resistance to antibiotics and weakens resistance to disease — at least that's my theory built up from my experience. People are then more susceptible to TB caused by malnutrition, and lack of sanitation.

Prostitutes have no access to health services. You can only go to a private doctor if you have any money. Otherwise, if it's a grave case, you have to go to the public clinic which is awful. Public hospitals will treat anybody whether or not they've paid their health contributions but they are under-equipped and understaffed.

Now we have a health project but we get no support from the State. We said 'there's already a health post but it doesn't treat us, we've no stamps. The public clinics come only maybe twice a week and you have to queue all night to have a chance of seeing the doctor.' When we did research into the history of prostitution in our area, we found that records show that prostitutes are seen as a health risk, transmitters of the plague, TB, syphilis — and now AIDS. That's the official attitude — that we're a health hazard.

What is the situation with regard to AIDS?

Official bodies, society, attempt to define it in terms of groups of people; prostitutes, homosexuals, the promiscuous, drug users. The political question is, what about the people who frequent prostitutes? They are not regarded as a high risk group. AIDS strips bare the questions of the totally inadequate health services, the blood banks which are run by a private Mafia, the government propaganda which spends millions on a national campaign and nothing on research. And it strips bare the hypocrisy and prejudice of society. Sure, AIDS kills, but so do many other things. Prostitutes have always been at risk of diseases and the government and health services have never lifted a finger before.

The number of clients has fallen off and women often insist on the use of condoms but the man often refuses to use one because it questions his masculinity. He says if he gets the disease it is the woman's fault. He never regards it as him transmitting the disease. But of course, if a woman gets it, it's from a man.

What are your relations with the feminist movement?

One of the main blocks which exists is between feminists and prostitutes. Feminists cannot accept prostitutes because they say prostitution exploits women and they won't enter into a discussion of what it is. They regard prostitutes as downtrodden women with no rights, by their very occupation. To overcome this is a fundamental thing. An examination of attitudes to sex and the hypocrisy which governs the laws on sexuality must include feminists among the hypocrites.

When I left prostitution I realised that the middle class feminists found great difficulty accepting my way of life, behaviour and history. As Proust said, 'I consider my enemy anyone who wants to control my liberty'.

What are your hopes for the future?

Now, as a prostitute, a woman has no human rights, they have no access to what health services exist and they are subject to arbitrary violence by the police. In an ideal world, unions of prostitutes would be accepted, but then we would be well on the way to the end of the reason for prostitution. In such an ideal world every worker could put his hand on his heart and say 'I am a prostitute' and every prostitute could say 'I am a worker'.

Gabriella Leite, a prostitute in Rio de Janeiro, was the inspiration behind the founding of the National Collective of Prostitutes. She formerly worked with a church organisation which assisted prostitutes.

John Magrath is the Senior Press Officer for Oxfam.

FEMININE PAIN

DAHABO ALI MUSE (SOMALIA)

(extract adapted from an English translation)

And if I may speak of my wedding night:
I had expected caresses, sweet kisses, hugging and love.
No, never!
Awaiting me was pain, suffering and sadness.
I lay in my wedding bed groaning like a wounded
    animal, a victim of feminine pain.
At dawn ridicule awaited me.
My mother announced: Yes, she is a virgin.

When fear gets hold of me,
When anger seizes my body,
When hate becomes my companion,
Then I get feminine advice, because it is only feminine pain
    and I am told feminine pain perishes like all feminine things.

The journey continues or struggle continues
    as modern historians say.
As the good tie of marriage matures,
As I submit and sorrow subsides,
My belly becomes like a balloon.
A glimpse of happiness shows,
    a hope, a new baby, a new life!

But a new life endangers my life,
A baby's birth is death and destruction for me!

It is what my grandmother called the three feminine sorrows.
She said the day of my circumcision, the wedding night,
    and the birth of a baby are the triple feminine sorrows.
As the birth bursts, I cry for help,
    when the tattered flesh tears.
No mercy, push! they say,
It is only feminine pain!

And now I appeal.
I appeal for love lost, for dreams broken,
For the right to live as a whole human being.
I appeal to all peace loving people to protect, to support
    and give a hand to innocent little girls who do no harm,
Obedient to their parents and elders, all they know is only
    smiles.
Initiate them to the world of love,
Not to the world of feminine sorrow!

OVERCOMING THE BARRIERS:
WOMEN AND PARTICIPATION IN PUBLIC LIFE

EUGENIA PIZA LOPEZ

In Costa Rica, women have played an important and sometimes decisive role in grassroots organisations; demanding services in the urban neighbourhoods, land in the rural areas and general improvement of their conditions at national level. However, their contributions and their right to lead struggles for change have not been recognised, nor has the need radically to transform the political agenda by giving women's issues their rightful place.

A participatory research project was set up to explore and raise awareness of women's marginalisation. Its objective was to strengthen the women's groups and organisations and enable them to identify the barriers they faced to full participation in the process of social change, and devise strategies for action.

At the time (1981-4), the quality of life in Costa Rica was deteriorating. The national debt was one of the largest per capita in the world. Economic packages negotiated between the government and the International Monetary Fund (IMF) resulted in radical cuts to state services. Politically, the climate was one of tightening control and restriction of the 'democratic space' available to organisations, especially labour unions and peasants' organisations. Barriers to women's participation had to be seen and addressed in that context, with the added dimension of the demobilisation and co-option on the part of the state of many grassroots organisations.

Methodology

The researchers/facilitators worked with women from three ethnic groups and from three sectors: urban poor, small farmers and landless peasants. The women all belonged to some form of organisation. These included small productive co-operative groups, community groups aimed at demanding community services, and trade unions affiliated to political parties. A few of the women participated fully in their groups but many had only a nominal degree of participation, with little or no access to information or decision making.

The women lived in very bad conditions, in one or two-roomed houses for an average family of six, with very poor provision of basic services. Two-thirds of them were married, and the remainder were heads of households. Alcoholism was common among the partners, who were in most cases under-employed with very low salaries, or unemployed.

The research project was a participatory one, over a three year period, which combined gathering data with consciousness building, and the women worked on and analysed the information themselves. The process was an integration of theory and practice, and enabled an understanding by women of the situation of women, starting from their everyday life and moving towards their wider environment of family, community, region and nation.

The first stage of the research consisted of intensive life-story interviews, where the women shared their personal experiences and reflected together on women's condition. The most significant factors preventing women's participation were identified, and guidelines for discussion were drawn up. Then, focused group discussions were held with 250 women in 12 groups, and the research team introduced the use of popular education techniques. Every theme was addressed through activities such as drama, music, mime, drawing and role play, to encourage women's creativity and allow a sharing of feelings, experiences and problems. The analysis was on two levels; feelings and emotions, and the interaction between women's experiences and their wider environment (family, community, organisations). By discussing the obstacles to participation, and working together to produce leaflets, films, radio programmes, songs and comic strips, the issues became clearer and better understood by all involved. The women took the message back to their husbands and families, organisations and political parties. Finally, the whole experience was evaluated and strategies developed to introduce the issues to other communities and grassroots organisations.

Domestic work and family responsibilities

Women have three distinct roles in society. These can be described as reproductive (everything that is necessary for reproduction of the work force), productive (producing goods and services as part of the work force) and community management (the tasks necessary for maintenance of social relations). The work performed by women at home has social, economic and political relevance, and yet it was hardly recognised as work, or seen as important, by women themselves, male relatives, or society as a whole. Women, whatever their class, assumed responsibility for tasks such as cleaning, cooking, shopping, and looking after their children, husbands, etc. They also played a key role in transmitting the culture, socialising children and caring for the ill and elderly. Domestic tasks were very varied and demanded constant attention. The total time spent doing domestic work was the same as, and sometimes more than, the time spent in income earning activities.

For poor women domestic work was particularly labour intensive and carried out under very difficult conditions i.e. no piped water, no electricity, no labour saving devices. Economic adjustment had worsened the situation; women had to increase the scope of their tasks and take on an even heavier work burden at home in order to fulfil needs which could no longer be met in other ways.

The double working day

Women had to carry all these domestic responsibilities whenever they participated in the public domain, be it in paid jobs, community organisations, or political parties. Women of the poorest groups did paid work as a result of economic pressures but found themselves discriminated against and facing opposition from their partners and other members of the household. Most were seriously overworked and tired — in practice, a woman's average working day was 14 hours, sometimes up to 17 — and they had little time to take part in other activities and/or participate fully in community organisations.

Involving others — especially the men — in the domestic work of the household and/or demanding the creation of services at the national level, such as creches and communal kitchens, were not seen initially as options by the women. They did not see the possibility that the state might be obliged to assist in alleviating women's burdens. Instead, they suggested that in order to participate more fully in community or political organisations they should organise themselves better, or cut down the hours spent on paid work, neither of which were really feasible. The research process enabled them to see the importance of demanding services directly related to their 'reproductive' role, especially creches and launderettes.

Women in paid jobs

There has been an increase in the number of women in paid work in Costa Rica in the last 30 years, but their jobs are mostly low paid, without social security and seasonal, and mostly in the informal sector of the economy. In the context of the economic crisis this situation worsened.

In the urban areas, women's opportunities for employment were limited to domestic work for others, petty trading and, in some cases, factory work. Young women found employment in Free Trade Zones (FTZs) in unstable jobs with very exploitative working conditions. For the few women in income generating projects, co-operatives or self-managed enterprises, although their incomes were very unstable, working conditions were a little better. They had more flexible working hours so that it was easier to cope with their double working day. In some cases they could bring their small children to the workplace.

In the countryside women were agricultural workers involved in food production. They provided cheaper labour in harvesting cash crops. Skills traditionally related to domestic work, such as weaving and pottery, were used for small-scale production and petty trade.

The changing structure of land ownership had important effects on women's employment. Large sections of the land had been taken from small land-owners as the expansion of *latifundios* (large estates) took place, and the peasant economy thus lost its subsistence base. The result was a process of proletarianisation of the peasant household, with rural-urban, rural-rural migration, mainly of males, to find paid work. Women were increasingly becoming heads of households. Women, too, joined the agricultural labour force, employed mainly as 'agricultural worker helpers', which in practice meant that they got one-third less salary for performing very much the same tasks as men. The problems for women were lack of adequate skills, low literacy and the need to find a job which fitted in with their responsibilities at home. The work they did was often temporary, and always low paid.

Machismo

The existence of sexist cultural patterns in the educational system, the mass media, religion and other social institutions, created cohesive ideological and cultural pressures which limited the effective participation of women. These pressures were present in political parties (across the political spectrum) and people's organisations.

Machismo exists across the whole structure of society and influences the law, social norms and attitudes, social and economic activities, cultural forms and personal relations. It affected the sexual, procreative, working and emotional life of women and determined the relationship they had with their partners, the relationship between the man and his family, and the expression of sexuality between the couple. Domestic violence was widely prevalent.

The unequal personal relationships between men and women reinforced women's feelings of insecurity. They asked their husband's permission to go out to work, meetings or other social events. They tried to avoid the public sphere to 'avoid problems with the *companero* (partner) in front of the children'. They saw these problems as individual and not social.

Women's perception of themselves

In the analysis of the obstacles to participation faced by women it was important to consider their self-image. The way in which women valued themselves was a reflection of their social and economic situation.

Even after recognising the differences in the way in which women perceived themselves, common patterns emerged which crossed geographical and ethnic divisions. The most important issue related to the problems and difficulties that women faced in fulfilling their roles as mothers and carers, at the same time as meeting their economic and community responsibilities. The concern about the well-being of their children permeated every aspect of their lives. It was present in their relationships with their partners, when they were working outside the household and particularly when they were involved in activities which did not bring an immediate income to the family. When they went out to work, in many cases they had to leave the children on their own or with the eldest daughter (sometimes as young as seven years old). They did not have enough time to spend with their children and they felt too tired to play and have fun with them. This made them feel guilty and prevented them from spending enough time in community organisations to take an active role in decision making.

Women expressed their frustration at not being able to realise their full potential. Because they did not finish their primary education, but married and started to have children 'too young', they felt that their choice of work was very limited and that they did not have opportunities to realise themselves through other activities.

The psychological consequences of their workloads, especially the domestic work, should not be underestimated. Tiredness and frustration at not being able to 'realise their dreams', isolation, and their limited ability to participate and gain recognition in the public domain, produced frustration and demotivation.

The character of organisations in which women participated

The women involved in income generating schemes expressed the importance of this in enabling them to obtain some economic independence. However, because these schemes were very often set up without proper marketing research or strategies, and with no training in accounting and management, they tended to fail, leaving the women disappointed. Failure was often seen as personal, due to lack of skills and education, and not as structural. This had a negative effect on women's involvement in the public domain. After economic failure came withdrawal from other forms of community and/or political organisations.

In community organisations, women took part in mobilisation and everyday activities but had no control over decision making and direction. However, collective experience provided a space for women to develop confidence and understand their rights within the organisation. They needed to develop leadership, public speaking, and organisational skills.

Although women from the cities and the Atlantic zone recognised the importance of unionisation, they questioned the effectiveness of the unions to meet women workers' needs. This was due to a number of factors. Firstly, women were employed mostly as temporary or home-based workers or in FTZs, and to organise a union in those conditions was very difficult. Secondly, unions were strongest in sectors where women were not employed. In addition, unions saw their main role as negotiators for improvements in safety conditions and salaries; while women felt that their immediate needs were for creches in the workplace, flexitime, enforcement of maternity leave provisions, etc. Women had little opportunity to assume leadership roles within unions, both because of their double working day and because they met overt opposition from male leaders and members.

Women who participated in left-wing political parties were more aware of national issues and were able to identify their social and economic problems and see possible solutions. However, their participation at local level and beyond was restricted, and their political work never focused on women's rights or issues affecting women's development. Women's main roles were preparation and distribution of food in meetings, leafleting, and attendance at rallies.

Conclusion

Through the analysis of the women's everyday life it was possible to identify the roles they played and their relationship to society as a whole. Their particular needs, their values and their self-image were identified. By looking at the realities of women's lives — heavy domestic work, low paid employment, the double working day, *machismo* — it was possible to identify with them the barriers to participation they faced. It was only when these barriers were recognised that work could be started to overcome them. It was a long process which still goes on. The transformation of unequal structures which discriminate against women is a difficult task, sometimes painful, sometimes rewarding.

Eugenia Piza Lopez is the Gender and Development Unit adviser for Asia and Latin America. Her previous experience includes research on images of the Third World in the UK, work on popular education with Central American women and participatory research in Costa Rica.

FROM 'MOTHERS OF THE NATION' TO WOMEN IN THEIR OWN RIGHT: SOUTH AFRICAN WOMEN IN THE TRANSITION TO DEMOCRACY

SUZANNE WILLIAMS

The transformation of South Africa into a non-racist, unitary and democratic state has been the rallying call and stated goal of the progressive movements in the country for many years. The fight against apartheid and racism has been a long and distinguished one, not over yet. Only very recently, due to the pressure of women's groups and some recognition of the importance of gender issues in the construction of a democracy, has the term 'non-sexist' been added to the list of aims of the struggle. But as groups and organisations, moving the emphasis from struggle to reconstruction and development, redraft their agendas, what place on them will be given to the realisation of a non-sexist society? The struggle for national liberation in South Africa has always been defined by race and class: gender inequalities have taken second place, and raising gender issues is often considered to be premature, and divisive. The place of woman has been to remain alongside her man, supporting him in the struggle, participating in the organisations, serving time in detention — but also almost exclusively responsible for the maintainance of the social fabric of home and children in the face of the terrible destructiveness of the apartheid system.

'The mothers of the nation', said Oliver Tambo, President of the African National Congress, the ANC, in 1987, 'the womenfolk as a whole, are the titans of our struggle... One of the greatest prizes of the democratic revolution must therefore be the unshackling of the women.' The ANC is committed to the emancipation of women in the new South Africa, and in August 1990 the ANC Women's League was relaunched in the country. But women are no longer content to be the mothers of the nation, the wives and daughters, defined by their relationships. Exiled ANC women said to *Speak* magazine on their return to South Africa: 'We must not assume that every woman is a wife or mother, or that she intends to be a wife or mother. This is a weakness, arising from our tradition. We need to address attitudes...' (*Speak*, no.30, 1990).

The legacy of women's subordination in South Africa is, some activists argue, even more difficult to deal with than the legacy of apartheid. Women from the Rape Crisis group and shelter for battered women in Cape Town, interviewed for 'Women Speak', a documentary video on South African women made by the producers of *Speak* magazine, said: 'It will take a lot longer to get rid of sexism than to get rid of racism, because there is a contradiction in the way people think. People of course reject assertions of black inferiority to whites — and yet will assert that women are biologically inferior to men.' The subordination of women — exemplified in traditional practices such as the payment of *lobola* (bride price), and polygamy — preceded the apartheid system but was immeasurably exacerbated by it and is inseparable from it. Gender oppression cannot be detached from other forms of oppression, and women in South Africa today insist that it has to be tackled as part of the process of national liberation, and not left until 'after the revolution'.

'In South Africa we find very stark examples of how different kinds of oppression are related to one another. The apartheid system has operated to discriminate against people classified as non-whites, and in so doing has less obviously bolstered and legitimated discrimination against the poor and against women — particularly poor black women, who are at the very bottom of the pile. Brittan and Maynard... discuss how different forms of oppression are, in a sense, modelled on each other, using very similar mechanisms — "the oppressive practices which occur in one sphere are never entirely encapsulated or constrained within that sphere alone". One kind of oppression serves as a model for other kinds.'(Segar and White, in *Agenda*, No.4, 1989).

This article gives an account of some of the achievements of women's organisations in South Africa and their plans to overcome the enormous obstacles faced by women in their struggle to ensure that a non-racist, unitary and democratic South Africa will be non-sexist as well.

Much of the material for this paper is gathered from the popular educational women's magazine *Speak*, which has a female and male readership of some 10,000. Shamim Meer, founder-member of Speak collective, was interviewed for her views on some of the issues.

I asked Shamim whether she thought democracy would bring equal rights for women in South Africa.

'We know that it won't be realised automatically, because democracy doesn't always include women's rights. But women's issues are not something you attach or leave out, they are an integral part of democracy or socialism. This idea is taking a long time to be accepted in South Africa. So women will have to continue the struggle for a long time still.'

The 'Titans of the Struggle'

Women have been central to resistance to apartheid from the beginning. although their own initiatives were not always given due recognition. In 1913 women launched a protest campaign in Bloemfontein in the Orange Free State against the pass laws, which controlled the movement of blacks in and out of 'white' areas, being applied to them. Their campaign led to the formation of the Bantu Women's League — the first national organisation of black women. Yet women were not allowed to become full members of the ANC, founded in 1912, until about 30 years later. Through these years women continued to mobilise against pass laws, and the local bread-and-butter issues that affected everyone's lives. Finally, in the forties in a climate of mass mobilisations, women were accorded full membership of the ANC and in 1948 the ANC Women's League was founded. Women from the League were instrumental in setting up the Federation of South African Women, FEDSAW.

In 1954 a conference bringing together women from all over South Africa, from trade unions, township and community organisations, Congress (ANC) organisations and any women's groups able to send a delegate, founded the Federation of South African Women, FEDSAW.

FEDSAW broke new ground as the first national women's organisation open to all races. The founding conference adopted a Charter of Women's Aims, which, while demanding equal rights with men in relation to marriage, children and property, full opportunities and equal pay at work, and the strengthening of women's participation in trade unions and people's organisations, nevertheless refers to women predominantly as wives and mothers. The Preamble reads: 'We, the women of South Africa, wives and mothers, working women and housewives, hereby declare our aim of striving for the removal of all laws, regulations, conventions and customs that discriminate against us women... ' The third section, Women's Lot, opens: 'We women share with our menfolk the cares and anxieties imposed by poverty and its evils. As wives and mothers it falls upon us to make small wages stretch a long way. It is we who feel the cries of our children when they are hungry and sick. It is our lot to keep and care for the homes that are too small, broken and dirty to be kept clean...'

Challenging men on the issue of law and custom, the Charter points out that large numbers of women are the breadwinners and heads of their families, and yet are given the legal status of minors. 'This intolerable condition would not be allowed to continue were it not for the refusal of a large section of our menfolk to concede to us women the rights and privileges which they demand for themselves. We shall teach the men that they cannot hope to liberate themselves from the evils of discrimination and prejudice as long as they fail to extend to women complete and unequalified equality in law and practice.'

Although the Charter as a whole was never adopted by the liberation movement, some of its demands and those of another FEDSAW document, the Women's Demands for the Freedom Charter, were incorporated into the Freedom Charter. This document, drawn up by the Congress of the People, a meeting of nearly 3,000 delegates who gathered in Kliptown, near Johannesburg, in 1955, laid out the demands and aspirations of South Africans for peace and freedom in their country, and has inspired the liberation struggle for the last 35 years. The FEDSAW Women's Charter too still stands today as an impassioned indictment of women's position under apartheid and under customary law.

In August 9th 1956 FEDSAW organised a march of 20,000 women to the government buildings in Pretoria to present petitions signed by hundreds of thousands of women protesting at the extension of the pass laws to women. When the Prime Minister refused to see them, the women stood in silence for 30 minutes before singing the national anthem and a new song, whose refrain has become synonymous with the courage and resilience of South African women: 'When you touch the women, you have struck a rock. You have dislodged a boulder, you will be crushed.'

This historic march, and the ensuing protest which spread all over the country, prevented the issuing of passes to women for another seven years. The powerful emergence of women on this national scale was finally recognised as giving new strength to the resistance movement. In September 1959 when the ANC held a special conference, a bright red banner proclaimed *Makabongwe Amakòsikazi* — we thank the women. (Bernstein 1975, p.49.) Then in the early sixties the state clamped down, banning the ANC, the Pan-Africanist Congress (PAC), the South African Communist Party (SACP), the Women's League and other political organisations, and FEDSAW fell apart as its leadership was banned, jailed or exiled.

The turbulent 1980s: women at the heart of the struggle

Resistance went underground, erupting in the seventies in widespread strikes and the rise of the Black Consciousness movement, and in the 1976 Soweto uprising when a generation of black schoolchildren were catapulted into radical politics by the force and brutality of police reaction to their protests against discriminatory state education for blacks. This is often seen as the beginning of the South African revolution, which gathered momentum through the eighties in popular organisation and mass resistance. The State brought its full weight to bear on this new surge of opposition through successive States of Emergency, giving itself sweeping powers to carry out mass arrests and detentions, to control meetings and the media, and to maintain army troops in the townships. But although many organisations were again crippled, as in the sixties, by the removal of their leaders, the force for change was by now unstoppable.

In the late seventies and during the eighties women organised at every level, in local, regional and national groupings. Bearing the brunt of the turbulence of the decade, struggling to keep homes and families going in the face of the breakdown of schooling, violence on the streets, forced removals, and mass arrests and detention of children, they had to rely on support from other women. Women's groups were crucial to the support of children being harassed and intimidated at school. Women were at the forefront of the rent boycotts, campaigns against high food prices, and issues around security in the townships. Women were, in every sense, at the very heart of the struggle.

The United Women's Organisation (UWO), formed in 1981, played a key role in the formation and launch of the United Democratic Front (UDF), the major oppositional force of the decade to which over 800 progressive organisations were affiliated. UWO broadened its base to become the United Women's Congress (UWCO), and other regional organisations were set up: the Natal Women's Congress (NOW),the Federation of Transvaal Women (FEDTRAW), while FEDSAW became re-established in the Cape.

Through the eighties women also became an increasingly active force in the trade union movement. Individual unions and the major trade union congress (COSATU) developed into formidable opponents of the apartheid regime. The strength of their political muscle was measured in May 1987 when an estimated 1.5 million workers responded to the call for a two-day strike in protest against the parliamentary election from which unenfranchised blacks were excluded.

The trade union movement is dominated by men, with few women in leadership positions. 'Women have had to fight every inch of the way, and still fight every day for their space in the unions,' says Shamim. But women have won some significant improvements in working conditions from within their unions and with the support of their male colleagues.

The campaign to press employers to provide PAP smears, tests to detect early signs of cervical cancer, for their female employees was started by the Chemical Worker's Industrial Union, which has a female membership of only 6 per cent. The Commercial Catering and Allied Workers' Union (CCAWUSA) has a predominantly female membership, and represents some 70,000 workers. It pioneered agreements on maternity rights, which have subsequently been won by other unions for their workers.

The South African Domestic Worker's Union (SADWU) represents almost a million domestic workers, the vast majority of whom are women, highly exploited by low pay and arbitrarily defined working conditions. Hidden in white homes, and unprotected by labour legislation, they can be subjected to every kind of humiliation, violence and sexual abuse. SADWU demands an end to child labour, and formal contracts from employers for domestic workers. These should cover a minimum wage, set working hours and sickness, pension and unemployment benefits. SADWU has the almost impossible task of trying to persuade employers to agree to these demands. However, public campaigns for just working conditions have strengthened the hand of domestic workers, while SADWU continues to fight for their legal protection.

In September 1990 COSATU organised a day of action on which thousands of workers took their children into work with them. This launched the National Childcare Campaign, which demands parental leave for childcare, creches, and childcare allowances for unemployed workers, and which aims to get childcare demands included in the 'living wage' negotiations at plant and national level. 'I think that today's action will lead men to be more interested in our kids in the future,' said Templeton Namdo of the Transport and General Workers' Union. 'As men we don't know how to raise children. We have a lot to learn.' (*Speak*, no.32, 1990.)

Women have also begun to organise separately within their unions, setting up branches where women can gain confidence, leadership training, and discuss issues which it is difficult to get on the agendas of general meetings, such as maternity leave and PAP smears. 'We hope that women's branches will train women to talk more in general meetings of the union. At the moment they don't speak so they are not selected as shop stewards.' (Refileo Ndzuta in *Speak*, No.29, 1990)

Towards the end of the eighties international political pressure, sanctions, disinvestment, and the military defeat which led to the independence of Namibia, all contributed to the weakening of the South African State, forcing it to begin negotiating with the opposition for peace. In February 1990 the ANC, South African Communist Party, and other political organisations were 'unbanned', Nelson Mandela was released and the tide had irrevocably turned. While the basic pillars of apartheid are still in place, and the country is racked by violence generated by white and black reaction to the negotiations between the government and the ANC, progressive organisations throughout South Africa are planning for the construction of a new democratic order.

Into the nineties: women's issues in a new South Africa

What are the issues that women have to address as they come into the nineties, into a climate of hope and fear, into the social and political turmoil which is the legacy of apartheid? Shamim Meer, of Speak: 'Although general political harrassment and detentions continue and we don't have real freedom to act yet, there is more space and openness to organise and get together and plan our activities. In the homelands women's groups are able to operate more openly. We are moving our focus from struggle to transformation and development, and women need to be prepared for this. They need information in order to be able to make judgements and decisions, about the new constitution, for example. And to understand the ANC's policy statement on women and be able to contribute to the ANC Women's League proposed charter of rights.'

With the relaunch of the ANC Women's League some of the regional women's organisations opted to dissolve in order to set up its local branches. Others, such as FEDSAW, may continue to exist under a planned broad alliance of women's groups, which are to include church and union-based women's groups and organisations outside the ANC like the Black Sash. Founded like the ANC Women's League in the forties, the Black Sash was until 1963 a white women's organisation, set up in protest against apartheid laws. The Black Sash now has a vast network of advice offices all over the country and performs an invaluable service to people struggling under complicated apartheid legislation and fighting forced removals. One of the ANC Women's League's first campaigns will be the canvassing of women's views and demands all over the country as groundwork for drawing up a Women's Rights Charter, to be part of the ANC's constitutional proposals.

Other major issues for women to tackle in the nineties, according to Shamim, are illiteracy, the need for broader skills training, affirmative action to ensure women take up leadership roles in political organisations, the continued need for women to organise separately from men to understand their own oppression, and poverty, particularly amongst rural women. At the Malibongwe Conference in Amsterdam in January 1990, organised by the ANC Women's Section, where women from within and outside South Africa met to discuss contemporary women's issues, a resolution was passed to set up a trust fund to raise money for education and skills training for rural women.

Rural women — at the bottom of the pile

Almost 60 per cent of all women live in the rural homelands or bantustans, the areas designated by the South African government for the black population, and into which millions of black South Africans have been forcibly dumped, removed from their homes in land reserved for whites. At least 60 per cent of households are women-headed. Here the responsibility for shelter, food and children is borne entirely by the women: men, migrant labourers in the towns, are only occasional visitors.

Conditions in the impoverished homelands are desperate: only the most rudimentary schooling and health services exist and there are almost no opportunities for women to earn money to supplement the uncertain remittances from husbands or fathers of their children. Sometimes the meagre pensions paid to old people are the only source of income to family groups, and even these payments are subject to corrupt or inefficient administration. Poverty-stricken women in the homelands form a reserve army of labourers, for homeland industries or seasonal and casual agricultural work. They are unprotected by labour legislation, and wages and working conditions are appalling, but the only other choice is to eke out a miserable living by brewing beer, selling vegetables or making brooms or baskets.

On white farms, women are the most vulnerable in the most exploited general category of South Africa's workers. Farmworkers, like domestic workers, are almost entirely unprotected by labour laws, some living in semi-feudal dependency on white farmers. A woman's right to remain on the farm usually depends on her husband, and her labour may be required as a domestic servant or seasonal worker, as a pre-condition of her husband's employment. This work is sometimes unpaid. On average women farmworkers work 60 to 70 hours a week. When they are paid, it is less than men for the same work, and their children are expected to work without pay. In addition to heavy farmwork, women work the usual 'double shift', fetching water and firewood and carrying out all the domestic duties of cooking, cleaning, and taking care of the children within their own homes. Child labour is common, and sexual exploitation of women and young girls widespread, at the hands of male workers as well as white employers. (Davies 1990, pp.24-29 and Vukani Women's Collective, 1985).

Training women for the future

The Grail, based in Johannesburg and staffed by Catholic lay-workers, is one of many organisations working with women in community level projects. The Women's Leadership Training courses were started in 1985. 'Competent, informed women are badly needed to help build a new South Africa, based on the values of care and concern for all citizens, meaningful work as an essential part of a thriving economy and the promotion of equality and basic human rights for both men and women and care for the earth as the primary source and sustainer of life.' (The Grail, Work Proposal 1990). For the past two years the Grail has concentrated specifically on gender issues, through courses on health, literacy and basic economics. The group is one of the few working with teenage girls (60 per cent of the population in South Africa is below the age of 20) and runs agricultural and production co-ops for rural women, as well as Woz'Obona, an early childhood learning service group working with predominantly rural pre-schools in the Transvaal and the Transkei.

Another church organisation working with women in training, education and economic projects is the Christian Women's Movement (CWM). Mary Mkhwanazi, CWM General Secretary and for many years regional organiser for SADWU, outlined her perception of some of the issues facing women. 'We must have equal opportunities in work, and equal pay for equal work. Women must be able to own property in their own right, not through their husbands. There must be provision for women to decide about issues like abortion. Shebeens [backyard bars, usually run by women, selling home-brewed liquor] are open 24 hours a day and cause problems for families. The men spend all their money there. These should be legalised, with restricted hours. Violence is a terrible problem. It is now spilling over into local projects and the work can't progess. I say to the women in our groups, and churches: "Our children are being killed by our husbands. As Christian women, what can we do about it?"'

Women and township violence

The violent clashes between ANC/UDF supporters and members of the Inkatha movement of the Kwazulu leader Chief Buthelezi have cost thousands of lives over the past few years, and continue unabated, particularly in Natal and in the areas around Johannesburg. While political solutions are being sought to the problem, women have tried to organise meetings between Inkatha women and ANC women to work on reconciliaton at community level. Women are particularly affected by the widespread destruction of homes. A member of the Natal Organisation of Women (NOW) interviewed on Women Speak said: 'As is usually the case, women are the ones who are faced with the responsibility of bringing about stability in the home, bringing about a situation where there is some kind of security, finding accomodation, feeding the children and things like that. This becomes increasingly difficult in situations of conflict because it means that the meagre resources that you had access to before the conflict situation have been dispersed or totally taken away.' The majority of the refugees fleeing from the conflict in the Pietermaritzburg area in 1988/89 were women and children.

Violence against women

Violence against women, rape, and sexual harassment are issues which have only recently been brought into the open, and women are struggling with them through women's groups, from within their trade unions and within the political organisations. Both white and black women are the victims of sexual violence, but black women are far more vulnerable. According to the Project for the Study of Violence, based at the University of the Witwatersrand in Johannesburg, white anger and fear after the release of Nelson Mandela led to an increase of attacks on domestic workers; black, female and at home they are easy targets for white aggression. The Project sees this as an extension of the extremely high level of intra-familial violence and killings in poor white households, where women are invariably the victims.

Rape Crisis in Cape Town, and People Against Woman Abuse (POWA) in Johannesburg both run shelters for victims of rape and battering. There are now Rape Crisis centres around the country. While violence against women is part of the violence which pervades all sectors of South African society, rape and sexual harrassment of women are sometimes masked by both cultural and political attitudes. A student interviewed by *Speak* on rape in marriage said: 'Immediately a man marries a woman, he has a right over her. Since *lobola* (bride price) still exists in our country, and a woman appears to be a commodity, then when a man has bought that commodity, he has a right to have sex with her. He should not be punished for this.' (*Speak*, no.26, 1989.)

'POWA believes that progressive organisations have a role to play in ending rape and violence against women. They say... these issues must be raised in our organisations. Most organisations state in their constitutions that they are against sexism, but issues affecting women are not taken seriously. The issue of violence and abuse of women should be put high on the agenda... rape and woman-abuse should be fought as seriously as racism is fought. Only in this way can we hope to end rape.' (*Speak*, no.29, 1990.)

Sexism at the centre: the most difficult challenge

The exploitation of women within progressive organisations is a highly sensitive issue. The most controversial resolutions to be put forward at the 1989 COSATU congress dealt with sexual harrassment within COSATU and 'bed politics', where senior males in the union exploited new female recruits in casual relationships. When these relationships collapsed, the women often left the union. The resolution, put forward by the TGWU, called for 'tighter discipline and that such discipline be part of a proposed code of conduct'. (*Agenda*, no.5, 1989.) The resolution was not passed, as the issue was considered to be too delicate, but deferred for further discussion about a general code of conduct. The ANC has such a code of conduct, which mentions sexual harassment, and the National Executive Committee of the ANC has approved policy which condemns wife battering. (*Speak*, no.30, 1990.)

Almost equally controversial was the resolution which called for the promotion of women leadership within COSATU. After much heated discussion, this was passed, with the recognition that factors preventing women from greater involvement in union business should be tackled. These included women's sole responsibility for childcare and housework and the problem of the danger of taking public transport late at night after night meetings. The issue of women's participation in progressive organisations is being taken up by the ANC Women's League, which proposes affirmative action to achieve at least 30 per cent female representation in delegations and in leadership structures within the ANC. Returnee ANC exiles interviewed by *Speak* affirmed: 'We have stressed there should be no token representation. A woman has to work three times as hard as a man to be his equal, because of women's triple oppression. The ANC must work to improve women's lives, so that women will be in a position to get the training and the skills.' (*Speak*, no.30, 1990.)

1991 will be a critical year for women, as it will be for South Africa's future. Activist women are under no illusions about the difficulties they face in the battle to establish the legitimacy of their demands. No longer content to put up with women's oppression in the name of the greater struggle against apartheid, women face strong opposition from men — as they do in all countries. A strong national women's organisation is recognised to be essential to give women the muscle they will need. As Firoza Adam, a delegate from FEDTRAW to a national women's workshop in March 1990 whose aim was to discuss the setting up of a national women's organisation, said: 'It is important for us now to unite women from all walks of life committed to a non-racial, non-sexist, democratic South Africa. Otherwise we could find ourselves in the same position as many other women from other countries in the post-liberation era. After having struggled together with their men for liberation, women comrades still found themselves in a situation where the position of women had not changed. We need to assert our position as women more strongly now than before and we can only do that effectively as one unified loud voice.' (*Speak,* no.28, 1990.)

'Women of my country, we are at war
Young and old, black and white
We are at war
The winds are blowing against us
Laws are ruling against us
We are at war
But do not despair
We are the winning type
Let us fight on
Forward ever, backward never.'

Gcina Mhlope

References

Agenda Collective (1989), *A Journal about Women and Gender:Issues* 4 & 5, Durban.

ANC, *Women March to Freedom,* London.

ANC (1984), *Women Organised,* a FEDSAW Commemorative Pamphlet, London.

Bernstein, H. (1975), *For their Triumphs and for their Tears, Women in Apartheid South Africa,* London: IDAF.

Davies, W. (1990), *We cry for our Land, Farm Workers in South Africa,* Oxford: Oxfam.

Russell, D. (1989), *Lives of Courage, Women for a new South Africa*, New York: Basic Books.

Speak Collective, Various issues of *Speak* magazine, and video '*Women Speak*'.

Suttner and Cronin (1986), *Thirty years of the Freedom Charter*, Johannesburg: Ravan Press.

Vukani Women's Collective (1985), *South African women on the Move*, London: Zed Press.

Suzanne Williams was born in South Africa. She joined Oxfam in 1977 as Deputy Country Representative for Brazil. Subsequently she was one of the founders of the Gender and Development Unit and its first coordinator. She is currently working as a freelance development consultant.

THE CHANGING LIVES OF SOMALIAN WOMEN

RHODA IBRAHIM

Somali women in the rural areas

Somalia is a country where the majority of the people live in the rural areas and nomads live in a harsh and demanding environment. About 46 per cent of the Somalis are nomads, another 29 per cent live in the rural areas and the remaining 25 per cent are urban based.

Somali women play a significant role in Somali society; the division of labour is clearly defined and heavily weighted towards women. Traditionally, the nomadic woman milks the animals, processes the milk, feeds the family, and cares for and watches the livestock. She also collects firewood, cooks, feeds the children, cleans the house and washes the clothes and the utensils. It is her responsibility to weave the mats and produce all the craftwork related to the Somali *aqal* (home) from the outside coverings to the smallest milk-pot. The nomads move from place to place in search of grass and water and women have the heavy responsibility of arranging the transport, dismantling the nomadic *aqal*, and loading it on the back of the camel. Before they start moving, women check and count all the animals and collect all the other artefacts and utensils so that nothing is left behind. When they reach their destination, it is again the woman's duty to provide the family with something to eat and drink, to erect the *aqal*, to check the animals and release the livestock for grazing. The husband only has to decide where to move, arrange additional transport from other families if they are short of transport camels, and build the pen for the animals.

In agricultural societies, women undertake local trading and other activities not related to their private household chores. During the farming season they help in land preparation, plant, weed, harvest, scare away birds from the fields, pack grain in sacks and store it in safe places. They carry the products to the market and sell them. Rural men may marry more than three wives in order to gain extra labour for their farms.

The women in rural areas are economically weak and dependent on their husbands. Livestock is owned individually by the nomadic people. But women's ownership is dispersed through inheritance, since men and women never share inherited property equally, and so female ownership is marginal.

In order to gain small amounts of money for themselves, rural women trade and sell small things. There is a traditional way that women save money called *hagbad*; at the beginning of each week or month, each woman in the group contributes a certain amount of money and all the money is given out to one woman on a rotating basis. This system gives the women a chance to start a small business without going into debt and gives them a certain amount of financial independence.

A girl is directly under her father's authority and is his responsibility. If he dies or is away the control passes to her brother or the closest male relatives. Marriage is negotiated between her father and the groom's relatives, and responsibility for her then passes to her husband. A Somali woman is brought up from childhood to be loyal and obedient to her father and then her husband. All the decisions concerning her life must meet her male relatives' approval.

Polygamy is commonly practised by men. Islamic law lays down strong rules about the extent of this practice: only four wives are permitted and they must be treated on an equal basis. However, polygamy almost always results in insecurity, jealousy and instability among the women as men tend to assist the later wives and ignore the first. In Islamic societies, divorce is the inalienable right of the male. He can release his wife whenever he chooses without any justification.

In traditional Somali society, the ideal Somali woman is the one who performs her household chores well and bears many children, especially male. In some parts of Somalia it is common to refer to the newly born daughter as *rarey* meaning load carrier. Since women are not seen as decision makers, they are considered to be intellectually weaker than men. One unscientific Somali proverb says '*Kal caano geleen kas ma galo*' which means 'the breast that holds milk could not hold intelligence'.

The forces of change and blocks to change

The role of Somali women is slowly changing. One of the first influences was the liberation movement of 1943-1960. Although women were not allowed to participate actively in meetings and decision-making processes they joined the movement, became recognised as nationalists and played a significant role.

Urbanisation has been another major force for social change. Opposition to urban migration became strong when single women started to migrate. Females migrating alone are seen as a problem by both urban and rural men. All female migrants are branded as bad and loose, and sometimes their male relatives punish and repudiate them, as they are seen as a blot on men's reputation. Branding female migrants as bad has been a strong weapon repeatedly used to discourage female migration. Men regard towns as a male world, which they control.

The adaptation of the written Somali language and compulsory education of 1972 and 1975 have provided a remarkable educational expansion in which girls participated. During 1974-1984, female enrolment in primary education increased and enrolment in secondary schools for girls increased from 17 per cent to 34 per cent. However, numbers of female students still decrease at higher levels of education and, especially in rural areas, girls traditionally spend most of their time from an early age helping their mother in household chores and caring for young brothers and sisters. This prevents many from attending school. Anyway, parents prefer to send their sons; many people believe that boys should improve their social status through education while girls improve their status through early marriage.

In town, there is now a network of family-centre schools run by the Women's Education Department under the Ministry of Education providing non-formal education for women. They provide courses in such subjects as food, nutrition, health, sanitation, textiles and handicrafts. Women are also taking literacy classes to learn to read and write. Since education is intimately related to employment opportunities, many women also want to attend adult education classes.

In the debate concerning the effects of female education upon social change, great indignation is expressed against women who believe education means emancipation and equality with men. Some men attempt to solve this problem by marrying women with little or no education whom they hope to impress and control by virtue of their superior station in society.

The impact of urbanisation

Traditionally, rural women know the number of livestock and size of land owned by their family. Urbanisation has made it difficult to know the wealth of their husbands. They rarely know their husband's income as the man deems it a weakness if he tells his wife, and they have practically no control over his financial resources.

Since everything in town costs money, survival in the urban areas depends upon some form of employment, and this economic necessity has led many women into different types of work outside their homes. Nowadays, a lot of women find themselves competing with men who regard them as a threat even in jobs requiring no great skills. The jobs most commonly undertaken by women are as teachers, nurses, clerks, street sweepers and office cleaners. Urban women are also involved in many kinds of self-employed work and 50 per cent of small-scale businesses are run by women e.g. trading cigarettes, fruit, vegetables, charcoal, cooking oil and home-made sweets.

Urban women increasingly choose their own husbands and then simply inform their parents of their choice. Others marry without telling anybody; the families regard this as a disgrace to their honour. The divorce rate in the urban sector is said to be high and I believe that this is due to men's inability to accept the social changes arising from education, employment and an increase in women's income which leads to their economic independence.

The rate of female-headed households is high in urban areas e.g. 66 per cent of the 60 women that we interviewed in Heegan village at Yaqshiid district were heads of households. Female heads of household include those who are widowed, divorced, first wives whom their husbands failed to support, etc.

Conclusion

I believe that urban women are freeing themselves, and migration and then decisions about their marriage are the first actions they undertake in this process. But there seems to be refusal on the part of men to accept the changes taking place in the society as a whole and a misinterpretation of the real purpose of these changes. Men nowadays always claim that the women are becoming 'thick-headed': 'They are not hearing our words'.

Any agency which aims to help the disadvantaged and the poorest must have women as a priority. It is important to explore and identify changes taking place and to implement micro-projects for low-income women in both urban and rural areas, and to tackle and monitor the effects on women of other projects in Somalia. In all agency work it is essential to 'think women' i.e. consciously to talk to and plan with women as well as with men, and to support women in these times of change.

Rhoda Ibrahim had experience in primary school teaching before becoming a development worker. She has worked in Somalia for Oxfam, PSP and Overseas Education Fund International. She is currently studying African women at the Institute For African Alternatives (IFAA).

3

GENDER AWARE PROJECT PLANNING AND EVALUATION

Introduction
Tina Wallace

In the previous two sections of the book, we have raised issues and highlighted some of the particular problems faced by women, especially poor women, because of their roles and responsibilities, and the constraints within which they operate. But we have also shown that, in many situations, women are finding ways to work to improve their circumstances and to challenge their position; and we have stressed the need for international agencies to be more responsive to women's needs.

Aid agencies, who have until recently been unaware of the specific problems and possibilities facing women, have now accepted the crucial role women play and the many real needs they have. But in order to work with women effectively it is essential to have appropriate tools. It is not possible to simply take tools and methods which have been developed in the past for men and use them with women. Women's lack of power, their often restricted ability to attend formal meetings, to act independently, or the fact that many women are not part of existing organisations mean that working with women is different and often more complicated. New methods and ways of working are required. So in this section we focus on ways in which agencies can develop their understanding of the needs of women. Staff need to be able to relate and talk to women, to learn from them and find ways to support them.

Appropriate methodologies for planning and evaluating projects and programmes for their impact on women must be developed. Only by understanding the effect projects and policies are having on women is it possible to know whether the quality of their lives is improving or worsening.

The issue of staffing is critical (and raised in the articles by Longwe, Munro, Mehta and Rubens), as is the need for an agency to have a commitment to working with women in every project and not just in 'women's projects'. It is essential to ensure that the staff employed are aware of the issues, that they do not work with imported gender concepts, and that time is taken to analyse and learn from experience. Working with women in this way is a relatively new, uncharted and at times difficult process, that inevitably involves questioning past development practices and challenging existing gender relations, within the agency, the project or the wider society. Mona Mehta explores how these issues were approached by one Oxfam office in India.

All the papers in this section stress the need to involve women at all stages of the planning and implementation of projects and programmes. This applies whether the project is deemed to be a 'women's project' or a community development, forestry, health or agricultural project. Sara Hlupekile Longwe's paper links the lack of attention that has been given to women's needs within the development process directly to a lack of awareness among those who plan and implement development projects. This has important implications for all development agencies.

Longwe, Moser, Munro and ZARD all propose different methods for finding out what women's situation is and how best to address it. They all emphasise the need to listen to women and respond to their articulated needs, and to involve them in planning and evaluation. Sara Hlupekile Longwe defines gender awareness as recognising that women have special needs, are disadvantaged as a group, and that ultimately their development requires equality with men. She provides a model for assessing how a project is affecting women. Using this five-point model, staff can judge how far they are meeting women's 'concerns', which Sara Hlupekile Longwe defines as the day to day needs for improving their existence within traditional gender roles; and how far they are addressing women's 'issues', which she defines as the need for more access to resources, and greater control over income; in fact, for equality between women and men.

Caroline Moser presents a different model, but one which also differentiates between women's needs relating to their present workloads and responsibilities (which she calls practical needs), and those which relate to changing gender relations and giving women more control and more power (which she calls strategic needs). She uses the distinction between 'practical' and 'strategic' which was originally made by Maxine Molyneux. Maxine Molyneux defined practical interests as those which arise from women's roles within the sexual division of labour and enable them to meet their basic needs. Strategic interests are those which challenge women's subordinate position by, for example, legislating against discrimination. She stressed that all women's interests — be they practical or strategic — are shaped by issues such as class and ethnicity, and can only be analysed and understood within each society.

Caroline Moser builds her model on this critical distinction between practical and strategic, but she moves away from the idea of interests to that of needs. Essentially her model focuses on the triple roles of women (reproductive, productive and community management), from which arise women's needs, classified as practical or strategic. Using these tools she looks at the ways in which practical and strategic gender needs can be met in policy and practice, and how they have been addressed or neglected by development agencies over the past decades.

Miranda Munro takes as her starting point the fact that agencies must meet the needs of the people they work with in order to do effective development, but suggests that in practice this can be very difficult. She describes ways of approaching the community that can help to ensure that a proper partnership is established between the agency and the people concerned, and that this partnership includes the women. She follows the work of Molyneux, and Moser and Levy, and stresses that, while it is important to identify women's practical and strategic interests, this must be done together with the women, and may in fact be a complex and sensitive process for the whole community. The agency must not impose their cultural ideas on the women or men involved, and defining interests may turn out to be a slow process of discussion. This initial process must also take into account which practical and strategic needs can actually be met within the political, social and economic conditions of the community.

To assist agencies in this difficult process, Miranda Munro emphasises the importance of improving awareness of gender relations among staff; of improving ways of consulting with women; and of improving the quality of information available for planning by using a range of different techniques, including rapid rural appraisal.

Another way of improving understanding of gender relations is to develop checklists on gender which are relevant to a particular society or country. There are many checklists available from international organisations such as USAID, ODA, Ford Foundation, and from academic sources. The one developed by the Zambia Association for Research and Development is presented in this section, as an example of a very wide ranging and helpful checklist. However, the real value of checklists is the actual process of drawing one up, in which people work out, in a participative way, the most critical factors affecting women in their particular country or situation.

Other models have been developed — and one developed by DAWN is presented by Peggy Antrobus at the end of this book — and in this section we have not attempted to provide a comprehensive overview, but simply to provide some ideas on staffing, project appraisal and planning from a gender perspective. This section closes with a short piece by Frances Rubin on evaluation and some of the problems experienced when undertaking project evaluation from a gender perspective. She highlights the need, if this process of evaluation is to be successful, to have clear and gender relevant terms of reference for the evaluation; to choose staff who understand the issues; and to ensure that women are consulted during the field visits. It is crucial to understand the gender implications in every project and throughout the programme, and to see gender issues as central to all development work.

ANALYSIS OF A DEVELOPMENT PROGRAMME

MONA MEHTA

Background to the programme

In 1984, Oxfam West India office made the decision to recruit a
Woman Project Officer for undertaking women's development
work. The office representative was strongly convinced of the need
for women's development and the decision was the result of
lengthy discussions between some existing staff members (all male)
and the head office.

The premises on which this decision was based were:

Women were not involved in the development programmes
which the office supported, especially in the decision-making
processes.

The male staff were unable to make any headway in changing
this situation, because the social reality made any sustained and
qualitative contact with women difficult. The male staff were also
less interested or competent in addressing the issue.

A woman project officer, who had some development experience,
would be better able to tackle gender issues.

Thus, in May 1984 I joined Oxfam as a woman project officer. At
that time I had only a year's relevant work experience, and some
formal training in development work, which had given me a
rational basis of analysis, communication and learning skills.

The brief of encouraging and supporting women's development
work was so vast and so vaguely defined that it was more a
question of finding a new approach; an approach which would also
fit in with Oxfam's priorities and structures. After six months of
getting to know the various areas, the project partners and to some
extent the 'invisible' women, the strategy adopted was to initiate
and encourage women's development activities and organisation at
the grassroots level in one of the poorest areas. The aim was to
develop structures which enabled women to come together and,

over time, identify their own needs and priorities and consequent development activities.

During the year that this strategy was attempted, it became increasingly evident that it was not working. The major reasons for this failure, apart from my obvious inexperience, were that, though this strategy had been in line with the West India office approach to the other programmes, it was not relevant in the context of women's development. Women's position in society was different from that of men and needed a new and different strategy. Also, I was unable to spend enough time in the area of concentrated grassroots organisational work, since this was not consistent with the priorities of Oxfam's work, which were basically that of a funding organisation.

The failure, however, enabled more reflection on the issue of women's development within the context of Oxfam's work. It was felt that women's development was not just about setting up a few separate women's groups while letting most of the development work remain male-dominated and male-oriented. It was important to make women's development central to all of Oxfam's work, and to initiate qualitative rather than mere quantitative changes in the programme.

Once accepted, the work strategy and my own role as woman project officer shifted enormously, from concentrating on the project level to working at three different levels:

at Oxfam organisational level, providing inputs on the issue;

at the office level, constantly questioning our work from a gender perspective and finding concrete ways in which qualitative changes could be initiated;

at the programme level, working with the project leaders, mostly male, and with the still mostly 'invisible' women.

This strategy was evolved and attempted over three years. In the following section I will attempt to analyse the basic assumptions and resultant experiences. I would, however, like to make clear that this narration is from my own perspective, and I was only one of the many actors involved, many of whom made far greater contributions to the whole process. Also, although in the above background I describe the three levels of my role, they were actually a product of a continuing evolution and at no time were so clearly defined. Here I will only analyse the levels of the organisation and its structures. This undoubtedly presents an incomplete picture as it omits the project work which is a vital aspect of Oxfam's work and priorities. This omission is not because the people are not important but because of the limited scope of this paper. It is also felt to be important to look at one's own house and try to put it in order before other societies or groups are analysed.

Analysis

The assumption that women's development could best be achieved through making gender central to the issue of development, and the subsequent need to initiate qualitative changes, was based on firstly, the negative experiences of the previous development attempts, which can now be analysed as attempts to apply the strategy of male-dominated development to women's development. This was, in its very basic premises, contradictory and self-defeating. Secondly, the belief that seeing women's development as just a separate and 'added' aspect to development in general was also self-defeating, as it perpetuated marginalisation and kept women's development work separate from what were considered to be the serious aspects of development.

The fundamental basis of the strategy was to make gender central to all the work of Oxfam, and this had far-reaching implications at the Oxfam organisational level. Even if it was attempted only within the West India office, many of the changes needed the involvement of structures beyond the individual office. To generate influence at this level a separate, informal structure developed within the overall framework of the organisation. This started in 1985, with a group of five women project officers who only had in common the facts that they were all women and had project-related jobs. The first meeting made apparent the different perceptions of women's development which came from the reality of differing backgrounds and different work roles; however, there was a commonality of interest in the issue and a commitment to it. Thus, accepting the differences, a common ground could be developed. In fact, in many ways exploring the differences gave the process of search a dynamism and strength.

The group as it developed decided to shift towards becoming an issue-based group. The decision was based on two assumptions: firstly, that it was possible that men could also be 'feminist', and secondly, that it would be strategically erroneous to make gender a sex-based issue, as it was seen as an issue concerning both men and women, and the unequal men-women relationship. Members of the group recognised that there were men in the organisation who were sensitive and gender aware, and that it was strategically important to involve them because of the reality of the hierarchical structure. Also, within the organisation there was a tendency to make women's development work sex specific, seen to be of interest to women only. This was seen as unacceptable and contradictory to the aims of the group.

The group also had to face the issue of 'Western feminism', especially given Oxfam's international structure and the support that the group received from the newly established Gender and Development Unit at the head office in the UK. This problem continues to arise from time to time, as threatened individuals try to dismiss the issue by labelling it as Western, and therefore of no relevance to the local situation. It is seen also as anti-tradition and anti-culture. The deeper assumption here is that any new ideas that challenge or question culture or traditions are taboo. Challenging gender relations, especially as they are closely linked to the household and thus central to the whole structure of society, is thought to be particularly subversive and interfering. Even in Marxist ideology, the issue of gender relations is taboo as it is seen as an imperialist weapon for diverting attention from the basic issue of the class struggle. Thus, the gender issue has to deal with antagonism from two levels, culture and ideology. It seems to be easier for many people to dismiss the issue as 'Western', 'bourgeois' and the work of a few urban, non-traditional women.

The structure of the group, named Action for Gender Relations Asia (AGRA), was outside the management hierarchy, and it emphasised the involvement of all levels of staff; this in itself also had implications for the organisation and the work, because it gave an example of the possible alternative ways of working for change within the organisation; it opened up issues of hierarchy within the organisation; and it brought up the question of the implication of gender issues within the organisation itself, and in the personal lives of the staff (especially in relation to their families).

It is fairly clear that AGRA has been successful in making gender relations an issue which all staff are aware of, though this does not necessarily imply that all staff are positive about the issue. Gender awareness-raising is a process of changing attitudes and, while it is possible to enable people to confront their own biases and attitudes, it is not possible to change these if the individuals do not wish to do so. This posed a number of problems. In the short term, any movement towards a more gender sensitive work strategy would continue to face obstacles put up by staff who do not believe in gender equality. This is very much a question that the present group has to face and work with. In the longer term, gender awareness and commitment to gender equality would be a necessary criteria for staff recruitment.

AGRA, though to an extent able to make gender an important issue in project work, was initially more involved with the organisation and its staff. An issue faced by many staff is the contradiction between their new gender awareness and the continuing reality of their own social surroundings. Many staff members find their attempts to practise gender equality a frustrating experience, especially where there is resistance from within their own families. Informal staff partners' forums have been initiated to spread awareness of gender and other development issues among the families; to foster an increased sharing between partners; and to create support structures among the staff. The experience of the forums has been extremely rewarding, though the process has not been easy. It is difficult to bring together people who come from very varied backgrounds and cultures and share only the fact that they are partners of staff. It is an experience, however, which is spreading among other offices and helping to overcome many other issues besides gender.

The impact of practical gender work strategies on development is still quite limited; this is partly due to the nature of the organisational structure and partly due to the difficulty of coming up with clear strategies or answers. Here it is very important to mention one of the major limitations of AGRA — only Oxfam staff are represented; there are no partners from among the people we work with. This gap automatically limits the contributions to practical change strategies at project level.

Several case studies of projects have been undertaken, with a view to understanding the processes experienced by project partners in addressing the issue. The studies involve both projects which have had a positive impact on women and those which have not. These studies are still continuing and so it is not possible to see the end result. The experience to date shows that suitable criteria for such studies need to be developed and this requires staff time and involvement. The organisation has to create the time for staff to undertake such studies. This is not easy in an organisation like Oxfam which generally places a lot of emphasis on action.

This emphasis on action has long-term implications for the development of further awareness, and the resultant changes in work strategies on gender issues. The studies may point to the need for major changes in the criteria for supporting projects, and possibly a shift, for quite some time, away from funding action programmes towards more supportive work, such as providing training and other inputs. This would, of course, require major policy decisions in the organisation, but at some point it may become essential if our work is to have any major impact.

Partners, group leaders and women

The West India office worked mainly with groups of poor and exploited people and more or less directly. The shift in strategy required that, instead of forming similar and separate groups of women as attempted earlier, the focus should be on working with already existing partner groups in order to influence them to undertake gender issues. This was easier said than done. Some of the contradictions of the strategy and subsequent experience are presented.

Many of the leaders personally found the issue extremely threatening and against their beliefs. However, since they saw the issue as a pressure coming from a funding agency, they made some token efforts, such as including a couple of women on the committee, etc. Some others were more open but, being essentially paternalistic leaders, they took this as an opportunity to extend their power. They came up with proposals for very traditional development activities for women, which would lead to women working, but under the control of male leaders. A few progressive young leaders took up the challenge of making gender inequality an issue in their work. They, however, still had to face the patriarchal structures in their own communities and groups. A majority of them thus followed the strategy of appointing women as community organisers to undertake women's development, while they provided support through their work with the men.

This strategy, though possibly the most feasible in the existing circumstances, had inherent problems. It assumed that the women workers, simply by virtue of being women, were interested and competent to organise women. In reality a number of the women were not interested in development issues at all and many were too young to have adequate experiences to enable commitment. The few who were interested started off with lesser awareness than their male colleagues, since very few women have any experience of development. This created a hierarchy in the group, with the male workers developing a paternalistic attitude towards the women and reinforcing the traditional roles in the community. Only a handful of women and men were able to challenge this set-up. If this strategy is followed the risk of paternalistic structures developing is very high. Conscious realisation of the danger of paternalism, careful selection of women workers, and adequate emphasis on training for both the women and the men would minimise this risk.

Another problem of the strategy was that most of the existing activities undertaken by the groups were in some ways related to economic goals, and this emphasis was further aggravated by the drought and consequent relief activities. In contrast, the approach to the organisation of women was very different, as various experiences had highlighted the problems of income generating projects for women; the emphasis was thus on conscientisation and organisation, so that women could then independently determine their priorities and consequent activities. The two approaches obviously did not match, and group leaders who were interested only in the first approach found it difficult to accept the second. Some of the Oxfam staff, too, found it difficult to accept this approach as it immediately showed up the contradictions in other programmes and implied the need to question all of our work in a new light. The contradictions still remain and will remain until Oxfam honestly undertakes major rethinking on its approach and priorities and the consequent implications for change in the nature of programmes supported. In the few situations where groups accepted the strategy, albeit limitedly, there have been positive developments and women's groups have evolved fairly independently.

The experience of organising women is also of high value. An issue that has repeatedly come up as being crucial in determining the success or failure of an organisation has been the class and ethnic differences between women. In many cases a group did not really form because poorer women had differing interests but could not articulate them, and so withdrew from the group. This culture of silence has also had an impact on the organisational process. It is not easy for women to put aside the views of men and develop their own views, based on their own experiences. They find themselves having to face the issues of class, race, and gender oppression; and their interests have to be articulated in the concrete reality of the constant struggle for survival.

Conclusion

The project analysed above has been a constantly evolving one, and more of a search for answers than an answer in itself. It has had some positive effects in terms of the impact on Oxfam's own organisational structure and work. It has also started a process of change and a search for ways in which women can be equally involved in the development process, and this with a number of women who until now have been treated as mere objects to be developed.

In conclusion, I would like to say that all of us who have been involved in this project started out with little more than goodwill and a commitment to gender equality. It is hoped that our experiences have in some way contributed to the understanding of gender issues and that it will help the work undertaken to combat injustice, inequality and oppression.

Mona Mehta is a development activist and was until recently a member of the Oxfam staff in India. She was a founder member and coordinator of AGRA. She has studied at the Institute of Social Studies in Le Hague, and has an interest in the problems of tribal people in Gujerat.

GENDER AWARENESS:
THE MISSING ELEMENT IN THE THIRD WORLD
DEVELOPMENT PROJECT

SARA HLUPEKILE LONGWE

Although development agencies and Third World governments are presently in the process of trying to formulate and implement new policies on women's development, success with these policies depends on increased gender awareness amongst development personnel. This paper looks at what gender awareness means in looking at women's development in the Third World, and defines this awareness in terms of an ability to recognise women's issues at every stage of the development project cycle.

The need for gender awareness

The general lack of attention to women's needs within the development process stems from a general lack of gender awareness amongst those who plan and implement development projects. The project target group is often treated as an undifferentiated group of 'people' without recognising the special needs of women; more likely, and worse, a male biased vocabulary is used to describe the target group which becomes 'men' rather than 'people': in this way the women of the target group actually disappear from sight — and from thought. Typically a project document describes the Third World farmer as 'he'; but in actuality, the Third World farmer is usually a woman.

Development in the Third World is not merely about increased productivity and welfare, although these things are important. Development is also about meeting the needs of those that are most in need, and about increased participation and equality. Development is therefore also concerned with enabling people to take charge of their own lives, and escape from the poverty which arises not from lack of productivity but rather from oppression and exploitation. The typical rural woman in the Third World is a hardworking producer of food who remains, with her children, short of food and malnourished: the food is consumed by the husband rather than the wife; by men rather than women and children; by landlords rather than tenants; by townspeople rather than rural people; by rich consumers rather than poor producers.

In this situation, the problem in women's development is not primarily concerned with enabling women to be more productive, more efficient, or to use their labour more effectively. These things may be important, especially in special situations. But the central issue of women's development is women's empowerment, to enable women to take an equal place with men, and to participate equally in the development process in order to achieve control over the factors of production on an equal basis with men.

There are three essential elements in gender awareness: first the recognition that women have different and special needs; second that they are a disadvantaged group, relative to men, in terms of their level of welfare and access to and control over the factors of production; third that women's development entails working towards increased equality and empowerment for women, relative to men.

Adherence to a policy on women's development may be assisted by referring to a standard checklist of questions to be asked at every stage of the project cycle. But a sympathetic and imaginative interpretation of policy for all situations will depend on a good understanding of women's development, a commitment to it, and the ability to raise questions of one's own.

Criteria for recognising women's issues

Gender awareness means being able to recognise women's issues. This section of the paper introduces five criteria which I have found useful as a basis for identifying women's issues, and therefore as an analytical framework for understanding women's development.

If the central issue in women's development is equality with men, then there is a need to spell out the different forms and levels of equality that constitute development. Much of the development literature on this subject is concerned with defining equality according to the conventional sectors of the economy and society: equality in education, employment, under the law, and so on. The difficulty with this system of analytical division is that it provides a focus on areas of social life, rather than the role of increased equality in the development process. I shall therefore introduce five different levels of equality as the basis for criteria to assess the level of women's development in any area of social or economic life.

WOMEN'S DEVELOPMENT CRITERIA

Level of Equality		
Control	↑	↑
Participation	*Increased*	*Increased*
Conscientisation	*Equality*	*Empowerment*
Access		
Welfare		

It is suggested that these levels of equality are in hierarchical relationship, so that equality of control is more important for women's development than equality of welfare. It is also suggested that the higher levels of equality are automatically higher levels of development and empowerment.

Any social situation becomes a women's issue when one of the above five levels of equality is called into question; it becomes a more serious issue when it is concerned with the higher levels, and a more basic issue when it is concerned with the lower levels.

Let us now look at each of these five levels in a little more detail to see what is entailed at each level:

i. Welfare:
The level of material welfare of women, relative to men, in such matters as food supply, income and medical care. This level of equality is not concerned with whether women are themselves the active creators and producers of their material needs: such involvement would suggest a higher degree of empowerment and development.

ii. Access:
Women's access to the factors of production on an equal basis with men: equal access to land, labour, credit, training, marketing facilities and all publicly available services and benefits. Here equality of access is obtained by ensuring the principle of equality of opportunity, which typically entails the reform of the law and administrative practice to remove all forms of discrimination against women.

iii. Conscientisation:
The understanding of the difference between sex roles and gender roles, and that the latter are cultural and can be changed;

conscientisation also involves a belief that the sexual division of labour should be fair and agreeable to both sides, and not involve the economic or political domination of one sex by the other. Belief in sexual equality lies at the basis of gender awareness, and provides the basis for collective participation in the process of women's development.

iv. Participation:
Women's equal participation in the decision making process, policy making, planning and administration. It is a particularly important aspect of development projects, where participation means involvement in needs assessment, project formulation, implementation and evaluation. Equality of participation means involving the women of the community affected by the decisions taken, and involving them in the same proportion in decision making as their proportion in the community at large.

v. Control:
A utilisation of the participation of women in the decision-making process through conscientisation and mobilisation, to achieve equality of control over the factors of production, and the distribution of benefits. Equality of control means a balance of control between men and women, so that neither side is put into a position of dominance.

A development project addresses women's development when it addresses a women's issue. The term 'women's issue' is here defined differently from a 'women's concern'. 'Women's concern' is here used to describe matters relating to women's sex roles, or their traditional and subordinate sex-stereotyped gender roles. By contrast, a 'women's issue' is one which relates to equality with men in any social or economic role, and involves any of the above five levels of equality. A main purpose, therefore, of the five criteria is to show whether one is dealing with 'women's issues' or 'women's concerns'.

In terms of the above criteria, poverty relates to basic welfare, where family income falls below the level necessary to meet basic needs and subsistence. There is nothing in this definition of poverty which necessarily means that poverty is a 'women's issue'. Poverty is, first and foremost, a 'general concern' which affects both men and women. It becomes more of a 'women's concern' where women have the main responsibility of producing the food crop, and where women have the responsibility of ensuring the welfare of children. Poverty becomes a 'women's issue' where food and income is not fairly distributed between men and women, and where women do not receive a fair share of the fruits of their labour.

The failure of development projects in the Third World to address women's development may be understood in terms of the above five criteria. From the 1970s there was the criticism that women were treated as invisible, and women's needs were not addressed at all. With the increasing attempt to address women's development, the common criticism is that the so-called women's development projects are addressing 'women's concerns', rather than the issues of inequality, and therefore the project intervention leaves the overall structure of inequality untouched. However, a small number of current projects are now trying to address real women's development; but usually such projects work only at the lower levels of welfare and access to the factors of production, and are not facing up to women's need for more control over their social and economic lives.

Assessing women's needs

Project formulation ought to begin with an investigation into the needs of the target group, both by considering the needs which are implicit in their situation, and by asking them about their felt needs and priorities. The first and perhaps most important reason why 'women's issues' are overlooked is that usually no needs assessment is carried out.

Typically a project is formulated by a consultant or programme officer who has no detailed or specific information on the situation or particular needs of the target group or affected community, but who identifies project objectives on the basis of knowledge of the overall national situation and development priorities and objectives. Typically, this background knowledge includes little or no information on the general situation of women in the country, or the main issues which need to be addressed in women's development.

The stage therefore is set for the formulation of a project which overlooks the position of women entirely. In so doing, a project is likely to have a negative effect on women's development, especially by increasing the burden of labour upon women, whilst allowing project benefits to be controlled by men. Such a project may well be set for failure, since many women will quietly opt out of project activities as they see the extra burdens put upon them, and the lack of benefit to themselves and their children.

My argument is that the needs of women in a target group and affected community must be assessed from the start of a project at all five levels: welfare, access, conscientisation, participation and control, with a view to suggesting how the project can make a meaningful contribution to women's development at each of these levels. It is also necessary to identify priority target groups, such as female heads of household or landless widows, who are more in need of development assistance, and who are more at risk if the project intervention does not take account of their special position and needs.

Women's issues in project identification

The usual situation is that women are completely overlooked when identifying the project objectives. If the agency responsible for formulating the project is asked why there is nothing about women's development in the project document, a typical answer is that 'This project is not concerned with women, it is a forestry project', or simply 'This is not a women's project'.

There is still a common perception amongst development personnel that women's development is confined to separate and special women's projects, and that these separate projects should be concerned with income generating activities, especially in women's clubs and in the sex-stereotyped activities of knitting, sewing and cooking. However, in terms of the five criteria introduced in this paper these 'women's club projects' cannot be seen as a contribution to women's development, but rather as a subtraction from it.

Women's issues in project design

Since the women's development component is typically missing at the stages of needs assessment and project identification, it follows that there is usually little to be found at the final stage of project formulation — project design.

Women's issues in project implementation

For the few projects whose design is seriously concerned with making a contribution to women's development, it is sad to see this concern evaporate at the stage of implementation. One reason for this is that the members of the implementing team are themselves not gender aware, and not committed to the process of women's development, and fall easy prey to the various forms of bureaucratic resistance which I have described elsewhere (Longwe, 1989). It is common to hear the excuse that 'we are trying to do things which are against the local custom, and nobody seems interested, so why should we bother?' At the stage of project implementation the most important level of the criteria is conscientisation — amongst the implementing team!

It is important to note that the five criteria see women's development as a process of women's increased access, participation and control, and not merely as the outcome of increased welfare, income, production and skills. The development project is part of this process, and must remain true to it. Therefore the strategies and methods of implementation must exemplify the process of women's empowerment in such matters as the proportion of women in the team concerned with implementation, the level of gender awareness within the team, the proportion of female members of the target group who are members of the project management committee, equal conditions of employment for men and women, and so on. Conversely, a male dominated and patriarchal style of project administration contains implicit lessons and messages which negate project objectives concerned with women's development.

Women's issues in project evaluation

It follows from the newness of policy formulation on women's development, as well as the general shortage of professional experience in this area, that there is a general lack of know-how on how to evaluate a project's contribution towards women's development. The lack of activity in this area is compounded by the confusion of different methodologies in project evaluation, as well as the domination of the field by cost benefit analysis — a method which has little relevance to the field of women's development. Cost benefit analysis is concerned with measuring project outputs, whereas the evaluation of a women's development project must be concerned with assessing whether the social and political processes of empowerment are taking place. The evaluation of women's development must take place at each stage of the project cycle.

Women's issues in a development programme

In some ways the individual development project provides too narrow a focus on women's development. I will therefore look briefly at some of the programme level concerns which need to be considered.

Typically the individual development project is part of an overall programme of projects being implemented by a government agency. Similarly a development agency has a programme of many projects which are supported in any one country — the so-called Country Programme. Such a programme is guided by overall policies, and has its own priorities and themes. The question here, therefore, is whether women's development is a strong element within the overall theme, or is seen as a side issue.

The Women's Development Criteria provide the potential basis for evaluating a whole programme of projects in terms of their contribution towards women's development. For instance, an appraisal of the women's development component within a programme may be done by using the five criteria to look at the level of equality addressed in the objectives of each individual project within the programme. The Country Programme of any development agency in any Third World country is likely to be very underdeveloped in that there are many projects which reveal no attempt to deal with women's development, and those that do mostly address the lower levels of welfare and access.

It is important for the programme as a whole to take account of the overall situation of women in the Third World country, to take account of the policies on women's development of the Third World country, and to work out feasible starting points for introducing into the programme more projects which address women's development.

Such considerations might suggest quite different sorts of projects from anything which arises from attempting to bolster the women's development component in general development projects. For instance, if the low level of gender awareness amongst development planners and implementers is an obstacle to progress, then a women's development project might take the form of providing training workshops for development personnel within the government implementing agencies. Similarly, a contribution towards women's development may be made by assisting with the improvement of the institutional capacity of the government bureaucracy to plan, implement and evaluate projects addressing women's development. Some governments have set up Women in Development (WID) units within the government bureaucracy; whereas these units may remain ineffectual and sidelined if they are starved of equipment and trained personnel, they do have the potential to become effective and influential if they become the focus for development aid and technical assistance.

However, it may be difficult for the individual multilateral or bilateral agencies to tailor a Country Programme around particular development priorities, and a Country Programme is always in danger of being a mere collection of projects without much in the way of inter-connections or common theme. The building of a balanced and purposeful theme concerned with women's development suggests close collaboration with other development personnel working in this area, not only within different government ministries and implementing agencies, but also within the different development agencies which are operating in the particular Third World country. It is this sort of close collaboration which will enable the local office of the development agency to achieve a better Third World perspective on women's development, and make a more appropriate and meaningful contribution to this area of great need, but small progress.

References

Longwe, Sara Hlupekile, 1989, 'Supporting Women's Development in the Third World: Distinguishing Between Intervention and Interference'. Paper presented at a Training Programme in WID Issues for FINNIDA Staff, Helsinki, January 30th to February 15th, 1989.

Sara Hlupekile Longwe is a consultant in women's development and an activist for women's rights, based in Lusaka. Her earlier struggles as a secondary school teacher and later as a university administrator, provided a sound training for a subsequent full-time career in resisting oppression.

GENDER PLANNING IN THE THIRD WORLD: MEETING PRACTICAL AND STRATEGIC GENDER NEEDS

CAROLINE O. N. MOSER

While the important role that women play in Third World development processes is now widely recognised, awareness of the issue of 'gender and development' has not necessarily resulted in its translation into planning practice. Indeed for many practitioners involved in different aspects of social and economic development planning, the lack of adequate operational frameworks has been particularly problematic. The purpose of this article is to contribute toward the resolution of this problem. It describes the development of a planning approach which, in taking account of the fact that women and men play different roles in Third World societies and therefore often have different needs, provides both the conceptual framework and the methodology for incorporating gender into planning.

Gender planning

Gender planning is based on the understanding that because men and women play different roles in society, they often have different needs. Therefore when identifying and implementing planning needs it is important to disaggregate households and families within communities on the basis of gender, identifying men and women, boys and girls.

The triple role of women

In most low-income households, 'women's work' includes not only reproductive work (the childbearing and rearing responsibilities) required to guarantee the maintenance and reproduction of the labour force but also productive work, often as secondary income earners. In addition, women are involved in community managing work undertaken at a local community level in both urban and rural contexts.

Because the triple role of women is not recognised, the fact that women, unlike men, are severely constrained by the burden of simultaneously balancing these roles of reproductive, productive, and community managing work is ignored. In addition, only productive work is recognised as work. Reproductive and community managing work are both seen as 'natural' and so are not valued. This has serious consequences for women. It means that most, if not all, of the work that they do is made invisible and fails to be rewarded. In contrast, most of men's work is valued, either directly through paid remuneration, or indirectly through status and political power.

Identifying practical and strategic gender needs

When planners are blind to the triple role of women, and to the fact that women's needs are not always the same as men's, they fail to see the necessity of relating planning to women's specific requirements. But if planning is to succeed it has to be gender aware. It has to develop the capacity to differentiate not only on the basis of income, now commonly accepted, but also on the basis of gender. It is important to emphasise that the rationale for gender planning does not ignore other important issues such as race, ethnicity and class, but focuses specifically on gender precisely because this tends to be subsumed within class in so much policy and planning.

Gender needs

Planning for low-income women in the Third World must be based on their interests, in other words their prioritised concerns. In the process of identification of interests it is useful to differentiate between 'women's interests', strategic gender interests, and practical gender interests, following the model developed by Maxine Molyneux (1985).

By identifying the different interests women have it is possible then to translate them into planning needs, in other words the means by which their concerns may be satisfied.

Within the planning context, women's needs vary widely, determined not only by the specific socio-economic context, but also by the particular class, ethnic and religious structures of individual societies. The distinction between strategic and practical gender interests is of critical importance, as is the distinction between strategic and practical gender needs.

Strategic gender needs

Strategic gender needs are those needs which arise from the analysis of women's subordination to men. The strategic gender needs identified to overcome women's subordination will vary depending on the particular cultural and socio-political context. Strategic gender needs may include all or some of the following: 'the abolition of the sexual division of labour; the alleviation of the burden of domestic labour and child care; the removal of institutionalised forms of discrimination such as rights to own land or property, or access to credit; the establishment of political equality; freedom of choice over childbearing; and the adoption of adequate measures against male violence and control over women' (Molyneux, 1985, p.233).

Practical gender needs

In contrast, practical gender needs are those drawn from the concrete conditions women experience, in their position within the gender division of labour, and come out of their practical gender interests for human survival. Practical gender needs therefore are usually a response to an immediate perceived necessity which is identified by women within a specific context. As Molyneux has written, 'they do not generally entail a strategic goal such as women's emancipation or gender equality ... nor do they challenge the prevailing forms of subordination even though they arise directly out of them' (Molyneux, 1985, p.233).

Policy approaches to low-income Third World women and gender planning

Throughout the Third World, particularly in the past decade, there has been a proliferation of policies, programmes and projects designed to assist low-income women. Identification of the extent to which such planned interventions have been appropriate to the gender needs of women requires an examination of the conceptual rationale underlying different policy approaches from a gender planning perspective. Each approach can be evaluated in terms of which of women's triple roles it recognises, and which practical or strategic gender needs it meets. Such analysis illustrates the utility of the methodological tools of gender planning evaluation.

Until recently there has been little systematic classification or categorisation of the various policy initiatives to help low-income women. Concern for their needs coincided historically with a recognition of their important role in development. Since the 1950s a diversity of interventions has been formulated, not in isolation, but reflecting changes in macro-level economic and social policy approaches to Third World development. Thus the shift in policy approach towards women, from 'welfare', to 'equity' to 'anti-poverty', as categorised by Buvinic (1983), to the two other approaches categorised here as 'efficiency' and 'empowerment', has mirrored general shifts in Third World development policies, from modernisation policies of accelerated growth, through basic needs strategies associated with redistribution, to the more recent compensatory measures associated with structural adjustment policies.

While the different policy approaches are described chronologically, it is recognised that this presents an over-simplification of reality. In practice many of the policies have appeared more or less simultaneously. Agencies have not necessarily followed any ordered logic in changing their approach, most frequently jumping from welfare to efficiency without consideration of the other approaches. Different policies have particular appeal to different types of institutions.

The welfare approach

It was First World welfare programmes, specifically targeted at 'vulnerable groups', which were among the first to identify women as the main beneficiaries. As Buvinic has noted, these were the emergency relief programmes widely initiated in Europe after the end of World War II, accompanying the economic assistance measures intended to ensure reconstruction. Relief aid was provided directly to low-income women, who, in their roles as wives and mothers, were seen as those primarily concerned with their family's welfare. This relief distribution was undertaken by international private relief agencies, and relied on the unpaid work of middle-class women volunteers for effective and cheap implementation (Buvinic, 1986).

The creation of two parallel approaches to development assistance — on the one hand financial aid for economic growth, on the other hand relief aid for socially 'vulnerable' groups — was then replicated in development policy for Third World countries.

The welfare approach assumes first, that women are passive

recipients of development, rather than participants in the development process. Second, that motherhood is the most important role for women. Third, that child rearing is the most effective role for women in all aspects of economic development. While this approach sees itself as 'family centred' in orientation, it focuses entirely on women in their reproductive role, and assumes men's role to be productive. The main method of implementation is through 'top-down' handouts of free goods and services. When training is included it is for those skills deemed appropriate for non-working housewives and mothers.

Although welfare programmes for women have widened their scope considerably over the past decades, the concern remains to meet women's practical gender needs in their reproductive role. They identify women themselves rather than lack of resources as the problem, and place the solution to family welfare in women's hands, without questioning their 'natural' role. Although the top-down nature of so many welfare programmes tends to create dependency rather than to assist women to become more independent, they remain very popular precisely because they are politically safe, not questioning the traditionally accepted role of women. Such assumptions tend to result in the exclusion of women from development programmes operated by the mainstream development agencies that provide a significant proportion of development funds (Germaine, 1977). The welfare approach is not concerned with meeting women's strategic gender needs in reproduction, one of the most important of which is the right for women to have control over their own bodies.

By the 1970s dissatisfaction with the welfare approach was widespread, with criticism coming from groups representing three very different positions. First, in the United States, a group of mainly female professionals and researchers were concerned with the increasing evidence that Third World development projects were negatively affecting women. Second, development economists and planners were concerned with the failure of modernisation theory in the Third World. Third, the United Nations designated a Women's Decade, starting in 1976. This was a result of the 1975 International Women's Year Conference, which formally 'put women on the agenda' and provided legitimacy for the proliferation of a wide diversity of Third World women's organisations.

During the 1970s criticisms of such groups resulted in the

development of a number of alternative approaches to women, namely equity, anti-poverty, efficiency and empowerment.

The equity approach

By the 1970s studies showed that although women were often the predominant contributors to the basic productivity of their communities, particularly in agriculture, their economic contribution was not referred to in national statistics or in development projects (Boserup, 1970). At the same time new modernisation projects, with innovative agricultural methods and sophisticated technologies, were negatively affecting women, displacing them from their traditional productive functions, and diminishing the income, status and power that they had in traditional relations. Findings indicated that neocolonialism as much as colonialism was contributing to the decline in women's status in developing countries.

On the basis of evidence such as this, the Women in Development (WID) group in the United States challenged the prevailing assumption that modernisation was equated with increasing gender equality. They asserted that capitalist development models imposed on much of the Third World had exacerbated inequalities between men and women. They recognised that women are active participants in the development process, who provide a critical, if often unacknowledged, contribution to economic growth. They started from the basic assumption that economic strategies have frequently had a negative impact on women, and acknowledged that they must be 'brought into' the development process through access to employment and the market place; they therefore recognised women's practical gender need to earn a livelihood. However, this WID approach was also concerned with fundamental issues of equality in both public and private spheres of life and across socio-economic groups. It identified the origins of women's subordination not only in the context of the family, but also in relationships between men and women in the market place, and hence it placed considerable emphasis on economic independence as being synonymous with equity.

In focusing particularly on reducing inequality between men and women, especially in the gender division of labour, the equity approach meets an important strategic gender need. Equity programmes are identified as uniting notions of development and equality. The underlying logic is that women beneficiaries have lost ground to men in the development process. Therefore, in a process of redistribution, men have to share in a manner that entails women from all socio-economic classes gaining and men from all socio-economic classes losing, through positive discrimination policies if necessary.

Equity programmes encountered problems from the outset. Methodologically, the lack of a single indicator of social status or progress of women and of baseline information about women's economic, social, and political status meant that there were no standards against which 'success' could be measured (USAID, 1978). Politically, the majority of development agencies were hostile to equity programmes precisely because of their intention to meet strategic gender needs, whose very success depended on an implicit redistribution of power. From the perspective of the aid agency this was identified as unacceptable interference with the country's traditions.

Similar antipathy was felt by many Third World governments who believed in the irrelevance of Western-exported feminism to Third World women. Many Third World activists felt that to take 'feminism to a woman who has no water, no food and no home is to talk nonsense' (Bunch, 1980, p.27) and labelled Third World socialists and feminists as bourgeois imperialist sympathisers.

In a climate of widespread antagonism to many of its underlying principles from development agencies and Third World governments alike, the equity approach has been effectively dropped by the majority of implementing agencies. However, the official endorsement of equity as one of the themes of the Women's Decade has ensured that it continues to provide an important framework for those working within governments to improve the status of women through top-down legislation, which has tended to meet potential strategic gender needs rather than actual needs.

The anti-poverty approach

The anti-poverty approach to women can be identified as the second WID approach, in which economic inequality between women and men is linked not to subordination, but to poverty, with the emphasis thus shifting from reducing inequality between men and women, to reducing income inequality. Here women's issues are separated from equity issues and linked with the particular concern for the majority of Third World women as the 'poorest of the poor'. Buvinic (1983) has argued that this is a toned-down version of the equity approach, arising out of the reluctance of development agencies to interfere with the manner in which gender relations are constructed in a given society.

The anti-poverty policy approach to women focuses mainly on their productive role on the basis that poverty alleviation and the promotion of balanced economic growth requires the increased productivity of women in low-income households. Underlying this approach is the assumption that the origins of women's poverty and inequality with men are attributable to their lack of access to private ownership of land and capital, and to sexual discrimination in the labour market. Consequently, it aims to increase the employment and income generating options of low-income women through better access to productive resources. There is also an increasing recognition that education and employment programmes could simultaneously increase women's economic contribution and reduce fertility.

While income generating projects for low-income women have proliferated since the 1970s, they have tended to remain small in scale, to be developed by non-governmental organisations (most frequently all-women in composition), and to be assisted by grants, rather than loans, from international and bilateral agencies. Most frequently they aim to increase productivity in activities traditionally undertaken by women, rather than to introduce them to new areas of work.

In the design of projects, fundamental conditions to ensure viability are often ignored, including access to easily available raw materials, guaranteed markets and small-scale production capacity (Schmitz, 1979; Moser, 1984). Despite widespread recognition of the limitations of the informal sector's ability to generate employment and growth in an independent or evolutionary manner, income generating projects for women continue to be designed as though small-scale enterprises have the capacity for autonomous growth (Moser, 1984; Schmitz, 1982).

Anti-poverty income generating projects may provide employment for women, and thereby meet practical gender needs to augment their income. But unless employment leads to greater autonomy, it does not meet strategic gender needs. In addition, the predominant focus on women's productive role means that their reproductive role is often ignored. Income generating projects which assume that women have free time often only succeed by extending their working day and increasing their triple burden. Unless an income generating project also alleviates the burden of women's domestic labour and childcare, through, for instance, the provision of adequate, socialised childcare, it may fail even to meet the practical gender need to earn an income.

The efficiency approach

While the shift from equity to anti-poverty has been well documented, the identification of WID as efficiency has passed almost unnoticed. Yet the efficiency approach is now the pre-dominant approach for those working within a WID framework — indeed, for many it may always have been so. In the efficiency approach, the emphasis has shifted away from women and towards development, on the assumption that increased economic participation for Third World women is automatically linked with increased equity. This has allowed organisations such as USAID, the World Bank and the Organisation for Economic Cooperation and Development (OECD) to propose that an increase in women's economic participation in development links efficiency and equity together.

The assumption that economic participation increases women's status and is associated with equity has been widely criticised. The identification of such problems as lack of education and under-productive technologies as the predominant constraints affecting women's participation has also been criticised. While the so-called development industry has realised that women are essential to the success of the total development effort, it does not necessarily follow that development improves conditions for women.

This shift towards efficiency coincided with a marked deterioration in the world economy. This occurred from the mid-1970s onward and particularly in Latin America and Africa, where the problems of recession were compounded by falling export prices, protectionism and mounting debt. To alleviate the situation, economic stabilisation and adjustment policies designed by the International Monetary Fund (IMF) and the World Bank have been implemented by an increasing number of national governments. These policies, through both demand management and supply expansion, lead to the re-allocation of resources to enable the restoration of a balance-of-payments equilibrium, an increase in exports, and a restoration in growth rates.

With increased efficiency and productivity as two of the main objectives of structural adjustment policies, it is no coincidence that efficiency is the policy approach towards women which is currently gaining popularity among international aid agencies and national governments alike. In reality this approach often simply means a shifting of costs from the paid to the unpaid economy, particularly through the use of women's unpaid time. Until recently, structural adjustment has been seen as an economic issue, and evaluated in economic terms (Jolly, 1987). Although documentation regarding its social costs is still unsystematic, it does reveal a serious deterioration in living conditions of low-income populations resulting from a decline in income levels. Within the household a decline in consumption often affects women more than men. The capacity of the household to shoulder the burden of adjustment can have detrimental effects in terms of human relationships, expressed in increased domestic violence, mental health disorders and increasing numbers of women-headed households resulting from the breakdown in nuclear family structures (UNICEF, nd).

The efficiency approach relies heavily on the elasticity of women's labour in both their reproductive and community managing roles, and only meets practical gender needs at the cost of longer working hours and increased unpaid work. In most cases this approach not only fails to meet any strategic gender needs but also, because of the reductions in resource allocations, results in a serious reduction of the extent to which practical gender needs are met.

The empowerment approach

The fifth policy approach to women is the empowerment approach; not yet widely recognised as an 'approach', although its origins are by no means recent. The empowerment approach differs from the equity approach not only in its origins, but also in the causes, dynamics and structures of women's oppression which it identifies, and in terms of the strategies it proposes to change the position of Third World women.

The origins of the empowerment approach are derived primarily from the emergent feminist writings and grassroots organisation experience of Third World women. It recognises that feminism is not simply a recent Western, urban, middle-class import. As Jayawardena (1986) has written, the women's movement was not imposed on women by the United Nations or Western feminists, but has an independent history. Since the late 19th century, Third World feminism has been an important force for change, but with women's participation more often in nationalist and patriotic struggles, working-class agitation and peasant rebellions than in the formation of autonomous women's organisations. Although the empowerment approach acknowledges inequalities between men and women, and the origins of women's subordination in the family, it also emphasises the fact that women experience oppression differently according to their race, class, colonial history and current position in the international economic order. It maintains that women have to challenge oppressive structures and situations simultaneously at different levels.

The empowerment approach questions some of the fundamental assumptions concerning the inter-relationship between power and development that underlie previous approaches. While it acknowledges the importance for women of increasing their power, it seeks to identify power less in terms of domination over others (with its implicit assumption that a gain for women implies a loss for men), and more in terms of the capacity of women to increase their own self-reliance and internal strength. This is identified as the right to determine choices in life and to influence the direction of change, through the ability to gain control over crucial material and non-material resources. It places far less emphasis than the equity approach on increasing women's status relative to men, but seeks to empower women through the redistribution of power within, as well as between, societies. It also questions two underlying assumptions in the equity approach; first, that development necessarily helps all men, and second, that women want to be integrated into the mainstream of Western-designed development, in which they have no choice in defining the kind of society they want (UNAPCWD, 1979).

A powerful articulation of the empowerment approach has been made by the Development Alternatives with Women for a New Era (DAWN). The new era envisaged by DAWN includes national liberation and also the transformation of the structures of subordination that have been so inimical to women. Changes in law, civil codes, systems of property rights, control over women's bodies, labour codes and the social and legal institutions that underwrite male control and privilege are essential if women are to attain justice in society. These strategic gender needs are similar to those identified by the equity approach. It is in the means of achieving such needs that the empowerment approach differs most fundamentally from previous approaches. Recognition of the limitations of top-down government legislation actually to meet strategic gender needs has led adherents of the empowerment approach to acknowledge that their strategies will not be implemented without the sustained and systematic efforts by women's organisations and like-minded groups. They highlight the need for political mobilisation, consciousness raising and popular education to bring about change.

The very limited success of the equity approach to confront directly the nature of women's subordination through legislative changes has led the empowerment approach to avoid direct confrontation, and to utilise practical gender needs as the basis on which to build a secure support base, and a means through which more strategic needs may be reached.

For example, in the Philippines, Gabriela (an alliance of local and national women's organisations) ran a project combining women's traditional task of sewing tapestry with the discussion of women's legal rights and the constitution. A nationwide educational 'tapestry-making drive' enabled the discussion of rights in communities, factories and schools, with the end product, a 'Tapestry of Women's Rights', seen to be a liberating instrument (Gomez, 1986).

A feminist group in Bombay, India, the 'Forum Against Oppression of Women', first started campaigning in 1979 on such issues as rape and bride burning. However, with 55 per cent of the low-income population living in squatter settlements, the Forum soon realised that housing was a much greater priority for local women, and, consequently, soon shifted its focus to this issue. In a context where women by tradition had no access to housing in their own right, homelessness, through breakdown of marriage or domestic violence, was an acute problem, and the provision of women's hostels a critical practical gender need. Mobilisation around homelessness, however, also raised consciousness of patriarchal bias in inheritance legislation as well as in the interpretation of housing rights. In seeking to broaden the problem from a 'women's concern' and raise men's awareness, the Forum has become part of a nationwide alliance of non-governmental organisations, lobbying for a National Housing Charter. Through this alliance, the Forum has ensured that women's strategic gender needs relating to housing rights have been placed on the mainstream political agenda, and not remained simply the concern of women. As highlighted by DAWN, 'empowering ourselves through organisation' has been a slow global process, accelerating during and since the Women's Decade, in which diverse women's organisations, movements, networks and alliances have developed. These cover a multitude of issues and purposes, with common interests ranging from disarmament at the international level, to mobilisation around specific laws and codes at the national level. All share a similar commitment to empower women. Experience has shown that the most effective organisations have been those which started around concrete practical gender needs relating to health, employment and basic service provision, but which have been able to use these as a means to reach specific strategic gender needs identified by women in particular socio-political contexts.

The potentially challenging nature of the empowerment approach has meant that it remains largely unsupported either by national governments or bilateral aid agencies. Despite the widespread growth of Third World groups and organisations whose approach to women is essentially one of empowerment, they remain under-funded, reliant on the use of voluntary and unpaid women's time, and dependent on the resources of those few international non-governmental agencies and First World governments prepared to support this approach to women and development.

Conclusion

The development of gender planning is intended to provide the conceptual framework and the methodological tools, relating to roles, needs and policy approaches, not only to assist in the appraisal and evaluation of current interventions, but also in the future formulation of more 'gendered' policies, programmes and projects.

This article is adapted with permission from World Development, 17:11, Caroline Moser, 'Gender Planning in the Third World: Meeting Practical and Strategic Gender Needs'. Copyright 1989.

References

Boserup, E. (1970), *Women's Role in Economic Development*, New York: St Martin's Press.

Bunch, C. (1980), 'Copenhagen and beyond: Prospects for global feminism', *Quest*, 5.

Buvinic, M. (1986), 'Projects for women in the Third World: Explaining their misbehaviour', *World Development*, 14:5, pp.653-664.

Buvinic, M. (1983) 'Women's issues in Third World Poverty: A policy analysis', in M.Buvinic, M.Lycette, and W.McGreevey, *Women and Poverty in the Third World*, Baltimore, MD: John Hopkins University Press.

Germaine, A. (1977), 'Poor rural women: A policy perspective', *Journal of International Affairs*, 30.

Gomez, M. (1986) 'Development of women's organisations in the Philippines', in *Women, Struggles and Strategies: Third World Perspectives, Women's Journal*, 6, Rome: ISIS International.

Jayawardena, K., (1986), *Feminism and Nationalism in the Third World*, London: Zed.

Jolly, R. (1987), 'Women's needs and adjustment policies in developing countries'. Address given to Women's Development Group, OECD, Paris.

Molyneux, M. (1985), 'Mobilisation without emancipation? Women's interests, state and revolution in Nicaragua', *Feminist Studies*, 11:2.

Moser, C.O.N. (1984), 'The informal sector reworked: Viability and vulnerability in urban development', *Regional Development Dialogue*, 5:2.

Schmitz, H. (1979), 'Factory and domestic employment in Brazil: A study of the hammock industry and its implications for employment theory and practice', *Institute of Development Studies Discussion Paper No.146*, Brighton: Institute of Development Studies.

Schmitz, H. (1982), 'Growth constraints on small-scale manufacturing in developing countries: A critical review', *World Development*, 10:6.

United Nations Asian and Pacific Centre for Women and Development (UNAPCWD), (1979), *Feminist Ideologies and Structures in the First Half of the Decade for Women*, Report from the Bangkok Workshop.

UNICEF, The Invisible Adjustment: Poor Women and the Economic Crisis, Santiago: UNICEF Americas and the Caribbean Regional Office, n.d.

United States Agency for International Development (USAID) (1978), *Report on women in Development*: 1978, Washington, DC: USAID Office of Women in Development.

Caroline Moser is a lecturer in Social Planning in Developing Countries at the London School of Economics (LSE). She is also a consultant to UN agencies and the World Bank. She has given training in gender planning at (SIDA), the Overseas Development Agency (ODA), (FAO), Oxfam and Christian Aid. She has also undertaken research in Colombia and Ecuador.

ENSURING GENDER AWARENESS IN THE PLANNING OF PROJECTS

MIRANDA MUNRO

Planning for rural development is too often shaped by a primary focus on the output of the plan at the expense of the process through which the plan is prepared and designed. This process involves people; their perceptions of how they fit into plans can take radically different directions. This fit between beneficiaries' needs, project performance and the role of the NGO (non-governmental organisation) begins with the learning capacity of the agency: how well it copes with mistakes and contingencies, how it uses its experience to strengthen institutional capacity and to what extent it shares the knowledge gained with the community.

This article identifies a number of useful factors that can improve the chances that a project will meet the needs of the people and lead to effective development. The way an NGO approaches and works with the community at the planning — and subsequent — stages is crucial; the importance of the entry strategy cannot be over-estimated. This strategy must be based on adequate knowledge, understanding and communication with the community, and women are vital to this process.

The importance of the entry strategy

A productive relationship between a rural development agency and a community will depend on the agreement reached between them at the planning stage, about the process of change. This will determine the entry strategy to be adopted. Three stages are important in deciding what this entry strategy should be (Fowler, 1988):

agreeing with the population on the values and goals which will guide the intervention (Roling),

negotiating an agreement on what the population and the agency have to offer each other; that is, how participation is to be organised and the role each will play in achieving the outcomes which are jointly planned (Oakley),

· arriving at a common analysis of the situation so that not just the problems and needs are identified but the reasons for them are jointly understood. (Chambers)

What must be avoided is the imposition of values important to the agency alone. For example, a Western feminist policy may not be easily or desirably transferable; but a commitment to security of livelihood for the poorest groups may stimulate development for both men and women which may bring about a desired shift in the balance of power between the genders, in favour of women.

Implicit in this approach is the establishment of a partnership in which the agency listens, learns and consults. This is important not just because the poorest groups in a community — particularly women — are easily overlooked, but because every community exists within a wider context. Developing an informed perspective on the links women have to wider environmental, political and socio-economic systems implies the agency's willingness, and ability, to appraise both women's practical and strategic interests.

Women's strategic interests have been defined by Molyneux as those which will facilitate a more equal and satisfactory organisation of society in terms of the structure of relationships between men and women. This could involve, for example, abolishing the sexual division of labour, removing institutionalised discrimination, and creating freedom of choice over childbearing. Women's practical interests have been defined as those which relate to women's daily concrete conditions and are often the ones most easily formulated by women themselves. They tend to be conceived through a focus on the welfare of the family and the women's importance to family subsistence, without questioning whether this constitutes equality of development for women. (Molyneux, 1985.)

However, identifying both women's practical and strategic interests must be a process which is sensitive to the community, and to the capacity of that community to work with the agency's different cultural perspective on relations between men and women, and vice versa.

Any jointly negotiated and agreed plan of action which details what it is possible to achieve for the benefit of women, should contain the ingredients for policy, project design and implementation. Moser and Levy (1986) identify two factors which are very important for a gender conscious entry strategy: the first is an informed judgement about which practical and strategic needs can be met in the socio-economic and political conditions of a particular place and time. The second is an assessment of the extent to which women have access to local institutions and whether these institutions can be used to meet some or all of the particular practical and strategic needs.

There are three approaches which an agency might consider in order to develop this informed judgement and accurate assessment. These are to improve its understanding of how gender relations work within the community; to improve the ways of consulting women and to improve the quality of information they use for planning purposes.

Improving awareness of gender relations

Understanding the relative access to and control over resources and benefits has to include an awareness of the differential access to power which is integral to the division of labour by gender. In conventional project appraisal the unit of analysis is the household, represented for purposes of estimating costs and benefits by assumptions about the behaviour of a male head of household. But it is a major misconception in project planning to see the household as a homogenous decision-making unit; this is clearly not the case in many rural societies where different members have separate productive and entrepreneurial roles and there are competing, unequal and often conflicting claims on resources and outputs for the satisfaction of basic needs.

There is an argument, therefore, for an increased understanding of gender relations within a household structure, whatever form the unit may take, in order to prevent a distortion of the entry strategy. There is a danger, of course, of being swamped by diversity and of looking at increasingly complex social relations without testing their impact on what happens outside the household. For example, women may have to get men's permission to work co-operatively with other women in an all-female organisation or they may want to receive men's sanction on their separate activities; this will not necessarily mean that the decision making is male dominated. At the same time, male control of financial gains from a women's group may be detrimental to the group's autonomy and growth and may also undermine individual women's decision-making power in the household.

How is it possible to arrive at an understanding of gender relations within a rural household? A key principle is to consult both men and women, most simply by documenting their different activities, resources and responsibilities which can then be compared. Indicators of how, for example, women and men experience changes to the environment, seasonality, access to preferred technologies, large family size, increasing costs of inputs for production, and an agency's style of intervention, can contribute to a body of qualitative information about women's activities, the resources they command and the responsibilities they manage. What has to be avoided is placing an exclusion zone around a target group of women, both during and after the planning phase, simply in order to reinforce their target-group status.

Improving ways of consulting women

Women are not a homogenous social group and their needs will differ according to their relative ages as well as their different activities, resources and responsibilities. A needs assessment should therefore take into account this social and personal heterogeneity. Women may well need support in defining their needs and various techniques have been employed to facilitate this process: documenting and sharing life histories; stimulating discussion around a series of photographs of the women themselves and other women; using a situational analysis or other data collection tools to highlight inequalities in the gender allocation of tasks. Needless to say this is also a learning process for the agency.

It is important that the context and style of discussion should be accessible for women for whom speaking out may be an unfamiliar event; the location, materials used, the size and membership of the group may all be significant. A group action may require organisational skills. Providing women with enabling skills for group management or supporting existing organisations that women use may be a vital investment in the development process even before the entry strategy is agreed.

As Moser and Levy say (1986), consultation on issues that perpetuate gender inequality, and the active participation of women in the planning process is desirable not only as a means of achieving development objectives, but as an end in itself. At the same time, women's expression of their situation and their demands for the fulfilment of certain practical interests may well provide a more accurate appraisal of what assistance would be appropriate than blueprinted objectives developed by outsiders based on strategic interests. How the meeting of practical needs is linked to longer term strategic needs must be decided as a result of frequent consultation and monitoring with the women concerned, and then a testing of solutions within the community.

Improving the quality of information for planning

A balance has to be struck between spending time on diagnosing gender inequalities and formulating proposals. Participative techniques that go beyond a dialogue with a target group can provide the means for the community and the agency to learn about each other's values and criteria. Testing this data in an interactive way is part of the process of building up a body of planning and monitoring information. The employment of Rapid Rural Appraisal techniques in a range of situations is beginning to show the importance of using a portfolio of methods. If these techniques can be aggregated, they can perhaps be used as an index of equity for women across particular profiles, to assess project performance and to highlight conditions which may improve the chances of success. Three of these techniques are as follows:

i. Direct matrix ranking and preference ranking:
Arriving at a common analysis of a situation has already been mentioned as an important stage in formulating an agreement for action in the community. In situations where women hold particular indigenous skills and knowledge, it is also important to understand the criteria leading to their decisions and preferences regarding productive or organisational practices. Ranking methodologies have been used with some success to identify local knowledge. Direct matrix ranking involves the respondent(s) listing criteria which are important to them when considering the value of a resource or when considering why one type of the resource is preferred to another. Scores are allocated to each criteria for each resource type and a matrix is constructed which can pinpoint the preferred type as well as indicating why one type, for example, a high yielding variety (HYV) or a traditional variety of the same crop, is not

preferred for that particular locality. The ranking of preferences can be conducted between two types of an item or between several types, thus building up a scoring matrix of ranked preferences. Having used the technique of direct matrix ranking for training village extension agents, I consider two characteristics of the method as potentially important:

> The quality of discussion required to arrive at a consensus within the group on the criteria to be ranked and then scored is a valuable learning process for all concerned, and yet one that is conducted under the control of the group.

> The criteria chosen by the group are often indicators of links in the system of resource management and decision making which might not otherwise appear. Once these links are known they can be a further reinforcement of a shared analysis.

ii. Situational analysis and food paths:

Gathering data through group interviews is a method requiring training and practice. A methodology which focuses on the stages and sequences of an activity can facilitate the process of acquiring gender sensitive data in a group interview. The situational analysis builds up a diagrammatic representation of a sequence of activities by focusing on the situation (e.g. introducing contour ploughing or allocating irrigation water). Each stage of the sequence can be examined and discussed to highlight the gender allocation of labour, resources and responsibilities. By using this technique for a 'food path', focusing on one crop, tracing the production of food from the purchasing and planting of the seed to the sale or preparation of the food, I have found it enables further layers to be added, such as hours spent, technology used, and seasonal variations identified, throughout an interactive process of discussion.

iii. Checklists:

Although checklists have become established as gender conscious tools for planning a project, the checklist can become a barrier to effective interaction between agency and community unless, like any tool, it is frequently refined and sharpened in the context in which it is used. Our understanding of this context is, after all, only the first step in the process through which women may come to realise the benefits from jointly planned interventions.

Conclusion

The importance of fitting projects to the real needs of a community cannot be over-emphasised; and to achieve this it is essential for agencies to discuss and negotiate fully with the community. In order to ensure that women are an integral part of the process it is important to improve gender awareness among all the participants, to find ways of communicating with the women directly and to base planning on the best level of information possible.

References

Fowler, A. (1988), 'Non-governmental organisations in Africa: achieving comparative advantage in relief and micro-development', *Discussion Paper* 249, Brighton: Institute of Development Studies, University of Sussex.

Molyneux, M., (1985), 'Mobilisation without emancipation? Women's interests, the state and revolution in Nicaragua', *Feminist Studies*, 11:2.

Moser, C. and Levy, C. (1986), 'A theory and methodology of gender planning: meeting women's practical and strategic needs', *DPU Gender and Planning Working Paper No. 11*, London: University College.

Miranda Munro is Research Officer in the Agricultural Extension and Rural Development Department of the University of Reading. She has worked and conducted research on gender issues in development in the Middle East, South East Asia and the Horn of Africa.

WOMEN'S STATUS CRITERIA

ZAMBIA ASSOCIATION FOR RESEARCH
AND DEVELOPMENT WORKSHOP

A woman's development project may be counted as improving the status of women to the extent that progress may be seen in the following indicators:

Basic needs:
Better provision for women of such basic needs as food, water, fuel, housing and health care; proportional distribution of basic needs between men and women.

Leadership roles:
Proportion of women to men in leadership roles in the community; involvement of women as women's leaders on women's issues.

Consciousness:
Awareness amongst women of women's needs and women's issues; awareness of discrimination against women; ability to analyse issues in terms of women's interests and women's rights.

Needs assessment:
Involvement of women in identifying the priority needs of the community, and in identifying the special needs of women.

Planning:
Involvement of women in project design, implementation and evaluation.

Sexual division of labour:
Level of involvement of women in tasks traditionally performed by men; level of involvement of men in tasks traditionally performed by women; number of hours per day worked by the average working woman, in comparison to the number worked by the average working man.

Control over the factors of production:
The level of women's access to, and control over land, credit, distribution of income and accumulation of capital.

The order in which these indicators are presented is not intended to imply an order of priority, nor a sequence of what should come first and what should come later. It is merely suggested that a successful project should be making progress across several of these indicators, and that a successful programme should include projects which seek to improve women's status across the full range of these indicators.

Lusaka, 12 July 1987.

WOMEN AND EVALUATION

FRANCES RUBIN

It is now nearly two years since I first coordinated an Oxfam Country Programme Review. The exercise gave plenty of food for thought about the difficulties that women can face in development work, and particularly in the process of evaluation. This note is anecdotal, but may illustrate some of the problems and give pointers to solutions, or at least steps that need to be taken to address the danger of excluding women from important moments of decision making.

Terms of reference

One of the first tasks to be completed was the drafting of the terms of reference (TOR) for the review in collaboration with the Country Representative. The programme staff had voiced concern about how to tackle gender questions within their work, and were trying to develop a country strategy where 'gender' was seen as an important issue. Following consultation with a number of colleagues, 'gender questions' were written into many aspects of the TOR. There was quite a strong reaction to this. Many people felt that such explicit mention of gender issues suggested that nobody, including consultants who might be contracted, were aware of gender issues. Because of these strong feeling the TOR were modified but remained explicit in terms of briefing the evaluation team members that gender issues were to be treated in an integral way throughout the evaluation. Above all, gender was not to be treated as a discrete issue in a separate chapter.

Contracting of consultants

At one time in the course of looking for members of the evaluation team it seemed possible that they might all be women. This raised reactions of alarm among some who suggested that an all women team might not be balanced. For how many years has Oxfam used all male teams without feeling concerned? At the end of the day the evaluation team was composed of two men and three women. At times they split up into different groups but these were always mixed.

Field visits

Even though gender was recognised as a central issue and there were always women in the visiting teams, we still encountered considerable difficulties in actually meeting women and hearing their views.

In a number of situations the male members of the team explained with confidence what women thought on a number of issues. To give one example, they explained that women could not participate in training courses because they needed to stay at home to look after the domestic affairs of the household. However, when we spoke directly with women, the women outlined various strategies that would enable them to leave their families and community, and attend meetings they saw as relevant.

On one particular day we were carrying out a programme of visits that had been organised by the village leaders. We asked if we (the visiting Oxfam team) could split up into two groups, so that the women on the team could talk separately to the women in the village. Since this was not on the agenda it took quite an effort to organise, and we were continually interrupted by people who wanted us to hurry so that we could rejoin the 'main' delegation.

Another time, I was reading the notes in the file, as we were on our way to meet a women's group. In one of the tour reports it was clearly stated on which days it was inappropriate to visit if you wanted to talk to the women — because the women were preparing for, and selling in, the market. Yet we found ourselves en route to this town precisely on market day! This happened again in another small community, where there was a very low turn out of women because they were all busy preparing manioc loaves for the market on the following day.

On our last project visit, committee members of a health post began to assemble for the customary discussion. One by one the committee members were introduced. There was one women member. Her name was read out 'Citoyenne (treasurer) — present'. 'Present?' I asked, 'but where?' The treasurer then popped her head into the inner circle of the crowd, bowed and disappeared.

After the round of introductions was complete I asked why the citoyenne who was present in the village was not participating in the meeting? The reason for her absence was that she was busy preparing lunch for the delegation. We politely suggested that she should be present at the discussions. She appeared, and in the course of the debates raised a number of issues of importance: issues related to the management and safekeeping of the finances that had been entrusted to her, as well as health issues that were of specific importance to the female members of the community, and which had not been raised by the other members present.

A plate of cold peanuts was handed round instead of a lovely meal: we had passed up on some culinary delights but we had enabled the treasurer to raise some important questions for the community; had she not been in the meeting these issues would not have been brought to Oxfam's notice.

Conclusion

It must be a rule that the TOR of all evaluations include gender as an integral part; that, except in very specific circumstances, there should be mixed evaluation teams and that, however difficult it continues to be, women evaluators must ensure that they get the opportunity to talk to women on their own.

Frances Rubin is currently acting Coordinator of Oxfam's Evaluation Unit, where she has been working since 1988, and has been directly involved in evaluation exercises in Zaire and Southern India. She started work with Oxfam as a Deputy Representative in Brazil in 1981, until 1986. She has also done a variety of research assignments for the Education and Public Affairs Departments, as well as working in Mozambique and Central Africa.

4

CASE STUDIES OF WAYS OF WORKING WITH GENDER

Introduction
Tina Wallace

In this section, we look at a variety of ways of working with gender relations. To date, the focus has tended to be on women separately, in income generation or health projects. While these approaches are important, they do have their limitations. Projects where women are the only participants often fail because men do not understand them and do not give necessary support e.g. where men are excluded from nutritional training they often do not understand the need for a new diet so women are not able to introduce it. Or women may lack the necessary resources of e.g. land, access to markets or transport to make the project successful. There are other ways of trying to work with women, and we have tried to cover some of the most innovative and successful in this section.

Less has been written about working with women and men together, where women are fully incorporated into the project, because less work has been done in this area and there is not much experience to record. However, four articles do touch on this area (Watson, Burgess, Mathew and Oxby). Brian Mathew describes the problems that are faced when projects which directly affect women do not involve them in the planning, decision-making, and managing committees of the projects. His focus is on water, but the lessons are equally applicable to a wide spectrum of development work — in agriculture, pastoralism and health, for example. While the women may well be seen as the target of the development, and provide the essential labour and time inputs, they are very rarely consulted, and are not trained in the use of new technologies. This often means that, not only does the project fail, but that women are further disempowered. They may actually experience a loss of control over water, land or animals with the introduction of a development project; and gender relations may be changed, to the disadvantage of women. Such projects are far from being gender neutral.

A number of articles in this section focus on work with pastoralist women in Africa. There are a number of reasons for this; first because until recently they were almost totally excluded from development thinking and development work which was all focused on the men. The women were virtually invisible and their often critical role in production as well as reproduction was overlooked. Second, some very interesting work has been undertaken recently in this area which illustrates both the problems and potentials of working with women who have always been neglected in the past. Many of the issues raised apply to women in agricultural societies and work with pastoral women was chosen as the main focus for some of the case studies because it is such new territory, and because their treatment in development projects highlights many important lessons which are widely applicable.

Cathy Watson's article on pastoral women in northern Kenya, illustrates the importance of research into the roles and responsibilities of women as well as men, before assumptions are made about appropriate development or welfare, particularly when working with societies where little is known about the pattern of gender relationships. Her research shows the critical roles, previously not fully understood, that women play within the Turkana economy, especially as the controllers of the food supply in the household. As pastoralist societies are undermined, the separate but complementary roles of men and women are changing, and women are taking on more work and added responsibilities. If agencies are not aware of this, emergency food and water supplies, and subsequent rehabilitation assistance, are distributed only to men, with profound effects on the relative positions of men and women and the success of the projects. Cathy Watson's research echoes that of Ann Whitehead (see Section One) on agricultural societies in Africa, and the conclusions they reach is that recent historical changes have adversely affected the position of women, and positive steps must be taken to counteract these.

Pastoralist women in Kenya are also the subject of Clare Oxby's article. While she emphasises the need to understand the roles women play and their many and various activities, she points out that research alone is not enough. Pastoralist women have suffered from the failure of agencies both to realise their involvement in animal production activities, and to involve them actively in the projects. Clare Oxby describes two innovative and successful restocking projects where women heads of households, as well as men, were targeted by the development agency.

In her article, Doris Burgess writes about a situation in which a whole society decided to address the structural inequality suffered by the women, and devised a programme which involved changing the basic social and economic structures, and the attitudes which discriminate against women. The focus of her article is health provision in Eritrea, but it encompasses a number of other critical issues that have to be addressed if women's subordinate position is to be transformed.

The other articles in this section describe work with women alone. Three articles have income generating projects and women's groups as their theme. This approach has characterised most of the work with women in recent years; partly because of the growing recognition that, because women have responsibility for the family, money given to them may be the most effective way of raising the health, nutritional and educational status of children, and, indeed, of the whole family. Agencies have been increasingly concerned to be seen to be working with women, and in many countries income generating projects are a familiar and acceptable way of doing so. Linda Mayoux, using case studies from India, gives a comprehensive overview of the problems that beset such projects. They often add to women's workloads without bringing any significant economic returns; poorer women have no time to participate in them; there are difficulties in acquiring raw materials, meeting quality standards and finding suitable markets. However, they may have other benefits for the women who participate in them, such as an opportunity to meet together and find ways of challenging existing constraints.

In contrast, Ben Pugansoa writes of an income generating project in Ghana, which was economically successful. The project assisted women to compete with large-scale male traders, who had previously bought produce at exploitative prices. This project was based on work the women were already involved in, and the market was known to be lucrative. It is important to recognise that some income generating projects can significantly improve women's income, and more work needs to be done to identify the factors that contribute to economic failure or success.

Betty Wamalwa looks at some of the political and economic issues around women's groups. She argues that these groups can only ever involve certain types of women — those with spare money and spare time — and will tend to exclude the poorest and youngest women; and that 'women's projects' per se are outside the mainstream of development, which goes on without regard to women. This theme is taken up again in the next section by Adelina Mwau. Women provide much of the work and energy on all projects, but they are effectively ignored in mainstream projects and are only targeted in women's projects, many of which are income generating projects, peripheral to their real needs.

The remaining articles look at a variety of different ways of working with women. There is research (which can be informal, participative and quick, or more detached and long-term); networking; drama and popular education work; counselling and group exploration of feelings and needs; management, literacy and business training; training in gender awareness; and training in new skills, previously reserved for men. Several of the articles in this part of the book are drawn from Latin America, where a great deal of innovative work, especially in popular education, awareness building around the issues of class and gender, and networking has been done.

There are accounts of two different awareness raising groups — one working through popular education using drama (*Les esclavas*) and one growing out of the mass movements around the church and the trade unions which organised mass meetings for women for study and recreation (MOMUPA). A testimony from Francesca in Brazil highlights the critical importance that women's groups based within the trade union movement can have for women.

Claire Ball's article describes a very different way of working with refugee women from the familiar one of seeing them as the recipients of food in refugee camps, images seared on to the minds of most people. She tells the story of a group of refugee women in

Mexico, working together to understand their history and to make sense of their present situation so that they can cope with the very difficult and painful conditions in which they find themselves. It touches on the vast subject of the psychological needs of refugees, and provides an example of how one group of women are tackling their problems together.

The section includes a case study from India, where women have been trained for the more lucrative jobs that are usually done by men. Many women work as building labourers in India, and this project aimed to give them the skills to work as masons and so earn higher wages.

The final example is drawn from Kenya: it is a graphic account of networking at the grassroots with pastoral women. Women were brought together to explore their cultures, their beliefs and myths about themselves; to look at their role in the economy and their place in development. There are other examples of networking in the book, both at the international level and the national level. It is a new and very powerful way for women to work together to explore their problems and also, more importantly, their potential.

THE PLANNER MANAGER'S GUIDE TO THIRD WORLD WATER PROJECTS

BRIAN MATHEW

Women are the principal collectors and users of water in the rural Third World. Indeed, the collection of water for domestic purposes is almost universally associated with women. Val Curtis in her book on women and the transport of water states: 'Water collection is an activity particularly reserved for women and children; in many countries for a man even to be seen collecting water would bring shame' (Curtis, 1986, p.8).

Yet the trend in much of the Third World has been that where technologies have been introduced they have been male-dominated. In effect a male monopoly of technology has developed which has excluded women. Thus water technologies have often been monopolised by men rather than the principal users. It is important that the water planner manager has a grasp of this so that he/she does not perpetuate the imbalance. This is especially important in water development because the success of any rural Third World water project rests on acceptance and understanding of the technology by the people who are going to use it. Therefore it is important that women are educated about the use and maintenance of the technology, and that they are freed from the widely held self-assumption that such work is somehow above or beyond them. This is not an easy process because women's access to resources, technology and literature is often restricted by culture, tradition, the attitude of their menfolk, and lower literacy and education levels than men (due to restricted access to school when children).

The exclusion of women from water projects

In many cases women have had little or no involvement in the implementation or planning phases of water projects. Of 18 randomly selected USAID water and sanitation projects in Carloni's 1973-1985 survey of USAID's experience with women in development over that period, the results show two things: firstly, that the projects showed a very low level of women's involvement (a criticism that could be levelled at many aid agencies); secondly, that they shared, with the energy sector, the lowest level of women's involvement of all sectors surveyed. Carloni's report mentions that a strong positive correlation was found between women's level of participation and the achievement of project objectives. Where women were involved, projects were highly successful; where they were not, projects failed to reach their objectives (Carloni, 1987). In this case women became involved in some of the projects, despite not being included in the initial project designs.

Other examples of the failures of water and sanitation projects to achieve objectives, resulting from the non-involvement of women, are numerous. One such was a water and sanitation programme in Tonga; this project, which claimed to be based on 'community involvement' principles, only involved the men. The project initially failed, but when women were involved, success followed (KPP and IDRC, 1985, p.13). In a similar project in Indonesia, women were excluded from the planning of a water scheme but were involved in the implementation (i.e. did the labouring). Here, too, the project failed. In this case the design of the water supply system was unsuitable for the needs and cultural habits of the women (KPP and IDRC, 1985, p.70).

An example from Iran shows the need for the involvement of women in the design of additional washing facilities. In rural Khuzistan, new communal laundry facilities were built with large rectangular sinks which rose to adult waist height. Iranian women, however, traditionally wash clothes in a squatting position, and as a result the new laundry basins were not used (Jahan, 1975).

In South India, a village level maintenance scheme for hand pumps on deep wells was initiated. Two years after the project began, 620 young men had been trained as caretakers. However, problems resulted because the women did not know who the caretakers were; and as the young men themselves did not collect water, they did not know when there were problems to sort out (Yansheng and Elmendorf, 1984).

Development projects can also act directly against the interests of women. In the case of a chicken farming project in Zaire, the project failed to recognise that water was scarce, that a great deal of water would be required, and that it was the women's job to collect the water. Thus the women had several hours of additional water carrying added to their daily duties (von Harder, 1975). This example, though not directly of a water project, illustrates the pitfalls that a project can encounter if women are not considered, consulted, or involved in the planning.

Where, in the past, water was drawn from an unprotected hole in the ground, it had a low status as did the women who collected it. A water project is more than an operation of installing new facilities; it is, or should be, a consciousness-raising process. If it is not, it will fail. Installations will become dirty, buckets or other parts will be stolen, broken parts will not be repaired, no one will feel responsibility, and the village women will return to their traditional sources for water. This sorry situation has been repeated too many times, purely because communities in general, and women in particular, have not been involved in the planning, implementation, management and maintenance of water facilities intended for their use.

(Extracts from A Planner Manager's Guide to the Socio-Economic Issues Involved in Rural Water Projects in the Third World, *Dissertation, Reading University, 1988.)*

References

Carloni, A. S., 'Women in Development: AID's Experience, 1973-1985', Vol.1 Synthesis paper. *AID Program Evaluation Report No.18.*

Curtis, V. (1986), *Women and the Transport of Water*, London: Intermediate Technology Publications.

Jahan, R. (1975), *Women in Bangladesh*, Dacca, Bangladesh: Women for Women.

KPP and IDRC: *Women's Issues in Water and Sanitation: Attempts to Address an Age-Old Challenge*, Ottawa, Canada: Kabalikat NG Pamilyang Pilipino Philippines, and International Development Research Centre.

von Harder, G. (1975), *Participation of Women in Rural Development in four villages*, Dacca, Bangladesh: Women for Women. As quoted in Nelson, N. (1979), *Why has Development Neglected Rural Women?* Oxford: Pergamon Press.

Yansheng, M. and Elmendorf, M. (1984), *Insights from Field Practice: How women have been and could be involved in water and sanitation at the community level*, International Task Force on Women and Water of the Steering Committee for Cooperative Action of the International Drinking Water Supply and Sanitation Decade.

Brian Mathew has worked on development projects in Central America, Southern Africa and the Sudan. At present he is an independent consultant based in Somerset.

TURKANA WOMEN: THEIR CONTRIBUTION IN A PASTORALIST SOCIETY

CATHY WATSON

Pastoral development has been one of the priorities for Oxfam's Kenya programme for several years. If this programme is to be effective, however, an understanding of the traditional social and economic structures, and the changes they are undergoing, is vital. Research, therefore, has an important role to play in pastoral areas. This is particularly true with regard to the status of pastoral women, who have frequently been overlooked in development projects.

In Turkana District, in northwest Kenya, women have on the whole been excluded from development planning (as indeed have Turkana men in many cases), and little is known of their needs and the effect which the many development inputs in the District are having on their lives. A research project was therefore established by Oxfam in September 1986, to examine the social and economic status of a sample of Turkana women. Oxfam provided funding and transport and work began in late 1986, continuing until May 1988.

A sample of 15 women was selected from three areas: Lokitaung settlement; a food-for-work camp; and the pastoral sector, in order to highlight the changes affecting the women and their families, particularly as a consequence of famine or settlement. The topics covered by the research were household economics; food supply; labour; society; and women and the law.

The research methodology involved the collection of both qualitative and quantitative data: three research assistants worked closely with the author throughout. One very important aspect of the work was the good personal relationships between the research team and the women in the sample, which enabled the latter to express their views freely. A second was the close contact the researchers maintained with a development project, the Turkana Water Harvesting Project. Many of the suggestions and recommendations arising from the research have already been incorporated into this project.

In this article the importance of women's labour in pastoral work and the critical role of women in controlling food supplies are highlighted.

Background

Turkana District is a semi-arid region in the northwest of Kenya covering an area of approximately 60,000 square kilometres. It experiences variable and erratic rainfall, with a high evapotranspiration rate and low humidity. The Turkana people, part of the Nilo-Hamitic Karamojong cluster, first moved into the District from the Ugandan escarpment some 200 years ago (Gulliver, 1951), and now number approximately 200,000. They are by tradition semi-nomadic pastoralists, herding a combination of animals (cattle, goats, sheep, donkeys, and more recently camels), although they have developed other strategies, such as sorghum planting, hunting and fishing.

Although cycles of drought and famine continually affect Turkana pastoralists, the worst crisis in living memory was the famine of 1980-81, called *lopiar* ('the sweeping', since it swept so many families clean of livestock). In response to this crisis, the European Commission, together with the Dutch Government, set up the Turkana Rehabilitation Project in 1981. After an initial phase of famine relief, this project established food-for-work schemes for the many Turkana who were in the famine camps.

The effect of this massive influx of food-for-work maize into the District cannot be underestimated. The economy, which had hitherto been principally pastoral, with a cash system operating in the settlements, was turned upside down, and maize became local currency, with which goats were bought and sold and social networks strengthened. A few family members stayed with the remaining livestock, while as many as possible worked in the food-for-work camps for maize, which they invested in more goats, and which also supported those herding the animals, so that the herds could be strengthened.

The level of food-for-work started to drop in 1985 and continued to decrease through 1986 and 1987, and increasing numbers of people returned to the pastoral sector; although some have been unable to return to pastoralism, because they lack either viable herds or the important social links. They have moved to towns in search of work. Most, however, rejoined their families or relatives who had been herding their remaining livestock. In 1988, there are some signs that the Turkana economy is returning to 'normal'; however, it is clear that the famine has left its mark, particularly on the marginal pastoralists, from whom the pastoral sample was selected.

Women's labour

In the pastoral sector, the family works hard as a unit, as all the family members are involved in the care of the livestock. In this way they share the workload more or less evenly; the workload lightens considerably in the wet season when herding and watering become less intense. The most arduous tasks for the pastoral women interviewed were building houses and *kraals* (enclosures), and watering the livestock.

In contrast, the food-for-work sample families appeared to work less cohesively as a unit. This is clearly shown in the difference in the workloads of the men and the women, the latter doing over 1000 hours per year more work. Since, in the traditional division of labour in the pastoral sector the men are responsible for herding the livestock, while the women are in charge of the food supply, when there are few or no livestock (as in food-for-work communities for example), some men leave the responsibility of providing for the family completely to their wives. In addition to this burden, women's work in the food-for-work schemes is generally more arduous than that of the men.

This fragmentation of the family unit, which is becoming a feature of some food-for-work communities, is seen clearly in the towns. Domestic labour requirements are on the whole lower in the settlements, so a man rarely provides for more than one woman (his current wife), as her labour is sufficient. Unaccompanied girls or poor women may be employed by wealthier households, to assist in the home: this is an example of the cash economy taking the place of traditional social systems.

The following extracts from case studies of women's days highlight the involvement of women in pastoral work, where men and women work equal amounts of time, and women's increasing workload in food-for-work settlements.

Women in the pastoral sector

Alim's day (dry season)

Alim rises just before dawn in the early dry season, and sits in her day hut churning milk. This process can take up to an hour, although as the dry season progresses and milk yields decrease Alim does it less frequently.

When the milk processing is completed Alim, with the help of her teenage daughter, goes into the *kraal* and milks the goats. Alim takes the milk to the day hut, where it is stored, so that it can sour ready for churning in the evening or next morning. She then shares the milk that she churned that morning, among the family members.

When the milk has been consumed, Alim and her elder son release the goats, and the boy sets off with his father to the grazing. Alim's daughter unties the cow-hides and goatskins from the roof of the night hut and arranges them on the floor of the day hut for sitting on. In the meantime, Alim is helping her younger son and daughter to release the kid goats, and, giving them each a small container of water, she sends them off with the kids.

In the dry season the goats are watered on alternate days. This is a watering day, so Alim and her daughter leave home at around 9.30am, and set off for the well; Alim carrying a large and a small *sufuria* (metal cooking pot) and her daughter a jerrycan. On the way to the well they join up with the women from a neighbouring home, whose goats will also be watered today.

The women arrive at the well before 10.30, and wait their turn while the previous people water their goats. This is a deep well (15ft), which requires at least three people to lift water from it, so Alim and her daughter team up with their neighbours to water first their own and then their neighbours' goats. Alim begins work at the bottom of the well, passing the water up over her head to another woman perched above her. After half an hour her daughter takes a turn at the bottom, and Alim sits on the lip of the well tipping the water into her large *sufuria* from which the goats drink. Alim's husband and son stand with the goats some way off, and release them to the well a few at a time so that they do not crowd. The younger son and daughter are on the other side of the riverbed, waiting with the kidgoats, which are to be watered next.

When the watering of the goats is complete, the donkeys of the two families are watered. The women then fill their containers and jerrycan and set off for home. The men and boys have already gone with the goats to find more grazing.

Alim reaches home at around 3.30pm, and rests with her daughter in her day hut. She sleeps for an hour, and then goes out with her axe to chop a new gate for the goats' *kraal* (the old one is very worn). As this is the dry season the goats do not return home until it is almost dark, by which time Alim has rebuilt the fire, and started to cook some maize she had bought the day before. The kid goats arrive first, and the children sit and drink some water while the elder daughter drives the kids into their *kraal*. When the goats arrive, Alim and her daughter again milk them, while her husband rests and takes some water. The younger children drink from the teat, and then tend the cooking fire, while their older sister arranges the hides on the night hut. When the maize is ready, the family eat together outside the night hut, before settling down to sleep.

The task of herding and watering livestock is both more intense and time consuming in the dry season months and is shared, with gender- and age-segregated tasks, by all the family. Men undertake fewer jobs which last for several hours at a time, while women's work is made up of many more fragmented tasks. Women are responsible for milking, milk processing, collecting domestic water, cooking and preparing food, building the enclosures, huts and fences at each encampment, collecting wild fruits and firewood and making utensils and leatherwork. Some women are also involved in agricultural work and a little food-for-work, though these patterns of labour vary between families of differing circumstances. Some women have taken up charcoal-making and selling, both non-traditional tasks, in order to make money to buy cereals.

The Kariwareng food-for-work camp

Akal's day

Akal's day begins at dawn, when she rises and, in the wet season, processes the previous evening's milk, before entering the *kraal* to milk the family's few goats. (In the dry season she does not process the milk, but gives it to the children to drink fresh.) When the family have drunk the processed milk, Akal helps her two children to dress, and then sends them off to nursery school in the centre of Kaalin. Akal's brother arrives from his home close by to collect the goats, which he will herd during the day with his own.

Akal and her husband, Loresi, set off at about 8am from their home to walk to the food-for-work site, about 6km away, where they are helping to build a sorghum garden. They work until 12.30, and then set off again for home. On the way, Akal gathers branches of dead wood, which she carries home on her head.

The children are already home from nursery school, and are playing with friends nearby, under the eye of a neighbour. Akal cooks some maize meal that she had bought the previous day into porridge, calling the eldest child (a girl of six years old) to come and tend the fire.

After the meal, the family rest a while, and then Loresi goes to visit one of his friends and drink beer. Akal takes her bundle of firewood into the centre of Kaalin to sell to one of the schoolteachers for Ksh2. She then walks to the other side of Kaalin, where her brother-in-law lives. He earns a salary as a school cook, and since it is still near the beginning of the month, Akal hopes that he will not have spent all the previous month's wages. She spends over an hour at his home, talking to his wife and drinking tea, before leaving with a gift of Ksh50. On her way home she calls at the shops and spends Ksh5 on a kilogram of *posho* (maize meal).

When Akal arrives home at 5.30pm, she cleans some maize and puts it in a tin of water, which she places on the rekindled fire. Her eldest child tends the fire, while Akal tidies the home and herds the goats, which have just arrived under the care of her brother, into the *kraal*. This done, she milks them and closes them up for the night.

The data from the Kariwareng food-for-work sample showed some seasonal variations, but these were on the whole less marked than in the pastoral sample, reflecting the latter's greater dependence on livestock. At Kariwareng, the men have a smaller workload than the women, a characteristic of sedentarisation, where the burden of providing for the family may be placed increasingly on the womenfolk, while the men chat and drink beer in the absence of livestock to herd.

Women's control of food supply

A woman is responsible for feeding her husband and children. The control she exercises over the food supply varies with the lifestyle/location. In the pastoral sector, and in the settlements, cash itself is controlled largely by the men. Their wives either request cash to buy food, or ask their husbands to go to the shop for them. Small amounts of money earned by the women (for example from charcoal making or selling skins) are usually spent immediately, even if the husband is not present. The women then report to their husbands on their return how much they earned and what they bought. In such instances, they often buy some tobacco for their menfolk as well as food for the family.

In contrast to cash, most foodstuffs fall directly under the control of the women. This applies equally to purchased cereals, food-for-work, and food gifts. Women are responsible for storing and preparing the food, and also make the decision of what to cook and in what quantities. They control the distribution, serving out the prepared food to their husbands, children and visitors.

Each adult woman in a pastoral home has milking rights over certain goats in the herd. She, or her children, milk these goats, and she processes the milk and distributes it amongst the family: the husband, wife and children all have a separate *akurum* (milk container), in which their allocation of milk is stored in the woman's day hut. Apart from the children, who may enter and help themselves, no-one touches the *akurums* except the woman. If a man wants milk for himself, or his visitors, he calls his wife to serve him.

Control over livestock products, milk, blood and meat — and purchased food — is largely in the hands of the women, whereas any decisions regarding the stock (slaughtering, sales, purchases) depend ultimately on the men. However, the greater the influence of cash on the household food supply, the greater the men's power, as is seen clearly in the example of the town women below.

As there are no livestock, a large proportion of the food supply for the town sample is obtained through cash purchases. As described above, cash is controlled on the whole by men. Small amounts earned for firewood or charcoal sales are exchanged immediately for food, but the women in town explained that if a wife receives a regular salary each month, the husband usually takes it from her, and she has to ask for it back, bit by bit, whenever she wishes to buy food. This causes many quarrels, they claimed, especially if the husband uses his wife's salary (or indeed his own) to buy beer instead. Several of the women present at this discussion said they preferred to live alone for this reason.

This shift of power into the hands of men has other consequences for the women. A woman who is largely dependent on her salaried husband for her income, is dependent on his goodwill to provide sufficient money for her to feed her children. If he is a fair man, there is no problem, but if he is not, and chooses to finish his salary in the bar on the way home, she is powerless to stop him.

Once food is obtained, town women exercise the same control over it as do the pastoral and settlement women, being in charge of the preparation, cooking, and distribution.

The status of women

Pastoral women can, through their husbands, have considerable influence in the home and in the pastoral community outside their own specific areas of responsibility, such as food supply. In the towns, women experience a loss of power: those with husbands or partners have little security or financial power; and those living alone, whilst having full control of their own (usually rather limited) income, have no social power, and lack the means to influence events through their husbands.

Turkana women have also been powerless (as have many Turkana men) in most of the development projects in the area. With the exception of the Turkana Water Harvesting project women have not been considered nor consulted and even those projects geared towards women have been conceived and organised by outsiders.

In addition to failing to transfer power, and consequently encouraging dependency on outside resources, most development projects have completely ignored the social and cultural setting in which they were established. This has meant that traditional knowledge, and in particular traditional institutions, have been overlooked in favour of imported systems and techniques, which are alien to the Turkana. Consequently, the projects' beneficiaries (men and women alike) have not been able — nor have they been encouraged — to take over the development process themselves.

References

Gulliver, P.H. (1951) 'A preliminary survey of Turkana', Report for the Government of Kenya, Capetown: University of Capetown, School of African Studies.

Cathy Watson has worked in Turkana for four years doing research firstly for the Intermediate Technology Development Group (ITDG) and then for Oxfam. She has a MA in Social Anthropology from Manchester University and is currently Sector Social Scientist in the Agriculture and Fisheries Sector of ITDG.

THE INVOLVEMENT OF AGROPASTORALIST WOMEN IN LIVESTOCK PROGRAMMES

CLARE OXBY

There is an increasing realisation that women play an important role in animal production: not only in dairying, but also in the marketing of dairy products, and in a whole range of animal husbandry activities, including the herding and watering of livestock, and caring for sick and young animals. The sexual division of labour, however, varies considerably from society to society: amongst the Twareg of Central Nigeria, for example, milking is seen as a man's job. In agropastoral societies, women may be performing duties related to animal production in addition to much of the agricultural work.

When planning interventions in agropastoral societies, therefore, it is of vital importance to know about the local division of labour; firstly, in order to target programmes to the people who are used to doing the job, and secondly, in order to gauge the impact of the programme on all members of the community, not just the participants. Specifically, we need to ask if women in the community are being expected to take on increased duties in addition to their normal routine of childcare, domestic water and firewood fetching, and, in many cases, animal production and agricultural chores; and are these extra tasks manageable?

There is plenty of rhetoric within non-governmental organisations (NGOs) about the need to involve women in all their programmes, at every level of decision making, and at every stage in the process of programme design and implementation. Some NGOs specifically mention agropastoralist women in this respect but, despite the rhetoric, the impact so far in terms of carrying out interventions is meagre. If agropastoralist women are involved at all, it is usually not in relation to animal production activities, but to other activities, such as primary health care, literacy, and handicrafts. For example, a consultant's report on the involvement of agropastoral women in Oxfam's Affolé Project, Mauritania, proposes project components for women, not in livestock-related production activities but in literacy, human health, and improved stoves — even though it is clear from the same document that women play an important role in animal husbandry (Oxfam Mauritania, 1988, p.24-27).

The main exception to this is dairy projects; in Western eyes, milking and the processing of milk products is an acceptable, even traditional, occupation for women. This attitude on the part of donors and planners is being reflected in a few African NGO programmes for agropastoralists. For example, ACORD's Mali programme has involved some women in the Unité Laitière Coopérative de Tin Hama. On the whole, however, such projects involve women as workers rather than decision-makers; the latter are nearly always men.

If the impact of the rhetoric on the type of projects which are being implemented is meagre, the same cannot be said about data collection in connection with NGO programmes. A number of NGOs are attempting to fill their information gap on agropastoralist women by commissioning special studies, with a view to using the findings in the planning of a further phase of programme activities: Mali: ACORD programme (ACORD, 1987); Sudan: ACORD Red Sea Hills Programme (McEwan, 1988); Kenya: Oxfam and ITDG Turkana Waterharvesting Project (Watson, 1988); and Mauritania: Oxfam Affolé programme (Oxfam Mauritania 1988).

In addition, Oxfam's Gender and Development Unit (GADU) has issued several articles by Oxfam staff on agropastoralist women in a number of the countries in which Oxfam operates: Erigavo, Somalia (Sulekha Ibrahim, 1987a; 1987b); Central Somalia (Graham, 1988); Turkana, Kenya (Watson, 1987; 1989); and Eritrea (Burgess, 1987). ACORD organised a workshop on Pastoral Systems and Social Change in Mogadishu in October 1988 at which two relevant papers were presented: one on the situation of ex-herder women in settled areas of Somalia (Fouzia Mohamed Musse, 1988); and the other on women's role in the Somali pastoral economy and related development issues (Amina H Adan, 1988).

There is thus increasing evidence that in agropastoral societies, women may be performing duties related to animal production, in addition to much of the agricultural work. Moreover, the by-products from their agricultural work may provide valuable nutritional supplements for the household animals. While not implying that we have sufficient information on such issues, this is one gap which is beginning to be filled.

The situation with regard to involving women in the subsequent processes of project planning and implementation, however, is far from satisfactory. One explanation is the inevitable time-lag between the data collection stage and the planning and implementation stages; and one can only hope that the next generation of livestock projects will reflect more closely, and build upon, knowledge of the division of labour operating in these societies which has now been collected. Another reason is the cultural constraints operating on many individual donors and planners. Although they may hold the most open-minded and radical views on other subjects, some people have, at the same time, highly unrealistic and stereotyped ideas on what women's role in society is and should be. They react in a deeply conservative and negative way when it comes to absorbing and acting on the results of recent research about women's roles in agriculture and animal husbandry, proposing and implementing improvements to women's lives, or even merely counteracting the damaging impact on women of recent changes in society.

One way to combat this is to create or strengthen special units (e.g. Oxfam's Gender & Development Unit) or special posts (e.g. ACORD's Women in Development Officer) at the NGO head-quarters, and to ensure that the organisation gives them wide support in translating the results of research on women's roles in agricultural production into project activities for women. This means encouraging such staff to comment on projects which do not have a special women's component, not just on those which do; for it is precisely in the former that gender issues may have been overlooked.

Following are brief descriptions of two rare NGO projects which have attempted to involve women in animal production activities. Both are restocking projects, and further project details are available in the full reports.

Kenya: Restocking projects (Wajir, Isiolo, Turkana and Samburu Districts) Oxfam

In Wajir, the restocked families were all headed by women; either widows or women whose husbands could not support them. In Isiolo, 8 of the 36 beneficiaries were women heads of household. In addition, there was a stipulation that each married man receiving stock would brand 10 for his wife or wives, who would retain this share in the event of divorce (this was not enforced by project staff). In Turkana District, 14 out of 50 beneficiaries were women; and in Samburu District, 17 out of 53 were women (10 of these were actually Turkana women, but living in Samburu District). In other words, about a quarter of beneficiaries were women in Isiolo and Turkana, and about a third in Samburu.

Although people said how well the restocked women were doing, in fact the flock performance figures do not show any statistically valid difference between the restocked men and the restocked women. The projects' evaluator explains this attitude to women's performance as surprise that women are performing well at all. She does point out that many women are in a more vulnerable social and economic position than men, particularly women who find themselves without a husband for a variety of reasons.

Mali: Programme d'apui aux actions associatives et coopératives (Timbuktu and Gao Regions) ACORD

The latest phase of this programme is targeting women for some of the restocking activities. In Gourma Rharous Cercle, Timbuktu Region, 30 of the 85 families restocked by September 1988 were female-headed. In Gao Region, there are separate restocking initiatives for men and for women; women beneficiaries are members of already existing women's groups in Menaka Cercle and in Bourem Cercle. So far, two women's groups in each district have been allocated small stock, together with a fund to contribute towards animal health and herding costs (ACORD 1988). Restocking is carried out in these projects in a rather different way from most other restocking projects, since the animals remain in a collective herd until they are fully repaid, rather than being transferred to the beneficiary's herd at the time the loan is agreed. ACORD has also taken the important step of recruiting a local coordinator of all the project components affecting women, in both regions where the programme is operating.

Recommendations

There is a continuing need for more data on the role of women in animal husbandry in specific societies and regions, and the impact of programmes on the community as a whole, not just the participants. For example, are some responsibilities in animal husbandry being taken away from women as a result of project activities directed towards men? We are starting to get some of this data, but the need is still great.

A distinction needs to be made between women who are dependents in households, as wives, daughters, mothers, or other relatives, and women who are heads of households. They are likely to have different roles in animal husbandry, and to need different types of support from NGOs. Female-headed households are becoming increasingly common, and especially so in some of the deprived communities in which NGOs find themselves working; men may be absent for long periods, or permanently, when they take up paid employment in the towns or when they are involved in fighting civil wars. Refugee camps are notorious for the proportion of female-headed households; husbands and fathers may be away tending livestock, on paid labour elsewhere, fighting, or dead. In Sablaale Settlement Scheme, Sablaale District, Somalia, for example, 25 per cent of households are female-headed. In such circumstances, women may be taking on extra responsibilities in animal husbandry, and this should be taken into account when planning livestock programmes.

The water-harvesting project, Turkana District, Kenya (Oxfam and ITDG) aimed to improve local techniques of rainfed cultivation through the construction of earthworks with draught animals. Initially, the project worked with men only, but after realising that women were in a majority in the food-for-work groups from which participants were recruited, the balance was redressed; by 1987, the majority of those selected for training in water-harvesting were women. The work of women was no longer limited to earth-moving, but included also surveying and construction control; and a quarter of the project staff were women (Cullis, 1987:6).

It makes sense to focus project activities for women around the more productive activities in which they are already involved. This should apply whether women are taking major herd management decisions as female heads of households, or helping with subsidiary tasks such as the care of young or sick animals. Supporting their contribution to animal husbandry will probably do more to revive the local economy than teaching new skills such as embroidery or even horticulture. Furthermore, it is often inappropriate to direct such activities as literacy, human health and hygiene, and family planning, exclusively to women: men may also be involved in taking decisions about such subjects and therefore the activities should in many cases be directed to men as well. All too often such activities are seen as the obvious means for NGOs to support women, whilst more productive activities are reserved for work with men. The time has come for a change, in response to the actual roles of men and women.

When introducing new technology in animal husbandry, for example in animal health or dairy processing, it is important to teach women as well as men, so that women do not end up being excluded from such activities, or merely providing the labour while the men take the decisions. Women should be involved, where appropriate, in decision making and managerial work.

The phrase 'cultural constraints' is often used as an excuse for not directing project activities towards women. One should ask what are the specific cultural constraints in the community in question and, at the very least, try to tackle them. One should also remember that many African societies are undergoing profound changes at the moment, including cultural changes, and attitudes to women's roles may also be changing. One should also ask who precisely feels these constraints, in order to make an appropriate response: is it all of the community, or is it particular individuals? Could it be some of the project personnel?

Depending on what exactly the problem is, and who feels it, different measures may be adopted. Would special women's projects be more acceptable than trying to involve women side by side with men? Would recruiting female project staff help? Would clearer messages to men about proposed activities with women help? Would a concentration on what are locally considered to be subsidiary animal husbandry activities rather than major herd management activities make a women's livestock programme less threatening? Or a concentration on small stock rather than large stock? The programme should be flexible enough to adapt to the particular local situation.

Existing women's groups may be used as an institutional channel for project activities with women. This is the approach that has been taken recently by ACORD in their Mali programme, so far successfully. It is also possible that ACORD's Sablaale Settlement Scheme for agropastoralists in Somalia, may be able to work through established groups. Surveys have pinpointed two types of groups which may be of relevance for future programme design: labour groups for agricultural operations, and savings groups to pool money (Spooner, 1989; El Bushra 1986).

Traditional women's livestock inheritance mechanisms may be used as a model for stock loans to women. In many livestock-keeping communities, women may hold stock in their own names, and pass the progeny down to their children. Some of these forms of ownership and inheritance have been eroded in the past few decades, as a result of the emphasis put on 'Western', male-dominant patterns. Even if these female-focused institutions are no longer operating, members of the community are likely to remember them. The Twareg are familiar with such a form of matrilineal inheritance of livestock, which was widespread until recently, and is still practised to a limited extent in some communities to this day. It is known by different names in different Twareg communities: one name is *akh-idderan* or 'living milk' (Oxby, 1987). In the area where ACORD is operating in Mali, this same institution is known as *ebatekh* (reported by Halatine, 1989). ACORD is considering this inheritance mechanism with a view to using it as a model for their women's restocking programme (Roche, 1989).

References

ACORD (1987), 'Note sur le volet d'appui à des groupements féminins dans le domaine du petit élevage', Annexe III of the Mali programme's 1987 Annual Report (Gao Region).

ACORD (1988), Annual Reports for 1988 on their programmes in Timbuktu and Gao Regions, Mali.

Adan, A.H. (1988), 'Women's role in pastoral economics and related development issues (Somalia)'. Paper presented at the ACORD Workshop on Pastoral Systems and Social Change, held October 1988, Mogadishu.

Burgess, D. (1987), 'Women of Eritrea', Oxfam GADU Newspack 5.

Cullis, A. (1987), 'Turkana Waterharvesting Project', Oxfam Project Report.

El Bushra, J. (1986), 'Programming for women's development in Sablaale, Somalia', ACORD Consultant's Report.

Fouzia, M. M. (1988), 'Situation of women (ex-herder) in settled areas (Somalia)'. Paper presented at the ACORD Workshop on Pastoral Systems and Social Change, held October 1988, Mogadishu.

Fry, P. with assistance from Herren, U. (1988), 'Evaluation of Oxfam's four restocking projects in Kenya', Oxfam Consultant's Report

Graham, O. (1988), 'Pastoral women and drought: social dislocation in Central Somalia', Oxfam GADU Newspack 6.

McEwan, M. (1988), 'Programming with women in the Sufayya area, Halaib District (Red Sea Province, Sudan)', ACORD Project Report.

Oxby, C. (1983), 'Women's contribution to animal husbandry and production', *World Animal Review* 48, Rome: FAO (also available in French).

Oxby, C. (1987), 'The "living milk" runs dry: the decline of a form of joint ownership and matrilineal inheritance among the Tuareg (Niger)'. Paper presented at the workshop 'Changing rights in property and problems of pastoral development', held at the University of Manchester, April 1987.

Oxfam (1988), 'Les femmes dans l'Affolé (Mauritanie)', Oxfam Consultant's Report.

Roche, C. (1989), 'Note on ACORD's experience of the role of livestock within the household: lessons from the Mali programme', May 1989, Memo to ITDG.

Spooner, B. (1989), 'Development Programming and Adaptive Research in Sablaale District, Somalia', ACORD Consultant's Report.

Ibrahim, S. (1987),'Enclosures and their impact on nomadic women in Erigavo' and (1987), 'Women's role in production in Erigavo, Somalia', Oxfam GADU Newspacks 4 and 5.

Waters-Bayer, A. (1985), 'Dairying by settled Fulani women in Central Nigeria and some implications for dairy development', ODI Pastoral Network Paper 20c, London: Overseas Development Institute.

Watson, C. (1988), 'The development needs of Turkana women', Report to Oxfam and to the Public Law Institute, Nairobi. See also short articles in Oxfam GADU Newspacks 5 and 8: 'Approaching Turkana Women' (1987) and 'Turkana Women: their workloads in a pastoralist society' (1989).

Acknowledgements

Thanks to the following, who made valuable comments on an earlier draft: Fatimata Oualet Halatine, Co-ordinator of the Women in Development component of ACORD's programmes in the Timbuktu and Gao Regions, Mali; Judy El Bushra, ACORD's Women in Development Co-ordinator, London; and Nicky May, Oxfam Country Representative, Kenya.

This paper is an extract from the monograph 'African livestock-keepers in recurrent crisis. Policy issues arising from the NGO response', prepared for ACORD (Francis House, Francis Street, London SW1P 1DQ) and published by the International Institute for Environment and Development, September 1989. (French version available shortly.)

Claire Oxby is a freelance development anthropologist, and a member of the Africa Committee at Oxfam.

WOMEN AND HEALTH IN ERITREA

DORIS BURGESS

It is no simple task to initiate a health service when the majority of the population is scattered, rural, and impoverished. Certainly, the isolation imposed by a 29-year-old war is immobilising; families have been separated, formal education interrupted, and the majority of the population has been displaced. War has become almost 'normal' — the core around which everything else revolves: it is in this context that women's worth is being reassessed.

The long-term effects of war and recurring drought leading to famine could have deterred any initiatives to improve the health of women in Eritrea, yet paradoxically the war seems rather to have focused energies and encouraged substantial progress in both health care and the position of women. For the Eritreans, it seems that war has created an agenda for mobilising the society around a recognition of the essential equality and value of human lives. The odds against survival and the primary need to keep up societal strength and numbers have generated the very conditions from which a system for meeting basic human needs can spring, reversing the cycles of poverty and degradation imposed by the war.

How has it been possible for the Eritreans to begin the slow process of developing the potential of a multi-ethnic, multi-religious society? One, moreover, in which not only the needs of the people are taken into account but an overall 'strategy' addressing those needs is formulated? Because of the necessity of winning the support of the people, grassroots-based initiatives have been developed in which health and education campaigns have become vital ingredients. The war and the consequent need for (wo)man power have provided the vital impetus for the empowerment of women themselves.

The initial advances in health care have been in the treatment of the many thousands of war injuries: burns from napalm, the devastating effects of cluster bombs, the loss of limbs, sight and hearing — all in a society that was already malnourished and suffering from the long-term effects of disease. The list of obstacles to developing health care and services were endless, yet out of this situation is emerging a thoughtful, integrated system which encompasses health and education geared to harness the potential of the people. It is as if the momentum and adversity of war have become the engine for building a meaningful and accessible health service.

Background

Eritrea is divided into eight provinces: Sahel, Senhit, Barka, Dankalla, Hamasien, Seraie, Semhar and Akele Guzai. The latter four are mainly highland areas while the first four comprise midland and lowland areas that are peopled by agropastoralists. The current (1987) survey gives a total rural population of around 2,500,000 of whom perhaps 60 per cent are agriculturalists who mainly live in the highlands, 30 per cent agropastoralists and less than 10 per cent pastoralists, living in the lowlands.

Briefly, the agriculturalists' livelihood depends primarily on the cultivation of crops; livestock are sometimes kept and oxen are used for ploughing. For the agropastoral people, crops together with livestock — including often camels, goats and sheep as well as cattle — are both essential to their livelihood. For the pastoralists, camels, cattle, sheep and goats are the primary means of livelihood, yielding milk which is also exchanged for grain; although occasionally some crops are grown.

'Conditions differ between lowlands and highlands. The lowland areas are inhabited by pastoralists who travel with their herds of camels, cattle, goats or sheep usually carrying all their belongings with them; women and children sleep in tents while men sleep outside... in some areas 80 per cent of the population have malaria. Families and livestock use the same water sources, often badly contaminated. The staple food is a porridge made from sorghum and salt, a little milk added by the better off.. vegetables are rarely included. The men eat first; the women and children eat what is left and when food becomes scarce, they are inevitably the first to suffer.'

'In the highlands, people live in settled villages of mainly subsistence farmers. Their diet is largely a fermented bread made from local grains. Vegetables and fruit are unavailable except near towns and irrigation schemes.'

Mobilisation of women

Most of the population of one million in the three largely liberated provinces are either pastoralists or agropastoralists and are Muslim. In each of the twelve villages which I visited in the Sahel, Barka and Senhit provinces and which form the focus of this article, there were a minimum of two cadres (political workers) in each, with special responsibility for coordinating activities amongst the women with the Department of Mass Administration. Recently, however, cadres responsible for women's activities have been placed directly under the National Union of Eritrean Women (NUEWmn). The cadres, usually Christian and from the highlands, are sometimes considered 'foreigners' in these localities and this makes the role of mobilisation and popular education often difficult, but it is crucial to the expansion of health care and health education. The programme of 'people's participation' is quite sophisticated, efficient and flexible and it is beginning to overcome the cultural gap between lowland and highland people; in each area traditions and cultures are studied so as not to offend local customs.

There are normally three steps taken within the guidelines for 'popular participation' — the process involving people in the democratic process. The first step involves the creation of People's Committees. These are generally formed on the initiative of the cadre sent to the area, but elected by the community, using customary methods, and hence are usually made up only of men. This confirms the position of local notables. At this stage, discussion about the participation of women usually goes on at the same time, but quite separately from the men's group and always with a woman cadre, usually meeting with women in their own homes. At first, in almost all cases it is the women themselves who are the most reluctant to step outside their cultural traditions, being seen very much as chattels to both their husband and children, and this initial contact with them is often the most difficult.

In one village, for instance, it took six years to get from the initial stage of a People's Committee on to the next one of the Challenge Committee. At this stage, villagers are encouraged to choose representatives from different levels of wealth and poverty, not just the traditionally influential. It is only at this point that women begin their direct participation with men in organising their villages. Throughout the process, the cadres are present to suggest what is possible, what support they can give and what the prospects are for overall development. Discussions around the need for and establishment of village clinics start at this stage, along with the education of women and children, which is particularly important in reducing the maternal and infant mortality rate. This constitutes the beginning of the village health programme.

Initially, the Eritrean People's Liberation Front (EPLF) send their own cadres into the villages; it is at the second stage that village cadres are elected and selected with the support of the EPLF. According to the NUEWmn, this is done on a regular basis, selecting women from various villages and districts. Courses are then held in political education, village administration, health care, and elementary agriculture; leadership and decision-making skills are also taught before the women return to their home areas. Priorities initially are education and 'consciousness-raising'.

When the cadres feel that the community as a whole is ready to administer the village themselves, they move them on to the final stage, the People's Assembly. According to Kaddija Ahmed, an elected member and organiser for the NUEWmn, it took four years to convince the men who made up the People's Committee that women were to be 'allowed' to attend the Challenge Committee and another two years for women to finally become part of the 'government'. This was the culmination, Kaddija said, of years of gentle persuasion, consciousness-raising, criticism and self-criticism, beginning with the women themselves who, at the outset, were extremely opposed to any outside interference: 'women should stay at home and look after their husbands and children'. But with the introduction of schools and clinics into the region, and during the process of educating the women — whose very customs made them the most disadvantaged — problems of resistance to change began to diminish slightly. Women still get shouted down by men during meetings, but at least they have the beginnings of self-confidence and the support of the women's association to start to answer back and not be silenced: to feel their equality.

In the People's Assembly, rich, middle and poor peasants are represented separately; the latter two groups are predominant so that their interests will come to the fore in the land reform programme which is introduced only at this third stage. The procedures for 'people's participation' are ultimately geared to a land reform programme designed to give more equitable access to land and also to provide the first stepping stone to improved agricultural practices and nutrition. Between 1976-1981 there was land reform in about 10 per cent of villages, affecting about 50,000 people. Of these, about a quarter received land for the first time; a tenth of these were women who had never had land of their own: 'if women are to be free they must be economically independent'.

The programme for women's self-reliance

It is within this third stage structure of the People's Assembly that women generally begin to play an increasing role. Nevertheless, as of January 1989, the proportion of women in these assemblies was still only 30 per cent.

In 1987 at the EPLF's Second Congress, eight women were elected to the Central Committee. This was no mere token gesture but had evolved out of the democratic process of 'nominations' and 'elections' taking place in the grassroots-based People's Assemblies. Given this opening, women have begun to take advantage of the commitment by the male leaders to enable women to participate fully, but as they themselves admit, they still have a lot of work to do. Being literate is not a pre-condition to being elected or participating in village organisation; women are helped to develop literacy skills while working within this structure. The political processes have enabled women to become involved in many ways: to learn the alphabet, have access to medical facilities and participate in the running of their village. But this hasn't happened overnight and in many areas is still in the embryonic stage.

Changes in the (self)-organisation of the village community and the awakening of the women within the village represent part of a broad, new emphasis on women. Prior to 1970, women in Eritrea were not organised in any formal sense. But as the war escalated in 1970-1974, a few women started to join the military, initially washing clothes or providing food for the fighters. Between 1976 and 1978 the Eritrean Women's Association was formed and in 1979 women began to organise on a national level and the National Union of Eritrean Women (NUEWmn) was set up.

In 1984 the NUEWmn produced a 30-page document on 'Study and Research on Women'. The introduction states that 'the goal of this study is to unearth and know properly the development of Eritrean society and the past and present social and economic condition of women so as to be able to place the current struggle of the founding of a new society on a scientific level'. There then follows the list of topics specifically on the agenda for research: the birth of a female and her upbringing; marital relations — betrothal, marriage, wedlock, pregnancy and delivery, rearing a child, divorce; production (work in and out of the home); handicrafts, religion, inheritance; death; the struggle waged by women going back to the Italian occupation of Eritrea during the Second World War. This extraordinary document is a clear example of the Eritrean women now setting their own agenda.

The consequences of the breaking down of the feudal structure, which had hampered the participation of all the people, include the growth of self-reliance, especially for women. The political processes together with the grassroots-based programmes have enabled many women to reconsider their worth. The responsibilities they are given by their peers to deal with the day to day running of their villages and to participate on a more equal footing with men, have been a crucial factor in rural mobilisation.

A springboard central to much of this activity has been the literacy campaign — for both men and women, separately to begin with — which can lead to advances in social services such as health care schemes. Because of the diversity of Eritrea's eight ethnic groups and geographical development, this process has been very uneven, reflecting the different needs of women from region to region.

Health

The health service that the Eritreans inherited was set up by the Italians in 1889 when, as Basil Davidson says, 'there was a European scramble for African colonies'. The Italians arrived and in 1892 drew up boundaries for what is now Eritrea, with the Emperor of Ethiopia, Menelik, who was then expanding his domain. The Italians wanted to develop the fertile areas for distribution to the newly-arrived settlers, using Eritreans as a cheap source of labour. They also built and controlled the ports, manufacturing, roads, railways and shipping. To service the increasing numbers of Italians, a health service was begun to protect the newly arrived from 'tropical diseases' but to provide only a limited service to 'indigenous' populations — ostensibly so disease would not be spread into Italian households. A hospital was built in Asmara and several small district hospitals and dispensaries were established in Italian settlements.

In 1941, the British ousted the 60,000 resident Italians; during their 50 years in the country, virtually no training had been given. The emphasis had been on the Eritreans learning Italian, Italian history and the basics of arithmetic. The health service that existed was staffed by Italians and closed when they left. With the arrival of the British as a transitional occupying force, only a few Italians remained to continue the day to day administration of Eritrea.

During the 22 years of Haile Selassie's over-rule, medical facilities for the Eritreans disintegrated amidst military atrocities. The health facilities were not servicing the rural civilian population but were confined to the cities and expensive private practices, supported by various aid programmes and staffed by foreigners — inaccessible to all but the privileged. The military takeover by Haile Mariam Mengistu in 1974 eventually diverted resources into a massive military campaign; the hospital staff changed and the emphasis on the surgical services increased to handle battlefront casualties. The exploitation of the rural population by successive forces left the Eritreans with the massive task of building a viable public health programme with their mobile teams.

The primary health care programme in Eritrea began in 1974 with an emphasis on the well-being of the rural population rather than on military injuries: it was a 'needs-based' health care programme. The aims were: promotion of proper nutrition; provision of adequate and safe water supplies and basic sanitation; promotion of mother and child health (MCH) activities including family planning and immunisation; provision of health education and curative services; and control of endemic diseases. The emphasis was clearly preventive rather than just curative. To this end much energy has also been devoted to feeding people during the successive famines that have occurred since 1974.

According to Dr Nerayo Teklemichael, Director of the Eritrean Public Health Programme, 'health planners in Eritrea have come out with a scheme that is considered appropriate for the prevailing situation: Community Health Service (CHS) for the village; Health Station (HS) for the sub-district and Health Centre (HC) for the district'. These units are backed up by regional hospitals and the central hospital at Orota where all the data is collected and assembled from outlying units. This 'pyramidal' structure is at its broadest in the least accessible areas with 40 mobile health units, hundreds of community clinics, 45 health stations (15 in 1986), 21 health centres and 25 regional hospitals.

The main hospital is at Orota; mostly built underground and into the rocky hillsides. It has the capacity to treat 1200 patients. While there I observed and photographed a thyroidectomy, intricate brain surgery for the removal of a bullet and an operation on a 45-year old man who had walked all the way from Sudan to have his varicose veins removed. There are facilities to carry out reconstruction surgery, operating theatres built out of shipping containers, teaching facilities with increasing use of audio-visual aids, the planning of a 'herbal remedy' garden, a solar-powered blood bank, laboratories for making ointments, infusions and tablets, and a mother and baby unit.

The Health Stations are units which aim to reach about ten villages or about 10,000 people. Each one would be staffed by four health workers including a laboratory technician.

At the district level, the Health Centres would serve 50 villages and be staffed by 15-20 people, including two or three nurses. They would deal with ante-natal, post-natal, and delivery services as well as immunisation and health education programmes.

This health care does not rely solely on the western pharmaceutical industry for basic drugs. The Eritreans are manufacturing over forty types of analgesics, vitamins, antibiotics, anti-malarial tablets, anti-tuberculosis, anti-intestinal parasites, vitamins, syrups and IV fluids. There is also a sanitary towel factory. Dr Nerayo goes on to say:

> 'Traditional medical practitioners could be the main competitors to proper PHC service... this does not seem to be the case in Eritrea... at present traditional medicine is widely practised by both the people and healers. However, it is recognised that there are some harmful practices and it is the policy of the Department of Health to identify the useful and harmful and to develop the useful and integrate them into the comprehensive health service. Re-training traditional birth attendants (TBAs) is a positive and practical example.'

By January 1987 there were about 309 TBAs, and the administration of their role is being increased to keep pace with the Eritrea Public Health Programme. Women are selected from their villages to train to be TBAs; the qualities being looked for are good health, energy, experience and the trust of the village. The number in each teaching group is 11 and classes are conducted in an informal manner.

Usually classes take place in the morning; the afternoon sessions are usually in the form of a tutor 'observing' the women discussing what they had learned in the morning. The course runs for five weeks and during this time some sessions are used to re-educate older midwives on 'inappropriate practices'. Because many of the women are not literate, they use visual teaching aids, for instance, in teaching anatomy. Hygiene and nutrition are also part of the course. They learn how to detect anaemia by looking at the eye, nails and gums. During this period, continual checks are made on their progress by the 'barefoot' midwife or doctor.

Since 1979, reports and records have been kept and are now designed in such a way that even illiterate women can document the sex of a child, and whether it be healthy or stillborn. There is a statistical increase in the birth rate, which might be due to more pastoral women giving birth in clinics or under the care of TBAs. Monthly reports of all births are sent to the Central Hospital at Orota. The maternal mortality rate is dropping but the infant mortality rate is the same as it was in 1984, due to gastro-intestinal infections, malaria and pneumonia as well as malnutrition.

Concluding comments

Within the structure of the PHC programme, Dr Nerayo discusses the target population that should benefit the most:

> 'It is generally accepted that children and women are the most vulnerable groups in any community and much more so in the developing world... in the case of women the most important step is to institute basic services of delivery and essential ante-natal and post-natal care. For children, revolutionary changes in health status could easily be realised if the six killing diseases of childhood are controlled by a vaccination programme.'

References

Food and Agricultural Production Study (1988), University of Leeds.

Firebrace, J., *Never Kneel Down*, London: Spokesman Books.

EPLF, *National Democratic Programme*.

Doris Burgess has spent ten years in Africa and has worked as a consultant for Oxfam and ACORD. She is a writer and editor and is currently Managing Editor of the Review of African Political Economy.

THE POVERTY OF INCOME GENERATION: A CRITIQUE OF WOMEN'S HANDICRAFT SCHEMES IN INDIA

LINDA C. MAYOUX

Over the past ten years Indian Government pronouncements have expressed a substantial change in attitude towards women's employment policy. Particularly in the last two Five Year Plans, the proposals are quite ambitious: measures include the modernisation of industries preferred by women, the promotion of self-employment through expanded credit and training schemes, and the breaking down of barriers to women entering new occupations through special training facilities. Nevertheless, women are still largely ignored in general development programmes. In practice, employment development for women has been mainly limited to 'income generation' in handicrafts and cottage industries through encouragement of self-employment or various types of small-scale organisation.

The aim of the research on which this article is based was to investigate a number of issues involved in these types of income generation schemes in the context of one particular area: Bolpur and Ilambazar Thanas in West Bengal. The schemes have largely failed in this area as elsewhere. The reasons for the failure were examined; in particular whether or not it was because of problems of design and/or administration of the programmes (which could be rectified), or a result of the socio-economic system in which the programmes were implemented (not soluble by changes in the schemes). Did the schemes have a positive effect on the position of the women involved? Possible solutions to some of the problems and the implications of the research for development programmes for women are discussed. Although the article only discusses research in India, other research has indicated that these schemes and problems are by no means unique and some of the solutions proposed may be applicable elsewhere.

A story of failure

The area was chosen firstly because it has a long history of handicraft development and rural extension. It is a popular tourist spot because of its association with the Bengali poet Rabindranath Tagore, and there is a flourishing and growing market for handicrafts. Secondly, previous research in the area indicated that unemployment and underemployment here are severe problems for women, as in the rest of India. There are few industries in the area apart from handicrafts. The economy is mainly agricultural, depending on monocropped rice cultivation.

There have been many attempts to develop handicrafts for women, going back to the 1920s. These have included training courses, bank credit and the setting up of women's organisations.

As in many other parts of India, there has been little attempt to diversify the types of training available to women, despite the stress on this in the Five Year Plans and other official policy statements. Training courses aimed specifically at women are in skills such as bag weaving, tailoring, and embroidery which are seen as particularly 'female' skills. Women also take part in mixed-sex courses in weaving, bamboowork, leatherwork, batik and other handicrafts. A number of courses are also run in villages at the request of women's organisations, including papad-making, blockprinting, hobbyloom and handloom weaving. There are in fact ample opportunities in the area for women to get training within a narrow range of handicrafts, provided they can either attend the centres or apply for training in their village through a women's organisation. A total of 146 out of a possible 618 trainees on four of the main courses were interviewed. Only 12 of them were found to be working in handicraft production after training.

Bank credit is provided under two all-India schemes — the Integrated Rural Development Programme (IRDP) and the Differentiated Rate of Interest Scheme (DRI) — which were introduced to enable the poor, both men and women, to get subsidised or low-interest loans for productive purposes. A number of women have obtained credit for handicrafts and livestock under these schemes. Loans are also given by some of the governmental and non-governmental organisations after training or as part of setting up women's organisations in the area. Out of a total of 205 IRDP and DRI credit beneficiaries on lists supplied by the banks, 100 were interviewed, only 10 of whom were found to be repaying the loans and working in the industry for which they received the loan.

Some women's organisations elsewhere in India, of which the Self-Employed Women's Association in Ahmedabad (SEWA), Working Women's Forum and Annapurna Mandal are the most publicised, have been reasonably successful in mobilising women and, to some extent, raising their income. In the area studied, however, there were no innovative organisations of this type at the time of the research. Instead, they were of the standard sort found in the rest of India:

Multipurpose small village organisations mostly dependent on the voluntary work of their members and operating with very low funds. Most of these have at some time tried income generating schemes and many have arranged training.

Co-operatives set up after training.

Larger organisations which are only concerned with handicraft production.

There were a total of 43 women's organisations in the area, though a number of others had failed to survive for more than a very short time. Apart from one hobbyloom co-operative and two embroidery production organisations, none of them led to any sustained economic activity. The only successful organisations provided women with reasonably regular employment but at low wages (Rs50-100 a month or Rs2.50-3.00 a day). Although these organisations had received government funding, they differed very little, if at all, from private establishments in the same industries in terms of pay and employment.

It is therefore reasonable to conclude that the schemes have largely failed. The sample of trainees and credit beneficiaries was limited because many of them had moved, married or addresses were incorrect. A lot of time was, however, spent tracing beneficiaries who had been said to be working. Although it is probable that of those not interviewed some were working, they would have been picked up in the course of the rest of the research if the numbers had been significant.

There were 35 successful loan and training beneficiaries. The majority were involved in tailoring and bamboowork, most of whom reported earning Rs50-150 per month on average and five over Rs250 a month. All those with the highest levels of income had been very poor prior to receiving the facilities and the schemes had obviously been of great help to them. These few cases indicate that poor women are capable of using credit and training of certain kinds for self-employment. The policy implications of this are discussed in more detail in the final section.

Reasons for failure: socio-economic structure or bad planning?

The failure of these types of scheme is not unique to this particular area. Self-employment schemes in handicraft and small-scale industry have had limited success for men as well as women. One must therefore ask whether the schemes are a complete waste of resources and should be abandoned to enable funds to be spent on some other approach, or whether their rates of success could be improved by certain changes.

It was often asserted at the local level that the problem was lack of funding and resources. However, although, as with most poverty alleviation schemes, the amount of resources involved is inadequate to the scale of need, amounts were not negligible. Expenditure on training was quite substantial, as was expenditure on credit, given the high levels of debt outstanding, and on some of the women's organisations. Greater resources are certainly needed for women's programmes and poverty alleviation schemes but it is not necessarily the case that merely providing more resources will improve the situation.

The failures were attributed by the administration to two main factors in the wider socio-economic structure and therefore not amenable to change. The position of women was seen to impose constraints on the schemes, and the nature of the particular handicrafts being developed — and indeed of handicraft development in general — was seen as uneconomic because of lack of markets. There was, however, no explanation of why, if this was the case, these particular schemes were being continued. On further investigation, neither of these two factors was found to be a major obstacle.

Women's position

As in the rest of India, most of the bureaucrats in charge of the design and implementation of income generation schemes at the local level are upper-caste, upper/middle-class, urban men. The few women involved also come from this background. They design the schemes based on two main assumptions about women's needs: firstly, they aim at work which can be carried on in the home because it is assumed that women are subject to restrictions on their movements outside the home. Secondly, income earning is seen as only a part, and often only a minor part, of women's activities. The assumption here is that women have to spend most of their time in unpaid work for the family, and also that there is a male wage which is more important to the family, and hence to women, than the female wage.

These perceived social factors make outworking in handicrafts appear the only viable employment for women, but are also seen as constraining their ability or their need to earn more than a minimal income. In consequence, women's schemes were often expected to fail.

Women are indisputably disadvantaged in many ways, because of discrimination in the labour market and the family as well as by the bureaucracy. This certainly affects their earning ability, particularly because of their lack of experience of marketing and of the world outside their village or particular urban area. However, both the above assumptions were found to be out of date, and suffering from middle-class and Hindu upper-caste bias.

Restrictions on women's movements outside the home are changing rapidly. Even in the past, Bengali women have played an active role in grassroots political activity, which led them to breach the norms of seclusion. In any case, the restrictions do not affect all women equally and have always tended to be less stringently observed, from necessity, by lower caste and tribal women and the poor, particularly older women, widows and divorced, or abandoned women in upper-caste and Muslim groups.

More recently a number of factors have led even undistressed upper-caste and Muslim women to question the traditional restrictions. Firstly, the increase in female education, particularly as much Bengali literature deals with various aspects of women's oppression, has led the best educated families to change some of the norms. Secondly, the increase in dowry payments has meant that there are a number of women (e.g. in families where the father is dead or disabled, or where there are many girls) whose families are not able to afford a traditional arranged marriage. This leads to an increase in love marriages, and also to certain women needing to find full-time employment to support themselves, and in some cases their families as well. These women are often leaders of change in their village. Thirdly, the extension of village bus services has been fully exploited by women of all ages to visit relatives, for other traditionally sanctioned activities, and for newer leisure pursuits. Fourthly, the Communist and other political parties have increasingly mobilised women for fund-raising and other activities and some women organisers have now begun to question their traditional role within the parties and in society in general. Over the past ten years the pace of change has gathered momentum.

The amount of unpaid work for the family is also very variable, depending on a woman's marital and social status, the number, age and sex of her children, and her family's economic status. Although women in all social status groups have to perform 'core household duties' — childcare, fetching water, cooking, washing, cleaning and mending — the amount of time needed is very variable, depending on the above factors and also the availability of resources. Landless Muslim women, for instance, generally only cook once a day because they have to save fuel, and the time required for their other tasks also varies. Women in small cultivator families, particularly from the lower caste and tribal groups, are overworked and perform tasks in cultivation, etc., which are an integral part of family production. These women do need part-time work. Landless women, however, have fewer tasks which cannot be substituted for if other opportunities are available. Even in the case of lower caste and tribal women, although their many gathering activities are essential to family survival when income is low or non-existent, many of the items collected, e.g.vegetables and fuel, can be substituted by purchased goods if the income is available. What these women need is full-time work at adequate levels of pay.

It was possible to identify four possible target groups of poor women whose needs differed, as summarised below. The only group for which the assumptions about women's need for part-time work held good was women in poor cultivator families where there was a male household head and a shortage of female labour, or where there were very young children. In no case were constraints on women's movements outside the home important, although women's lack of experience was a more significant difficulty.

The four groups were:

Educated women from poorer households. Some of these women are trying to support their families where the father is ill or dead. Many are unlikely to be able to marry because there is not enough money for a dowry and they are not able to secure well-paid professional employment but are available for any non-manual work in or outside the village.

Landless women from upper-caste and Muslim households. These women have little housework and few traditional means of employment. They also have a number of handicraft skills. They could take full-time non-manual work outside the home.

Landless women from scheduled-caste and tribal households. These women would need manual or non-manual work to give a higher income than the work they are already doing, or employment at times of the year when other work is not available, particularly February to June and August to October.

Women from poorer cultivator households in all groups. This is the only group where the main demand is for part-time work in the home. Even in this group, full-time work outside the home can be taken by women from joint families or where there is another relative to do the main housework.

Because of the assumptions made in the design of the schemes, and the lack of seriousness in their implementation they have failed to involve those women most able and motivated to use the facilities for production, i.e. landless women. The women from the poorest groups were the most likely to use both training and credit for production. Of the twelve trainees who were working, ten were landless and levels of outstanding debt were lowest for landless women.

The numbers of landless and non-upper caste women in the schemes were disproportionately low. The IRDP and DRI credit schemes and a Block Development Office (government rural development organisation) tailoring course were the only schemes explicitly targeted at the poor. Only a third of all trainees were landless, and even in the tailoring course less than half were from the poorest group. In the credit schemes only half of beneficiaries were from the landless or low-income urban families. Only a quarter of women's organisation members covered by the research were landless, although there was some variation between organisations. The majority of beneficiaries of all the schemes were from the upper castes, although these form only a third of the total population in the area.

This was an important element in the failure of the schemes since a great many of the better-off beneficiaries had no intention of working in production afterwards. Many had taken the courses, for example, in order to gain an advantage in the marriage market or a certificate for professional work. Some had simply wanted the stipend.

This failure to reach the poorer groups cannot be blamed on their lack of participation in handicrafts. Of the sample in the study of the private handicraft industries the majority were landless, 23 per cent were Muslim, 39 per cent scheduled caste and 12 per cent scheduled tribe. A number of other reasons were responsible, which may be acting separately or together in specific cases. Firstly, women from the target groups have difficulty in getting access to the facilities because of administrative barriers and discrimination, particularly when there is a high demand from more privileged groups. Secondly, specific features of the design of the programmes make them inappropriate to their needs.

It is important to point out that this does not imply that middle-class women have no problems. The increasing incidence of dowry deaths and other forms of discrimination facing them contradict such an assumption. However, it is not clear that handicraft schemes are the best way to improve their position. Other measures such as changes in the educational curriculum, legal aid services to enforce property and other rights, and the extension of professional employment for women are desperately needed and would probably be a better use of resources.

Economics of handicrafts

The second factor mentioned by the administration was 'the uneconomic nature of handicraft production'. There are undoubtedly problems with a focus on self-employment in handicrafts and small-scale industry as the major means of poverty alleviation or employment creation, and in many areas of India the prospects for this type of employment are certainly not bright for women or men. However, in this particular area the failure could not be explained by lack of market or expansion prospects for handicraft production in general, or for the specific industries introduced.

Four industries were studied in detail: bag weaving, embroidery, bamboowork and tailoring. All were found to be reasonably successful in the private sector. The area is unusual, though by no means unique, in offering local marketing opportunities for self-employed producers as well as organisations. The tourist market is expanding, with close to 200,000 visitors a year, 1,000 a day during the tourist season, to one tourist site in the town. In addition, there is a large middle-class population attached to the university which forms an important market for handicraft products. Entrepreneurs reported no lack of a market and shopkeepers complained of problems getting goods rather than of marketing problems. Many of the tourist products sold are mass-produced imports from Calcutta or Darjeeling but, as most tourists wished to buy 'Santiniketan goods', it would be possible for local produce to be sold, even at higher prices.

Although earnings are generally low, a few women in all four industries were able to earn enough for a minimal level of subsistence for themselves and their families by working eight hours a day or more. A very few self-employed women reported earning Rs7-9 a day in bag weaving. Tailoring was the most lucrative industry and some male tailors were earning Rs400 a month. No women were earning this level of income, although two women tailors reported earning Rs7-10 a day on a fairly regular basis. Incomes and conditions in the private sector are better or no worse than those achieved in all but a handful of cases by the income generation schemes.

Administrative problems and bad planning

Neither of the main reasons cited by the bureaucracy for the failure of the schemes was found to be a major explanation. The most immediately obvious problems were bad administration and planning which led to ineffective targeting even in targeted schemes, and irrelevance in the context of the industries concerned. Many of the schemes are introduced in an *ad hoc* manner and it is not surprising that they fail.

The tailoring training course was a particularly glaring example of bad planning. It was aimed at tribal women, but it started just before the rice transplanting season in which these women are a major part of the labour force. Consequently, many of the trainees had to leave and did not return to the course. The lack of tribal applicants led to a number of richer educated women, with contacts in the bureaucracy, entering the course, resulting in a class of forty to fifty trainees with only one trainer and four machines. It was not therefore surprising that none of the women learned enough to work after the training, or to take advantage of the bank loans which were available. The costs of this scheme were not negligible and it was a total failure, but it is still being continued.

The bamboowork training course, although partly successful, was not immune from bad planning. The course taught bamboo and cane work, despite the fact that cane was not readily available in the area. For much of the course there were problems of supply, whether a result of mismanagement or general supply problems was not clear. Consequently, the trainees had either to supply their own materials or, if they could not afford this, sit idle for about three months; they had to turn up to collect their stipend. In this situation it would have been much more sensible to place greater emphasis on teaching with plastic, which was the material the most successful trainees used after the course.

Credit schemes

Administrative problems accounted for a major part of the failure of the credit schemes. An important factor was the failure of the institution arranging the loan to provide subsequent employment. Sixty-six loans had been arranged for bag weaving by employees of Visvabharati after a training programme. Employment was offered but for various reasons this was on an irregular basis and at a very low level of income (Rs2 per day), and most of the women stopped work after a couple of months. They did not repay the loans and the banks were not pursuing the matter. The training had not equipped them for self-employment.

A second important element in loan repayment was found to be the relationship between the bank or intermediary organisation and the beneficiary. Interviews showed that a number of beneficiaries could have repaid without significant hardship, and much of the low repayment could be blamed on the banks' inefficient collection methods. This is partly understandable in view of the large amount of work involved in lending to 'weaker sections' and the high administrative costs and low returns on many small loan accounts.

It is unlikely, however, that beneficiaries will repay without either more effort by the banks or some incentive, e.g. the prospect of a further loan. Members of one bambooworking community were not repaying their loans because they could see no benefit in doing so, though they were repaying another loan arranged by someone they respected in the community because they did not wish to betray his trust. Members of another bambooworking community at a similar level of poverty were repaying their loans because they had been promised a repeat loan if they did so.

Thirdly, bank loans are used by the major political parties as a means of patronage, and political leaders are in fact plagued with demands for such arrangements. The selection of beneficiaries for their party political affiliation rather than their productive capacity and motivation to repay is obviously not likely to lead to satisfactory repayment levels, particularly when people are specifically told by certain political leaders that they will not have to repay. This aspect of loan usage was very much resented by the banks.

Women's organisations

Most of the women's organisations in the area were village organisations dependent on voluntary management. The more recent Development of Women and Children in Rural Areas (DWCRA) and other schemes elsewhere in India also envisage reliance on voluntary effort. However, unpaid organisers rarely have either the time or the expertise to do the marketing and organisation of production efficiently, and even the *gram sevikas* (women village workers) operating from local government headquarters lacked the facilities to keep in adequate contact with individual villages. Given the problems and the lack of entrepreneurial expertise on the part of the women involved, it is not surprising that most of these organisations fail.

The failures, therefore, in the area studied were not due to aspects of the socio-economic environment blamed by the administration, but to specific cases of administrative failure and bad planning.

Effects of the schemes on women's position

It is relevant to ask whether the schemes have nevertheless led to positive changes in women's position which could justify their continuance even in their present form. Although there is generally no explicit mention in the official policy documents of any aims of women's equality, freedom to decide their own future, etc., it is assumed that some improvement in their position will automatically occur as a result of the provision of income generating projects. The research took two indices of this: access to the world outside the home, and control over economic resources in the family.

The restrictions on women's access to the world outside the home are both variable between women and changing in the area studied. Employment in private handicraft enterprises had a significant impact on women's lives in many cases, although they were low-paid and exploitation was often apparent. Although they worked at home many of them went to collect orders, raw materials and finished products from the entrepreneurs or from the market, often because there was no male relative to do these tasks. It was obvious from the interviews that this had led to a change in their confidence and knowledge of the outside world.

A particularly striking example of this was in the lives of Muslim women embroidery workers in one village who worked for a middlewoman in Santiniketan. Village women who a few years ago were in purdah are now using the buses and walking long distances to town to fetch their work. Initially the work had all been brought by a man and a divorced woman in the village; but it was subsequently found that they were not handing over all the money, so more of the women decided to breach tradition and fetch the work themselves. At first they were criticised in the village but gradually as more women began to take part the criticism became less.

To the extent that most of the training programmes and banks required women to go to the town, they can be said to have added to a change which was already occurring. Where training courses and women's organisations already existed, this required much less of a change in women's attitudes. However, these changes have been small and other developments such as education, improved bus services, and cinemas, have been more influential.

The degree of control over family income was in fact very variable but did not depend on whether or not a woman was working for a wage. It was more common for women to decide how the household money was spent in poorer households, particularly in non-upper-caste groups, regardless of whether they were employed in waged work or not. Women, however, were not free to spend more on themselves, although they were more aware of how money was spent and thus more able to voice their opinion. Most of the women reported spending the majority of their income on the family, as dictated by their poverty.

Thus, although the current schemes have had some impact, this is not significantly more than that from employment in private industry. Other factors such as education and improved communications have probably been more influential. Several studies of large organisations elsewhere in India report quite marked changes in women's self-image, attitudes to social issues like caste, family planning and their status in the family and community, where this is a stated aim of the organisation. Other data suggest that many large women's organisations elsewhere may in fact merely replicate the class and gender hierarchies in society at large.

Women's programmes tend to 'mollycoddle' women more than private industry does. This is not necessary for poor women and it is in fact extremely unlikely that income generation schemes can yield women any significant income without challenging their subordination. The paternalistic model of altruistic social workers fulfilling all the difficult tasks accomplished by middlemen/women often means that the organisations collapse once the social worker has got tired or has been forced to take up some more lucrative activity. The assumptions about women's needs have to be changed, otherwise the failures will continue, reinforcing prejudices and cultural stereotypes about women's capabilities.

Possible solutions: greater commercial orientation and relevance

The research found that the schemes were largely irrelevant within the context of the industries at which they were aimed. They are introduced without sufficient technical knowledge and there is a complete lack of commercial orientation. Specific commercial changes might include the following: firstly, there is a need for more information on new designs, products and technology to permit greater diversity in the industries and products promoted. A great deal of variability was found in levels of profit between different items and designs. Some research is conducted in certain urban centres like Calcutta but the extension work is inadequate, particularly as far as women are concerned. Secondly, there is a need for major changes in the design of training courses. The main focus has been on basic skills training. In fact, this sort of training is largely redundant and frequently leads to serious oversaturation of skills in certain industries. Women often teach each other skills or learn traditional caste skills from male family members, and in many cases this informal training, even in tailoring, is better than that given by the courses.

What is needed is serious skills-upgrading courses to allow existing workers to produce a wider range of products; training for new industries and on-the-job training in commercial and marketing aspects of production as an integral part of both the above types of training. In the present courses on offer there is no training in marketing or linkage with organisations which could help with marketing or supply of raw materials. It was noticeable that many women (and even men) working in the industries studied had no knowledge of how to assess profit and loss or the relative profits from different types of articles. Equally important, women need to be shown the possible markets for their products, to learn about the variation in pricing, and to be encouraged to gain experience and confidence to go to new places and develop new contacts. Thirdly, the provision of bank credit needs to be more flexible to take account of the reality of the lives of poor self-employed workers.

Credit should take account of certain consumption needs. The main purpose of credit schemes has been to help workers obtain capital assets for production and raw materials. However, this is not necessarily what is needed by the poor to set themselves up in self-employment and in some industries these requirements are in fact quite low. In many cases studied, even where beneficiaries were working and repaying the loan, they had not used the bulk of the money for production needs but for basic consumption. Certain types of consumption expenditure are in fact a very rational use of resources, e.g. purchase of stable foods in bulk just after the harvest when prices are low. The money thus saved can then be invested in production or used as a buffer to prevent distress sales of produce, thus increasing income.

There is also a need to counter a certain amount of seasonality in the handicrafts market. Also, since shops often do not pay until the produce has been sold, capital is needed to tide workers over this period. Lack of capital has meant that workers' bargaining power is weakened *vis-à-vis* the shops and they cannot hold stocks to bid for the highest price. Lastly, capital is needed to enable producers to take risks in, for example, design innovation and to develop new markets.

Repeated injections of capital may well improve repayment levels. A new loan should only be given when the previous loan has been repaid, not to cover bad debts; but people would be likely to improve repayment levels if the loans had been sensibly allocated in the first place. Not only are poor workers more likely to use their first loan productively when they may get further finance if they repay it; it also improves their image of the banks and this is crucial in motivating them to repay without being pressured by expensive investigations and prosecutions.

It is more difficult to specify the ways in which women's organisations could be improved. A lot more research is needed on the types of organisation most economically appropriate in specific market and production situations and on how safeguards could be built in to prevent the corruption, mismanagement and exploitation which are currently so frequent.

Targeting poor women

The issue of targeting is far from straightforward. Poor women have a number of other requirements which need to be accommodated in the schemes if their participation is to be increased; particularly their need to improve their generally low levels of education, though not necessarily of skill; the need for income generation schemes to integrate with, or be sufficiently remunerative to substitute for, work they are already doing; and their need for more resources. These have implications for the design of the different schemes, in particular for higher levels of stipend and credit, and more flexible timing.

Higher levels of stipend and credit are, however, likely to aggravate the problem of targeting because of their attractiveness to women from the better-off groups. A possible solution is to try to make schemes 'self-targeting', i.e. attractive only to those groups for whom they are intended:

> The present emphasis on work exclusively in the home which does not require women to engage in marketing and mixing with

men should be reconsidered since the restrictions on these activities do not apply to poor women.

Targeting women already working and helping them to improve their income would reach more women from non-upper caste groups and also significant numbers of landless women.

Integrating income generation training, marketing, credit, etc., with other targeted schemes such as literacy, numeracy or health projects would be likely to improve both women's ability to earn an income and their position in the family, and also would be unlikely to attract the better-off, better educated women.

Conclusions and implications for women's development programmes

Although the changes outlined above are necessary to improve the success of the schemes, they can be only part of a programme for women's development. Handicrafts can have an important role in employment creation but this sector alone cannot solve the unemployment problem for women, any more than for men. Even in the area studied, with its potentially favourable environment for handicraft development, there is a need to diversify the industries in which women are involved. There are also limitations on what can be expected from self-employment and employment in small-scale industry, and the desirability of confining women to these sectors is open to question.

It is unlikely that the changes required in these schemes can be made without quite far-reaching changes in the attitudes of the bureaucracy towards women's issues and poverty alleviation in general. Although the cases described above can be seen as specific instances of administrative failure, poor planning occurs fairly systematically and the problems are intrinsic to development planning in India as elsewhere. They are even more pronounced in women's programmes because of the lack of seriousness with which these are generally treated. A new degree of flexibility and sensitivity is required on the part of bureaucrats to the local needs both of small-scale industry and of poor women — a transformation which would demand profound changes in their training and incentive structure.

Successful implementation of the schemes also requires the target groups to be more aware of and empowered to demand their rights, both as women and as workers. The wider women's movement, the education system, political activists and non-governmental organisations have an obvious role to play here, as well as the government administration. There is a need for income generation schemes and poverty-alleviation measures to be seen in this wider framework and for possible roles of these agencies to be more fully considered. This is particularly the case with women's programmes because of the importance of social and ideological factors to the success of the programmes, and the prejudice which exists at all levels.

(Note: this article is based on research done during a three-year ODA-funded research project in 1984-7. The research was supported by the Department of Anthropology, University of Cambridge, UK. The views expressed are, however, those of the author.)

Dr Linda Mayoux is a researcher on issues of women and development and small-scale industry policy. Her other work includes research on women in co-operatives in Nicaragua and Africa. She is currently based at Glasgow University, working on problems of development in the Indian silk industry.

RESOURCES FOR WOMEN:
A CASE STUDY OF THE OXFAM SHEANUT
LOAN SCHEME IN GHANA

BEN PUGANSOA AND DONALD AMUAH

The Oxfam loan scheme for women's sheanut purchase in the Northern region of Ghana was instituted in August 1986. Loans of various sizes were distributed to existing women's groups. The philosophy of the scheme was in line with the overall philosophy of Oxfam, which is to work with the underprivileged with a view to raising their quality of life and promoting greater social justice. The motivation for the scheme was a strong desire to encourage women to stand up for themselves in the face of what looked like an organised and determined attempt by local businessmen to dislodge them. The rural women required credit to enable them to assert their traditional role as pickers, processors and users of sheanuts and shea-products. It was anticipated that increased off-farm income would lead to increased consumption of goods and services, better nutrition and consequently overall improvement in family well being.

After the scheme had been running for eighteen months a workshop was organised for the resource persons and the participants to learn from each other. Attendance was better than expected, and the gender representation was 3:1 in favour of women. This paper highlights some of the issues discussed and some resolutions made to improve the scheme. It also includes the findings of a rapid field survey conducted among seven women's groups, all but one of whom were beneficiaries of the scheme.

Background to sheanut picking

The year for the rural women in the Northern and Upper East Regions of Ghana is divided into four production periods;   sowing (April/May); weeding (June/July); harvesting (September/October) and the fallow period from November to March which is devoted to construction work and off-farm income generating activities. All women's income generating activities have to fit into this production cycle. Sheanut picking reaches its peak in the heart of the 'lean season', the hunger gap spanning February to early July, and so is of crucial importance to the survival of the family.

Sheanuts may be picked by women from their husband's cultivated plots — the oldest wife regulates access where the husband is polygamous. Fallow plots (land abandoned temporarily because of soil exhaustion) are open to the wife or wives of the previous owners. Sheanut picking on uncultivated plots is open to all women. Late in the day, after the main picking is done, women, especially the old and widowed, glean the fields for any remaining sheanuts.

Sheanut picking is arduous work, requiring muscle, stamina and courage. Pickers wake up at dawn and trek distances of up to ten miles. Sheanuts are carried in pans or headloads of about 20kg from the bush to the house. After a suitable accumulation of several day's pickings, the nuts are parboiled, dried and processed into sheabutter or sold. The work is also dangerous. The main hazards are accidents associated with stumps and bites from snakes and insects, including scorpions; the women wear very little protective clothing. A survey carried out in the middle of the picking season found that anti-snake serum had run out about six months previously.

Recent government policy in Ghana, giving monopoly to the Cocoa Marketing Board (COCOBOD) for the handling of sheanuts and sheanut products, has made the sheanut industry very lucrative. Women who undertake the heavy workload and run all the risks deserve to benefit; however, it is not easy for women to obtain a license to trade with COCOBOD and the bulk of the profits are taken by urban-based men with influence. Local business men invariably employ women to purchase sheanuts from other women at small village markets and to take the nuts to bigger villages for bagging and transport to Tamale, the regional capital, where they are sold by these men to COCOBOD at great profit. The bad state of the roads and transportation means that the women undertaking sheanut collection also have to take personal risks.

Other income generating activities

Women are engaged in other productive ventures, financed partly from the money from sheanuts. The main activities identified were charcoal making, cutting firewood, local craftwork (mainly weaving straw baskets and hats), farming of groundnuts, maize and vegetables and trading in food. Women may also own small livestock and poultry. Several groups carried out some form of agro-processing such as groundnut, sheanut and vegetable oil extraction, or spinning. Oil extraction was undertaken all year round depending on stocks of raw materials. The problem of vegetable oil production and craft work is essentially one of the availability of raw materials; credit is needed to build up stocks at the time when materials can be bought cheaply.

In certain areas where land is abundant and accessible, women have increasingly taken on the role of independent farmers, in addition to their other roles. Many women are in fact heads of households. The burdens on women have increased in the context of static or inappropriate technology and policy frameworks that still consider women as mere appendages to men.

Disposal of women's income

Women's income is critical to the overall quality of life and standard of living in the family. It is mainly used to provide food (in times of scarcity), soup ingredients to complement the grain that is normally provided by the husband, cooking utensils, clothing for themselves and the children and to help with dowry requirements. Any spare income is invested in small livestock, and used for purchasing grain, seed and sheanuts for retail or production later.

Women have a large measure of control in the disposal of sheanuts. In one area, sheanuts picked on cultivated or fallow plots are shared with the men. Those picked from the 'wild' may be disposed of as the women please. In the disposal of the sheanut income, top priority is accorded to the food security needs of the family. Sheanuts are sold off, often cheaply, to buy food for the family. Women in better family circumstances have more choice in the disposal of sheanut income whereas those families at the margins of existence will normally sell sheanuts off very fast to buy food. It is in this context that the sheanut scheme provides an opportunity for women to hold sheanut stock as a group, as well as to purchase from the village market to retail later through COCOBOD, or to process into oil for retail and family consumption.

Most groups used the income from sheanuts to purchase and store grain which operates as a buffer for the rest of the village. As one woman said, 'Because we have corn in our group barn the village do not have to walk to Walewale to buy grain. Our only remaining problem is how to grind the grain, we have no cornmill. We have, at times, slept with hunger when we were not able to walk to Walewale to grind grain.'

Involvement of men

The women said that men had a genuine interest in the off-farm income generating activities of women and must be consulted if the cohesiveness of the family unit was to be preserved. Men often contributed the initial capital and also provided labour for the harder tasks, though women have to pay men to undertake such vital activities as weeding, digging and fencing. There were traditional arrangements whereby men's projects enhanced the income earning potential of women; for example, it was common practice for a man to make a plot available in his garden or farm for the women to cultivate food for the kitchen or the market.

As managers of the main production cycles, the men's management and timing of agricultural work determined what time was available to women for their income generating activities. The women felt that it was often necessary to consult with male members of the community when designing projects for women and that it was not unreasonable to try out pilot projects with the family unit as the major focus of attention.

The goals and aspirations of groups

The major concern for individuals and groups was for food security, shelter, clothing and health. Groups had to reinvest money quickly in order to make sure that their initial capital was not lost. Additional income would be used to provide the means to reduce the drudgery associated with women's activities. Donkey carts, grinding mills, oil extraction machines and even tractors were mentioned. There is also a quite legitimate long-term vision for the acquisition of bicycles to help mobility.

Women often have to travel long distances to reach cornmills (on average about five miles), and in six of the seven groups surveyed, they expressed the need to have their own cornmill for grinding grain and other food items used for the making of 'tuo saafi' (thick porridge). Women did not think it was beyond the ability of their groups to manage such facilities effectively.

Money was not the only form of support that they needed; small livestock, poultry and groundnut seed could all contribute towards greater self-sufficiency for women and be used as back-up security to be easily disposed of in times of pressing need. Discussions with women during the field survey suggested that, although the women were generally aware of the opportunities for generating more income, they could still benefit significantly from inputs on animation, credit extension and credit management. Such inputs should be seen as complementary to the provision of credit.

Generally, women appreciated the need for some protective clothing and equipment for sheanut picking, but they did not know where to buy gloves, and wellington boots seemed too heavy for the distances they had to walk. They said that they would be willing to buy appropriate protective clothing at reasonable prices. Lamps and torch lights are available but are very expensive and many women did not even know about them.

Profile of women in their groups

In the rapid field survey it was found that most of the women belonging to groups were aged between 25-60 with the majority around 45 years old. Births to younger women averaged four; older women had seven or more deliveries. Marriage is valued and most women were married; over 50 per cent were involved in polygamous marriages. About 30 per cent were unmarried, mainly widowed. Women's burdens increase with the size of family. In polygamous families, resources are stretched thinly and women have to assume greater responsibility for feeding and clothing children, and meeting medical bills and school fees. Widowed and other single women faced even greater economic problems. The profile suggests some relation between membership and marital status or circumstances, though this finding must be treated with caution due to the small sample size.

Most group members were virtually illiterate; well over 90 per cent of the women had never set foot in a formal classroom. All the group secretaries except one were male. None of the women, either as individuals or as members of a group, had previous experience of credit with a bank or similar formal financial institution.

Group structures

For five of the rural groups surveyed the sheanut scheme had contributed greatly towards food security for the whole community.

The other two groups organise production on a collective basis and whatever income is generated is ploughed back in a bid to build social capital; for example, one group had used some of its profits to put up a shed to house a cornmill provided by UNICEF. It is the consensus among members of these two groups that the loan scheme has not yet benefited them personally. Members expressed a desire to operate as individuals within the group framework so that they would be able to derive appropriate benefit from personal business initiatives.

Logistics of the scheme

Women have frequently demonstrated that they can be safely entrusted with productive credit. Banks, however, have been constrained in their ability to make loans to rural populations because of massive loan default rates by urban dwellers. Banks are mostly located in towns and lack understanding of the situation of rural people. Banking procedures are unfamiliar to rural people, and the requirements for collateral cannot be easily met.

Oxfam supplied a grant as a loan portfolio to the Bank for Housing and Construction (BHC) who administered the scheme. A Small Project Committee, which included representatives from the National Council on Women and Development, acted as a management committee, and was charged with legal title to the money in trust. The scheme was administered on normal banking principles with an interest rate of about 23 per cent. It was thought self-defeating to subsidise the scheme, which should at least cover its operating costs and also allow for moderate growth over time in order to extend its benefits.

The sponsoring agencies introduced clients to the Bank but further screening and selection were the responsibility of BHC. Clients had to be registered with COCOBOD and have a licence for sheanut purchasing. They were required to open an account with BHC into which payment by COCOBOD was made. BHC recovered the loan and interest from such payments. Coordination was achieved through periodic review meetings, seminars and workshops.

The role of the bank

The sponsoring agencies all considered it important that the bank administered the scheme. This left them free to concentrate on group development and the provision of extension support. It also insulated them from the tensions and temptations associated with giving and recovering loans. They felt that credit administration was a specialised field which required broad experience.

The women's groups complained that banks were inaccessible and women had therefore to travel long distances and incur other costs in order to secure credit. They also claimed that the banks were insensitive to their lack of familiarity with banking procedures. (They agreed that the intermediaries did a lot to minimise their inconvenience, and experience with other banks indicated that BHC was very accommodating.)

BHC decided to deliver services more promptly by appointing a Field Officer. A scheme to provide mobile support to supervise intra-group administration of loans was also under active consideration. This would provide an opportunity for BHC project staff to supplement the extension efforts of sponsoring agencies in the area of credit management. It was felt that this outreach should take place at least twice a year, at the beginning and towards the end of every loan season. The mobile banking service could also provide basics like rubber boots, hand gloves, torches, cutlasses, etc. for sale to women.

With regard to the question of the readiness of groups for self-management status and independent standing with BHC, it was contended mainly by the sponsors and BHC that, as groups established their credibility with the bank, BHC would not need to use the Oxfam loan portfolio as a security. A maturity period of 3-5 years was proposed but rejected by many groups who contended that credit was a way of life and could be extended to worthy members of the family through generations. It was decided not to press the issue of maturity for groups too hard as it might affect loan recovery. Groups might decide to build private capital at the expense of loan repayment for fear of losing continuous support.

The first loan season

Once a loan facility was granted, intra group distribution was effected in three ways. Some immediately shared the money among group members. In other groups individuals drew on the loan according to the amount of sheanuts they had purchased. Other groups spent the money on joint ventures. Most groups initially used the loans for purchasing sheanuts to sell to COCOBOD. Some of the most efficient groups quickly arranged for the collection of their purchases, got paid and bought more sheanuts which they resold. They turned the cash into grain or groundnuts for retail later on the open market. Two groups used some of the sheanuts for extracting oil which had a much higher value.

The scheme was instituted late in the sheanut season, so most groups missed the windfall profits that could have been reaped earlier in the season. There were also delays in the collections of purchases by COCOBOD resulting in losses from spoilage by rodents and over-drying of nuts. The next loan season was instituted earlier and COCOBOD said that they would try to solve the transport problems. Warehousing was recognised as a key to the success of the scheme: the groups requested COCOBOD and Oxfam to help them put up simple sheds from local materials.

The bank's view

As stated in the BHC report to the Oxfam Loan Scheme seminar in March 1988:

'The operation of the scheme for the first loan season has been successful. A loan recovery rate of 99.98 per cent was recorded. Delays and short repayment of outstanding loan balances were the result of failure of BHC counter staff to advise clients of interest charges. These issues were resolved at the First Review Meeting of the Scheme held in April 1987. That review meeting also provided an opportunity for group leaders, sponsoring agencies, CMB and BHC to assess the performance of groups in respect of application of loans, to educate womens' group leaders on how interest charges could be kept low and interact generally to resolve outstanding issues...

From the perspective of BHC, the scheme has been immensely successful. We also have taken notice of and approved of the flexibility with which some groups applied loans for activities other than sheanut purchases. It enabled some groups to make a turnover of over 300 per cent.

It is also our opinion that groups that were closely supervised and benefited from educational inputs from sponsoring organisations performed better. We recommend that sponsoring agencies intensify this aspect.

Advancing loans to groups rather than to individuals within groups has kept our administrative costs low.'

Some conclusions and recommendations

The loan scheme has been beneficial to precisely those women who need support most. It has contributed significantly to the needs of participating groups for productive credit which was otherwise not available. Loan repayments have been extremely high, and group turnovers healthy. The scheme has provided women's groups with the opportunity to build 'buffer' food stocks which are essential to food security; this has extended the benefits to the whole community. The women's groups are unanimous that Oxfam should increase the loan portfolio, gradually expand the scheme and start pilot schemes in other regions.

Women should be allowed to use the money to take advantage of other business opportunities not related to sheanuts. An extension programme of credit management should support such a Rural Women's Loan Scheme. The agencies should enhance the systematic growth and development of women's groups participating in the scheme. Field animation support could act as a catalyst for a wider programme of conscientisation of women. In the meantime the groups' development should be encouraged through training via conferences, workshops, meetings. The meetings that had been held had been a very important element in improving the scheme; resource persons and women's groups had learnt a great deal from each other; problems and misunderstandings had been discussed and solutions proposed.

Case study compiled from the following reports:

Amuah, D. (1987) 'Report on First Review of Oxfam Loan Scheme for Women's Sheanut Purchasing', Small Project Committee internal report.

Amuah, D. (1988), 'Resource Mobilisation for Development: The Role of Credit in Increasing Household Incomes through Off-farm Income Generating Activities of Rural Women. A Case Study of the Oxfam Loan Scheme', Small Project Committee internal report.

Pugansoa, B., 'A Supplementary Report on the Effect of the Oxfam Loan Scheme on the Operations/ Activities of Women's Groups Beneficiaries', Oxfam internal report.

Ben Pugansoa is Oxfam's Project Officer in North Ghana with a particular interest and involvement in this project. Donald Amuah is the Secretary of the Small Project Committee.

LIMITS OF WOMEN'S GROUPS AS A VIABLE CHANNEL FOR THE DEVELOPMENT OF WOMEN IN KENYA

BETTY WAMALWA

There was a time when development experts were satisfied with very little in terms of concrete Kenyan Government policy with regard to women. Researchers concerned with promoting the ability of women to participate in the development process could state:

> 'It is noteworthy that a token sum of £10 has been set aside in the 1975-76 financial year for activities pertaining to women in development. This is significant as an indication of Government recognition of the women's programme. It will now be possible to submit budget requests for expanding women's programme activities in this and subsequent financial years if convincing proposals are made.' (Pala A.O. *et al* (1975), *A preliminary survey of the avenues for, and constraints on women in the development process in Kenya*, IDS.)

During the 1970s the Kenyan Government placed greater emphasis on women's activities in the agricultural sector. Women's role in food and cash crop production was now officially recognised and explicitly associated with the country's economic development. Women's groups came to be seen more and more as the key to empowering women, particularly at the grassroots level, in the development process.

Women's groups: a history

Women's groups as an institution trace their roots back to traditional society: the *ngwatio* among the Kikuyu, the *risaga* among the Gusii and the *saga* among the Luo. In the traditional setting, they were concerned with mutual aid efforts. Through them, women engaged in joint agricultural labour, social welfare activities and recreation and entertainment.

It was on this foundation that the earliest formal, government-sponsored programme aimed at promoting development for women was based. This programme, started in the early 1950s, involved the organisation of a national body called *Maendeleo Ya Wanawake* which co-existed with the traditional base community self-help groups. As an organisation, it was a reflection of the view held in the colonial era that women in particular should contribute to improving the welfare and well-being of the family. *Maendeleo* functioned in the form of 'women's clubs', with primary emphasis on domestic crafts such as embroidery, and improving the family diet particularly for the children. This can be seen as a reflection of the concerns and preoccupations of the initiators — the wives of European colonists — who attached great importance to these activities as being conducive to raising the African family's living standards. Within the national historical context the 'women's clubs' are a reflection of one of the ways in which African women were to be 'domesticated' while being displaced from agricultural production.

With a new appreciation of the crucial role played by women in agriculture, activities in women's groups came to reflect this new vision. In the 1970s the Government initiated the Women's Programme in six of the Special Rural Development Programme areas. This represented the first attempt by the post-independence Government to link women actively to the development process. The programme functioned by building on the foundations provided by existing indigenous groups and, to some extent, *Maendeleo Ya Wanawake*. It served to initiate a new orientation for women's involvement in development. It did so by beginning to institutionalise the women's groups as the channel for information and material and technical resources to women who had hitherto been neglected. In an overall positive review of the programme, A.O.Pala *et al* found the major flaw to be that it 'generated new orientation but did not generate resources towards the groups and women to meet new expectations'. (Pala A.O. *et al* (1975), *op. cit.*)

The most important era for the women's group began in 1975 with the formation of a government agency charged with dealing with women's issues in Kenya; the Women's Bureau. With the formation of the Bureau, we see greater policy commitment to women when measured by relative material, financial and informational resources made available to women through women's groups.

The Women's Bureau

The Bureau had a mandate to focus on the development and integration of women in national development. Over the next ten years or so, the Bureau initiated the formation of an enormous number of women's groups. In 1976 there were 4,300 registered women's groups with a membership of 156,892; by 1984, the number of groups had risen to 16,500 with a total membership of 630,000.

The principal objectives of the Women's Bureau as identified in the 1979-83 National Development Plan were the formation of relevant programmes to meet the needs of women, and the coordination of all women's programmes in the country. Most specifically, and in accordance with the women's development programmes in the Department of Social Services (of which the Bureau is a division), the Bureau was to involve itself in the encouragement of women, through women's groups, to engage in income earning opportunities in agriculture, small industrial and commercial business; and the provision of relevant training in leadership, craft development and other special skills as a requirement for a successful women's programme.

In view of the above stated policy, it is not surprising to find that, although the Bureau had four articulated programmes, namely, research and evaluation; communication and liaison; assistance to organised women's groups; and training and education of members of organised groups and government extension, the assistance programme received the bulk of the Bureau's financial resources. Of the K£ 1.19 million available in development funds during four financial years, about K£ 1.03 million, representing 87 per cent of the available funds, went to organised women's groups. Furthermore, in accordance with the implicit view that income generating projects were best, 76 per cent of these funds went to such projects. The other programmes therefore received very few financial resources, despite their stated importance.

An assessment of the women's group movement

Women's groups are evidently seen as the principal vehicle for the involvement of women in the development process. The viability of this form of organisation must, however, be examined from three perspectives to determine the potential of the movement for the empowerment of women in the development process. For this purpose, the three following perspectives have been identified: women's groups at the local level; factors determining women's participation in women's groups; and the women's group in the national development context.

The women's group at the local level

The women's group movement is widespread in Kenya. Through these self-help groups, women are able to assist one another in times of need, such as during illness or childbirth; with agricultural work and major tasks such as thatching of houses; and in other social welfare efforts by which individual group members can benefit directly from a reciprocal relationship.

Women, through these groups, are also engaged in 'social investment' in education, health and the provision of social facilities. Although this category absorbs rather than generates resources in the short term, the long-term investment can be viewed as the creation of a community with increased productive potential. Women's groups have, in addition, become engaged in income generating projects and activities. These are projects aimed at generating further resources in a self-sustaining process. The projects include animal husbandry, handicrafts, agriculture and so on.

Women's groups have been particularly important for the women of Kenya because they have replaced traditional women's organisations. It was through these organisations that women expressed themselves on a social level. Of greater importance is the fact that the groups are viewed by women as a means through which the individual member can appropriate resources for immediate transfer and use within her household. Thus, 88 per cent of all group activities are aimed at the generation of rapidly distributable and disposable resources to individual members. It is fitting, then, that the most widespread activity among the groups is the 'merry-go-round' or rotating loan fund.

Women's groups have also helped to give women in Kenya an unprecedented visibility on social, cultural, political and national economic levels. Hardly a week goes by without women, through their groups, being mentioned in some context by national leaders in the press. On national television a programme called 'Women in Development' has devoted a substantial amount of time to the presentation of women's groups' activities.

Women's groups can further be of great importance in the local political equation. In electoral campaigns in some constituencies, their support, or lack of it, can mean the success or failure of a candidate. For example, in Kiambu, where women form a significant majority, their votes are obviously important and more so when their votes are organised. These groups can empower women to participate in public life by giving them collective confidence, bargaining power and pooled resources.

Who participates and why

Despite the national scope of the movement, total membership covers only a fraction of the eligible women in Kenya. The tremendous growth of 68 per cent experienced during the 1978-1983 period suggests a great potential when taken at face value. But when we examine what can be called the 'anatomy' of the women's group we see that this growth may not be sustainable. The sociological composition and finance and resource capability of women's groups suggest that over 60 per cent of the women in Kenya will be excluded. The distribution of benefits to members further suggests that only the social welfare type of project benefits members directly.

Sociological composition

A sociological investigation of the women's groups is particularly important because it indicates who participates and why within a given community. Further, it can help in determining the possibility of expanding participation to those excluded. It is thus important in gauging the viability of this particular approach to development, for the women in Kenya.

The typical group member is a middle-aged married woman from the middle peasantry. To participate in a group it is evident that a potential member must have certain minimum resources i.e. financial, labour, time, material, social standing, independence and so on. It was estimated in 1984 that, for effective participation, the minimum resources were Kshs.45 per month and five days per month. This automatically precludes the 60 per cent of women who live well below the officially defined poverty line. The majority of those excluded for lack of the above resources are young women, whose exclusion is further compounded by the peculiarities of age hierarchies found in most African communities. These women make up the highest percentage of the labour force and so are most in need of the organisation. In the final analysis, only 9 per cent of the female labour force is involved in groups.

Financial and resource capability

Women's groups rely primarily on members for raising financial and other resources in self-help endeavours. Contrary to popular belief, only 1.1 per cent of financial resources are generated from outside sources. Groups engaged in income generating projects and social investment activities (building halls, schools, dispensaries, etc.) are heavily dependent on outside assistance in direct contrast to those undertaking mutual assistance self-help activities. Very often investment capital in the form of land or machinery will be provided by donations and grants from local councils, government and well-wishers.

Group benefits for members

The distribution of financial and other resources is in two principal areas, namely, servicing members' direct individual needs, and investments in group projects (some income generating and other social investment projects and savings). The first category reflects very closely the reasons for initial group formation for the women in cases when they have initiated its formation. Various researchers have found that these groups do provide real and tangible benefits. In the second category, however, the potential benefits are rarely realised because of factors already enumerated.

Women's groups, *harambee* and development

The women's group movement in Kenya can be seen in relation to the national *harambee* movement. *Harambee* (which means 'let's unite') has been defined as the process whereby rural development projects are undertaken by communities on the basis of some sort of community or group consensus and initiative. *Harambee*, as an 'alternative' approach to development, becomes important in a country such as Kenya because of the inadequacies of the prevailing institutional mechanisms for generating growth and development. *Harambee* cannot, however, be expected to replace these institutional mechanisms. And in most cases it does not — except when it comes to women. In this case it can be seen that although policy holds that the economic position and status of the Kenyan woman has to be improved, it must not be done at the expense of groups that have already attained some degree of prosperity or status. Policy has accordingly placed emphasis on that which the women can undertake together, in groups, on their own initiative, with little or only token assistance.

Through the women's group, women's ambiguous status in the development process is played out most eloquently. The average rural woman in Kenya is a farmer producing subsistence and cash crops. However, conventional wisdom reinforced by the prevailing new 'cultural' attitude, finds it difficult to reconcile itself with this scenario. It prefers to see women as domesticated, dependent consumers. Channelling women's development through the women's group can be seen as a way of satisfying both the real role of women and the imaginary one. On the one hand, mobilisation through women's groups serves to recognise the important place women have in national development in their own right. On the other hand, emphasis on the women's group as the primary channel of mobilisation for women, secures their marginalisation and prevents them from participating as equal partners in mainstream development.

Conclusion

Women's groups are viable institutions for women at the local level. They offer members opportunities which can only be obtained when resources are pooled. At this level, women through such groups can even be an important part of the equation in the local politics of development. They can be the backbone of Kenya's *harambee* self-help movement, and hence catalysts for rural development.

At the national level, however, the anatomy of women's groups presented indicates that this institution cannot be the principal vehicle for the empowerment of Kenyan women in the development process. Socio-economic factors preclude 60 per cent of the women in any community from participating. The peculiarities that govern women in most African communities exclude the young and the poor woman. It is only those women who are able to command a certain accepted social status and who have also the finances and time, who are able to participate.

The women's group is voluntary and self-help in nature, using meagre locally available financial and material resources. The implication, then, is that the women of Kenya are gaining very little from the formal economic sector which they help to build through their productive and reproductive efforts. They are therefore being shunted into an alternative form of development which should and can only assist institutionalised official avenues, not replace them.

References

Maas M. (1986), *Women's Groups in Kiambu, Kenya*. Research Report No.26, African Studies Centre, Leiden, The Netherlands.

Pala A. (1974), The Role of Women in Rural Development: Research Priorities.

Pala A. (1975), *A Preliminary Survey of the Avenues for and Constraints on Women in the Development Process in Kenya*, IDS, University of Nairobi.

Ngau P. (1987), 'Tensions in Empowerment: The Experience of the Harambee (Self-Help) Movement in Kenya', *Economics Development and Cultural Change*, Vol 35.

Thomas B.P. (1987), 'Development through Harambee: who wins and who loses? Rural self-help projects in Kenya', *World Development*, Vol 15 No 4.

Women's Bureau Ministry of Culture and Social Services, *Annual Reports from Districts, 1985*.

Betty Nafuna Wamalwa is a freelance consultant with a research background in environmental affairs, resource management and women and the law. She has worked mainly in Kenya, although she has also studied in the USA and Norway. Her recent work has been for Oxfam, NORAD, the World Bank, Clark University and the African Centre for Technology Studies.

LAS ESCLAVAS DEL FOGON:
A POPULAR EDUCATION GROUP IN THE
DOMINICAN REPUBLIC

EUGENIA PIZA-LOPEZ

La Romana is one of the largest states in the Dominican Republic, growing sugar cane for the international market. The production of sugar cane started in the 1950s and has brought with it extensive socio-economic and cultural disruption. La Romana became a Free Trade Zone in the mid 1980s for the production of electronics, clothing and tertiary industry. The workforce (15,000-20,000) is composed mainly of women in their early twenties, with no formal organisation. Popular organisations face overt repression and there is opposition to workers' unions from employers, multinational corporations, landowners and the state.

'*Las esclavas del Fogon*' started nine years ago as a cultural group of women from the popular sector of La Romana trying to redefine and recover their national and local culture, which was threatened by foreign cultural products and customs. They felt the need to go back to their own roots in music, painting, dancing and poetry and translate these into 'popular art', incorporating the demands and needs of the community. In spite of many problems they have managed to establish themselves as a respected and legitimate group working for the popular arts in La Romana.

They are organised as a collective of eleven women. They define themselves as feminist and recognise the need for women to come together and work out the nature of their oppression. They feel that a collective provides a structure in which women can work together, respecting ideological differences and establishing relations which are truly democratic and non-hierarchical.

Since the start they have decided to work as a women-only group which, in a small rural, Catholic town, has posed some problems. The local press and church groups have labelled them as 'lazy, lesbian and anti-men'. *Las esclavas del Fogon* feel that their group represents an important space for women to grow and develop consciousness since women have only a limited or token presence in other organisations in La Romana. Their group is unique in the town in promoting women's rights, discussing women's status and linking these issues with other forms of discrimination, particularly that of racism against Haitians. At one stage they tried to work in the Bateyes (areas for Haitian workers only) but they faced repression by the local multinational employer and suspicion from the workers both because the group members were Dominicans and more especially because they were women. The management of the multinational initiated a campaign against the collective and they had to withdraw.

The group is organised in four areas: publicity, general coordination, popular education and finances. The popular education group works on cultural events in the *barrios* (neighbourhoods), preparing two *jornadas culturales* each year (large cultural events usually in the town centre aimed at the whole community), running workshops and training courses on popular and folk music, dance and poetry, organising *campanas de rescate cultural* (campaigns to reinstate traditional culture) and joining in the celebration of festivals and the carnival. The group is financed both by NGOs (especially for specific projects) and by the community through raffles, donations, etc. The group is just about self-sufficient and has three part-time employees. The other members of the collective work as volunteers, with the support of the membership and 14 committees in the *barrios*.

A number of unsuccessful projects have been an important part of the group's learning process. 'Only through many mistakes and failures can one build the necessary experience and learn how difficult it is to work in an organisation', explain members of the collective. They learnt that the group needed to go out and work closely with the communities themselves; they needed training in popular education techniques; to develop more campaigning and communication skills and to have a more complete understanding of their social environment. They redefined their strategies in terms of promoting organisation and decided to concentrate initially on women.

They started by organising committees of five women in each neighbourhood to celebrate 'Mother's Day'. They also promoted exchanges between women of different communities and friendly discussions about women's issues and the aims and nature of the group. Currently they have approximately 200 members who are working in 14 *barrios*, most of them from the popular sectors (housewives, workers and some professionals and university students). They also have nine cultural groups for young boys and girls who are working on folk dance and music. They organise a monthly cultural event in each *barrio*. This event takes place on the streets and uses the techniques of popular theatre, ensuring a high level of participation from the community. They present activities devised by the cultural groups and, with the use of improvisations, engage the community in singing and responding to songs which are based on issues of interest to the community. They also provide courses on poetry, dance and theatre to its members.

A street play, created during a one-month course on participative theatre and based on the life and hardships of peasant women, represents the most important activity for the group. Using the results of a study by *Centro de Investigacion para la Accion Femenina* (CIPAF) on women in rural areas, they produced a 90-minute play based on Boal's techniques of the theatre of the oppressed. A peasant woman from the South was invited to participate in the experiment and to have the role of main actress. The group feel that the course has provided them with new tools, revitalised them, and gave them the opportunity to become professional artists. It was a very successful experience, with enormous participation from the community. They will start using this experience in their own workshops and courses and share it with other groups in the Dominican Republic.

WOMEN ORGANISING THEMSELVES

AUDREY BRONSTEIN

The story of MOMUPO illustrates a process of discovery experienced by hundreds of poor urban women in Chile from the early 1980s to the present date — a process that has come to be called 'popular feminism': an awareness of the condition of double oppression of the *pobladora* (the shanty town of Santiago are called *poblaciones*, and the residents, *pobladoras*), as a member of the working class in a capitalist economic system and as a woman in a patriarchal society. This process has developed slowly, overcoming many obstacles, not the least of which are fear and repression, two of the most effective tools used by the Pinochet regime to crush popular resistance to the military dictatorship.

How MOMUPO started

A small group of socially committed and politically conscious working women were involved in a church-initiated popular education workshop with trade unionists in 1980. The aim of the workshop was to examine the needs of the workers, and the urban poor in general, within the context of the military dictatorship, then seven years old. The women, a minority in the predominantly male group, suffered constant frustration at not being able to discuss in any meaningful way with others in the group, the specific problems and needs of poor women. Most of the participants were union leaders and political leaders, and the discussion always centred on traditional political issues. In an attempt to establish their needs as a priority, the women formed a *'comision femenina'* (women's committee), and not finding much response within the main workshop, they began to contact other women from other groups, both union and non-union oriented. A number of activities were organised over the next year or two, ranging from discussion groups to arts and crafts exhibitions of items produced by the women. Gradually, and with the continued rejection of 'women's issues' by the central workshop body, the initial group of women, and the others who had joined them, became increasingly more independent of both the church and the union organisation.

They formed a coordinating committee with the objective of involving more women, particularly those who were not involved in any kind of community organisation. On the basis of their own experience, the founders of this coordinating committee realised that few women were going to get involved in groups that concentrated on global political concepts and showed little interest in the specific problems and needs of poor women. They also realised that if the popular movement for social change in Chile were to grow both in numbers and strength, efforts would have to be made to move beyond those who were already socially aware and politically committed. As the leaders of MOMUPO say:

'They [the union leaders] never understood the work we wanted to do with the ordinary woman, the ordinary housewife... we wanted to get them out of the house... have them take that first step, and then develop an awareness of themselves as people, as women and *pobladoras*, of the working class. After that, to work with them to develop a political and social consciousness. We were working towards developing a space where the *pobladora* could achieve an awareness of her identity, not just a class awareness, but also a gender awareness, through a process of personal and social development, and through looking at her own daily life.'

How MOMUPO functions now

MOMUPO was officially constituted as a movement in 1982, and still maintains its original structure: a loose federation of 12-15 base groups (about 25 women on average in each group), with each group maintaining its own autonomy and programme of activities, as well as forming part of MOMUPO. Most are subsistence oriented, including *ollas comunes* (small community-based kitchens which operate in people's backyards at lunch time) and small scale productive workshops (sewing and handicrafts). Each group elects a representative to the coordinating committee of MOMUPO, which meets once a week for general discussion, planning and evaluation. In addition, a five-person executive, elected from the coordinating committee, is responsible on a day-to-day basis for general management of MOMUPO's activities (including financial control, communications, public relations, etc). MOMUPO operates with minimal funding, the major expenditures being the cost of public transport for the members, and the rent and upkeep of a small house where they meet (funded by Oxfam).

Examples of MOMUPO's activities

Every few months, MOMUPO organises *'ampliados'*, which are mass meetings for the members of the affiliate base groups. The focus of these events ranges from the educational (health, legal rights, political analysis, theories of feminism, women's identity) to the purely social and recreational. In addition, they organise campaigns (usually once a year) on a specific theme:

1984 Against Hunger and Cold, including both the setting up of *ollas comunes*, and educational workshops analysing the structural causes behind the growing poverty in Chile. A number of marches to local municipalities and health authorities were also organised.

1985 Health (mental health problems, public and family hygiene, women's health problems).

1986 Women's Reproductive Rights, both to teach women about the reproductive process and family planning, and to expose increasingly common birth control abuses by the Government (e.g. forced removal of IUDs in state clinics).

1987 The Law in Chile Today, women's legal rights and the political context of the new Chilean constitution. Emergency aid programme due to heavy rain and wind storms (funded by Oxfam).

In addition, MOMUPO organises a 2-3 week summer school every January for its affiliate groups. Contents usually focus on three basic themes: popular feminism; the current political/economic situation; and practical skills (e.g. carpentry, appropriate technology, crafts and sewing skills, use of medicinal plants, etc). External workshop leaders are invited to cover those areas which the MOMUPO members cannot cover.

Achievements

MOMUPO's major achievement is its continuing survival as an independent grassroots women's movement within the context of a military dictatorship. Work with unorganised women is slow under the best of conditions, but it is made that much more difficult where there is a generalised fear and rejection of anything considered 'political'. MOMUPO has managed to create a recognised and legitimate space amongst those groups working for social change in Chile, where the *pobladora* can develop her understanding of the structures of society, and her own role within that, from the dual perspectives of class and gender.

Difficulties

It is in fact the success of MOMUPO which has brought them to a point of redefinition and analysis of their role. With the increasing politicisation of the popular movements in Chile, and the re-emergence of political parties, along with the effectiveness of MOMUPO's own work in class and gender consciousness, a number of external and internal pressures and conflicts began to appear in 1986. MOMUPO now has within its ranks women of varying levels of consciousness of gender and class, with some of the more advanced wanting to take MOMUPO more and more into the overtly public political forum, rather than reinforcing its work with unorganised and less aware *pobladoras*. At the same time, external pressures have been felt from political parties, middle-class feminist groups and professional development institutions, attempting to take advantage of MOMUPO's *poder de convocatoria* (pulling power), thus putting both their autonomy and self-sufficiency at risk. Along with this, there have been many demands for MOMUPO's presence in a great number of social and political coordinating bodies which began to appear in 1984/5. Attending to these requests has occasionally led to neglect of MOMUPO's own work as a movement, producing highs and lows in both the quantitative and qualitative aspects of their activities.

Having identified some of these problems, MOMUPO has dedicated a substantial amount of time during 1987 to a system-atisation of their experiences since 1980. Helped by an external facilitator (funded by Oxfam), they have tried to produce a clearer definition of the movement, its objectives, structure, etc. Part of their recent difficulties is also due to a tendency to operate spontaneously, with little recording of discussions, activities or decisions. This system worked reasonably well when the group was small and relatively unknown but as they have grown in size and public profile, their former system (using the term loosely) is no longer sufficient.

Out of this process of analysis has come a declaration of principles and a clear statement of their objectives as a movement. They continue to work on finding the kind of organisational structure which is best suited to their needs.

12 November 1987

Postscript

From September 1973, to early 1990, Chile was run by a military regime notorious for its general abuse of human rights, and, more specifically, repression towards independent community activities and community leaders. MOMUPO was established in the early 1980's, partly as a response to a severe economic depression, and partly through the growth of a broad-based grassroots movement for social change. Now, with the change to a freely elected, civilian government, with relative freedom for almost all traditional political parties, and a state that would appear to be promoting independent community activity, MOMUPO must continue to adapt to the changing situation, as must many other organisations, born out of repression. This is not an easy process given that MOMUPO must take account of the dramatic shift in the socio-political context, but at the same time, recognise that the needs of the poor continue to be substantially neglected as a result of the classic free market economic model, introduced by the military regime and strictly maintained by the new government. MOMUPO's activities have grown in number, and they now provide a focal point for hundreds of women during any given year. Even so, they continue to work with the same outside facilitator, examining the issues of internal leadership and structure, and their role as an organisation within the new political context, but within the same structural economic constraints.

August 1990

Audrey Bronstein has worked for Oxfam since 1982, first in the Andean Regional office covering Oxfam's programme in Paraguay and Chile. Since 1989 she has been based in the UK, as Acting Area Coordinator for the Latin American desk, Acting Head of the Public Affairs Unit, and now as Deputy to the Communications Director. She is the author of a report on Latin American peasant women for the UNDP which was published by War on Want under the title The Triple Struggle.

FRANCISCA: A TESTIMONY FROM A WOMAN RURAL TRADE UNION LEADER IN BRAZIL

INTERVIEW BY EUGENIA PIZA-LOPEZ

'When I discovered myself it was like maize growing in the field. First you have the leaves, green, tender, so timidly emerging out of the heart of the plant. Then the whole plant is geared towards producing *la mazorca* (maize cob), strong, bright yellow. It's a process I've gone through.

'I decided to open my eyes, to go out of this house and the fields five years ago. When I first went to meetings I sat at the back, embarrassed to talk or even look people in the eye. It was such an effort to speak, I felt so uncomfortable. My husband has been a trade union leader for a very long time, he encouraged me to participate in the union. Then we had our first women only meeting. I learnt a lot. We all talk the same language. It is so easy to say "we talked about being women" and yet it was such a difficult process for all of us. Any change in this world starts from the inside. How you value yourself and respect the dignity of a human being. Recognising your right as an individual to exist is so important as a starting point to join in the struggle.

'It was a total reversal of my feelings towards myself and the whole world. I learned to fight and engage in a struggle which will bring respect for the peasants. I want to be treated with respect myself, and any form of exploitation goes against our dignity as individuals and peasants. That's why I have been so involved in land issues. The land belongs to those who work it, not to the absent landlord.

'You see, so little has changed in my everyday life, and yet I am a totally new person. I still cook and clean and do most of the housework. But at least, at the very least, I and my children know the value of that work. No-one takes it for granted any more! I have had more than ten pregnancies and that is very hard work. I work the land about eight hours a day. Sometimes I even forget to have lunch! When I'm back at home I cook, do the washing, prepare the beans, play with the children. In addition twice a week I fetch firewood to make charcoal. I do it with the older kids. Those are the two hardest days of the week. We go to bed about one in the morning. When I prepare charcoal I don't wash the clothes, you see it would be too much work.

'Water? Water is so precious in this place. After years of drought we have to look after the water! It only takes us 40 minutes each way to fetch the water. Sometimes I do it myself, sometimes I send the girls. The girls are my extended hands. They work at home and in the fields. They are strong. I sometimes feel sorry for them, following the same pattern. I have tried, and will keep trying, to involve the boys in the housework. That is hard — they don't like it. They feel embarrassed and uneasy. My husband is setting an example. He now takes on some of the domestic chores. It's taken years for this change!

'Perhaps the most radical change is in his support for my development both as a woman and as a peasant leader. He knows that my heart is in the struggle. Although he used to push me to participate in meetings, when I first began to develop my own ideas independently of him he did everything to restrain me. He even forbade me to attend meetings. But I decided, with other women, to challenge these attitudes both at home and in the community. I believe in our organisations and I feel women are reshaping them quite drastically. It's just a question of giving us a chance.'

WHEN BROKEN-HEARTEDNESS BECOMES A POLITICAL ISSUE

CLAIRE BALL

(revised by Barbara Harrington)

There are currently some 200,000 Guatemalan refugees in Mexico, of whom only a quarter are legally entitled to be there. The other 150,000 are scattered throughout the country. Many end up in Mexico City, a bewildering and often hostile environment for undocumented refugees who are trying to battle with the paradox of having to conceal their nationality, their language, their traditional dress and yet desperately needing to seek out fellow Guatemalans with whom they can share, and try to make sense of, their experiences in exile.

The *Comité del Distrito Federal* (CDF) was formed in 1982, with the dual purpose of responding to the needs of Guatemalans in Mexico City and of collaborating in projects in the southern states of Mexico. Since then, more of the CDF's work has been directed towards helping people inside Guatemala itself. Oxfam has supported the work of the CDF, providing grants for salaries and for specific projects such as the House of Hospitality and the training of Guatemalan refugee women as community mental health promoters.

The House of Hospitality in Mexico City, set up in 1982 by the CDF, can only touch the tip of the iceberg. By 1987 it had provided temporary accommodation for about 200 refugees and their families. The House can receive up to 25 refugees at a time for temporary shelter. But those who have lived in the House and participated in the projects initiated by the CDF are in no doubt about the crucial contribution being made there towards understanding and interpreting the experience of the refugees and enabling them to channel those experiences actively into the process for change in the immediate circumstances of their lives as refugees in Mexico, and in the longer term to create conditions suitable for their return to Guatemala.

In September 1984, the CDF decided to include, for the first time, an explicit focus on the perspective of women. The people working with the CDF had long recognised the particular needs of Guatemalan women refugees as victims of the type of repression operating in the country through counter-insurgency programmes. But the way that this interlocked with the other systems of patriarchy which controlled the women's lives had still to be explored.

A group of twelve women — Indians and *latinas* (mixed Spanish and Indian descent); peasants, workers and housewives — came together in October 1984 to help each other find ways of dealing with the problems facing refugees in Mexico City. It was difficult for the women to trust each other, since distrust had been used as an instrument of repression in Guatemala, but they were determined to break through the distrust. In forming an action and reflection group they wanted not only to help each other but eventually to communicate with other women in the same situation. First, they had to overcome their communication problems within the group. Speaking in Spanish was not easy for the majority of the twelve, for whom it was their second language. However, with 22 different indigenous languages in Guatemala, the majority of Indian women were obliged to speak Spanish even with each other. The difference in levels of fluency and confidence in Spanish between the Indian and *latina* women further complicated communications problems within the group.

The women spoke about the contradiction of becoming invisible and concealing their identity for security's sake while also needing to become visible to give testimonies and to receive economic aid from agencies and charitable organisations. They were further pressed into hiding by having to become 'another', abandoning their traditional dress, which in Guatemala identifies them as a member of a particular village or community.

Having to grapple for the first time with unfamiliar zips and fasteners and cumbersome city dress; having to twist their bodies to carry babies across their breast instead of on their back; carrying bundles under their arms rather than on their head; are only the physical manifestations of the trauma of not recognising oneself and feeling as one who has no rights; of the total loss of cultural and personal identity which Guatemalan women refugees experience in Mexico City.

Talking about shared health problems, not the least of which is the gastro-enteritis associated with the high levels of air and water contamination in Mexico City, was the catalyst which eventually broke down the communication barrier within this group of women. One particular symptom which they all recognise and immediately identify with is *'tristeza de corazon* — literally, broken-heartedness. This is the most tangible and persistent characteristic of their experience as refugees, forced to flee their country, often having had to leave family and friends behind to an uncertain fate. Barbara Harrington, a Northamerican Dominican sister working with the refugees used this identification of 'health' problems engendered by their situation to encourage the question 'Why?':

Why are we poor?
Why do we get sick more easily than you, who came to be with us?
Why are we malnourished?
Why was our land taken from us?
Why did the Army burn our village and all our crops?
Why did we have to flee our country?

By beginning to analyse their poor health in the context of repression, the women started to question the reasons behind their present situation. They looked for constructive means of action, rather than seeing themselves as helpless victims. Identifying so many shared fears and anxieties, as well as tangible health problems, fostered a growing confidence. With this grew the women's realisation that, far from going quietly mad in isolation as many of them feared, they were in fact reacting and behaving normally under incredibly abnormal circumstances.

Wanting to translate these experiences into constructive help for the large numbers of refugees still coming into Mexico from Guatemala, the women decided to produce a booklet 'Sharing our Lives'. This not only suggested ways of dealing with the problems they were facing in adapting to life in Mexico City, but also broadened the definition of the 'political'. It gave the women's perspective on the need for change in Guatemala and their own role in that process. They divided their work on the booklet into three different aspects of their experience:

the events that had prompted them to leave Guatemala;
getting out of the country and crossing the border;

the problems that they found in adapting to life in Mexico City, and solutions.

There was much discussion about the repression in Guatemala and the women's perceptions were very different. The differing interpretations of the situation in the country and the feelings associated with their leave-taking provided insight into the specific problems of adaptation to Mexico. For example, when one woman living in Mexico City in a huge apartment complex spoke of missing her flowers, gardens, Guatemalan food and being at ease with her neighbours, another promptly retorted that she didn't miss Guatemala at all. She had had to flee the invasion of the Guatemalan army into her village: she saw it burn, spent weeks crossing the mountains to reach Mexico and lost members of her family in the brutal ordeal. To her, Mexico meant life!

Work on the project was slow. It took eight months to produce a 12-page booklet. Many of the women were illiterate and had to learn to use the alien medium of pencil and paper. By depicting their experiences in drawings the women recalled the trauma of the time. The project, as it existed at that time, was not geared to cope with the psychological consequences of this. The trauma had to be relived and assimilated rather than suppressed before the women could incorporate and use their experience effectively. They needed to articulate and use their experience, both for their own well-being and as a contribution, providing a women's perspective on the situation in Guatemala.

In taking part in any process of change, mental health is of fundamental importance. We need to suspend temporarily our own concepts of psychiatry with its emphasis on 'mental illness' and to consider instead the need of people in exile to be 'mentally well'. They need to be healthy in the broadest sense in order to be able to participate actively in a struggle of liberation, in which the rhetoric of the left is sometimes intolerant of any sign of psychological 'weakness'. The project committee thus initiated a training scheme for mental health promoters. It was anticipated that this would develop women's perspective on their own ability to participate in the process and to further the participation of other men and women.

The mental health promoters' project was written up in the summer of 1986, after consultation with the Guatemalan community in Mexico. The aim of the training course was to develop a core of eight to ten mental health promoters who would work specifically with Central American women refugees and their children. This core group would be composed of refugee women themselves. Integrated into the course were women, endorsed by organised groups of Guatemalans, who recognised the need, had a constituency, and were respected by the organisations committed to the liberation of their country. In this way the training was assured of a multiplier effect.

The course, first envisioned as a year-long process, now encompasses five distinct phases. The entire cycle is completed within a year and a half to two years. It relies on the participants using their own experience, group work and psycho-social and political perspectives. The women are finding healthful ways to help reconstitute what repression seeks to destroy: the joy of working for a just society.

Now, three years later, the original group of women is working not only with other refugee women but also with children, parents' groups and small community gatherings. They have been invited to work in the Guatemalan refugee camps in Chiapas and Campeche and also to give workshops for Central American refugees in the United States. The women continue to meet regularly in order to receive supervision, mutual support and feedback as well as to develop methodologies appropriate to the people with whom they work.

A second group of eight were introduced to the programme last year. They are currently developing a second booklet which deepens and broadens the analysis of the previous one.

This is a significant project in that it represents the determination of the women refugees not to be defeated by their circumstances. They learn not to let the horror stories control their lives but to exercise their own control over the stories; how to assimilate and use their experiences to provide practical help for others living through similar situations. Their stories and the exploration of their own mental health are making an important contribution to the political analysis of what is still happening in Guatemala, the country where their broken-heartedness began.

Claire Ball worked on Oxfam's Central America Desk from 1986-89. She is currently Assistant Desk Officer for Latin America and the Caribbean at Help the Aged and is particularly interested in the issues affecting older women in the region.

BREAKING THE MOULD:
WOMEN MASONS IN INDIA

RENU WADEHRA

In India's construction industry the strict division of labour means that women do the unskilled, tiring and backbreaking jobs of lifting and carrying concrete, mortar, bricks and sand and breaking stones whereas men do skilled work as masons, technicians, etc. Women never get an opportunity to upgrade their skills, therefore the myth that 'soft hands and nimble fingers' cannot do complex jobs needs to be changed.

According to the Indian labour law, at least 20 per cent of the labour force involved in the construction industry should be women, and as a step towards achieving this goal the Dutch Environmental and Sanitary Engineering Project set up a project to train women construction labourers in masonry work. This was the first attempt of its kind in the area. Under the Ganga Action Plan considerable construction activity was anticipated but the requirement of a minimum of 20 per cent women would be only a slogan unless women were properly trained. Otherwise, as soon as a skilled labour force was required, women would be out of work. The sanitation component of the plan, undertaken by Sulabh International, an implementing agency for low-cost sanitation, was found to be a suitable entry point for skill training since it was a long-running project. Applying their skills in this programme would give the women practical experience, confidence and credibility to take up work outside the project in the future.

The training was planned for fifteen women of Jajmao, Kanpur and fifteen women of Mirzapur in Uttar Pradesh where the Indo-Dutch plans were to be implemented. The three week training programme was planned to include one week's training in the class room and two weeks on site, with further on-the-job training for three months.

Women for training
It was decided to select women who had experience in working on

construction sites and were able to understand and speak Hindi. They should be residents of Jajmao, where the project was in operation and should be between 25 and 40 years old; priority would be given to women heads of households, widows and married women.

General group meetings were organised with women construction workers at the construction sites themselves after 6.30 pm, since the women left their homes during the early hours of the day to reach the construction site and normally returned after 6pm. Initially, local men and women volunteers and ICDS teachers were also involved in locating women. No women were excluded from taking part in the meetings because it was felt important that as many women as possible should understand the issues and become supportive.

The intention was to select women from different areas but during the course of the selection process it was decided to restrict the selection to a couple of areas only — the reason being that meeting too many women would raise hopes and expectations. Moreover it was thought that the women would find it easier to be supportive and encourage each other if they all came from the same area.

The men of the community had reservations about women being trained as masons. 'Why don't you give them sewing machines or introduce cottage industries for the women?' was the general opinion in the slums. Others simply laughed.

After the first round of discussions with the community, a second round was initiated with the women who were willing to work and a third round was with the selected women only. As the rapport increased and the selected women became acquainted with each other, it was decided to hold meetings every week.

We could not expect the women construction workers to be literate but many could write numbers and their name. Those who could not were asked to learn the basics and were advised to attend an adult literacy school in the area run by local men. Later, in consequent meetings we learnt that some had learnt from their school-going children, one had learnt from the ICDS teacher of the area, and one woman had learnt from her co-worker during the free time at work.

Among the women a 'we' feeling emerged very strongly. For example, one of the women said that she had forgotten how to write her name because she had only learnt it as a child. The immediate reaction of the women in the meeting was: 'How can we make the programme a success if you don't put an effort into learning?' All women learnt to write their names and read the measuring tape — these were the minimal skills required for the training. Everyone came prepared for each meeting, having made necessary arrangements for their family's food the day before.

The discussions in the meeting were not only centred around skills training; various issues emerged such as the status of women, and the question of equal wages. Films on Ganga pollution and Jag Sakhi (women's awakening) were also shown and discussed. It became clear that women were certainly fed up with unwanted children.

During the meetings, we learnt a lot from the women — their determination to learn, and their openness; and that they knew a lot about masonry. They had been working with the masons at the construction sites but had never had the opportunity to implement their skills. The confidence and determination of the women gave us courage.

Formal training

In November 1988 the training programme was started, led by a team of Sulabh personnel; one engineer, two supervisors and one mason. They also prepared the training materials, including an instruction video on latrine construction and visual aids which were displayed at the training venue. The classroom and demonstration training was conducted on the premises of a school where the trainees went on to construct three latrines as part of their training. Today all the three latrines are functional and elegantly made by women masons.

On-the-job training

The three months on-the-job training was on a low-cost sanitation programme undertaken by Sulabh. All the fifteen women started construction work on individual latrines and slowly some of them moved on to the construction of community latrines in Jajmao.Throughout the training period each participant's performance was assessed both through supervision on site and through group discussions at the meetings which started to take place every fortnight. Each trainee worked very hard and wanted to prove herself to be a good mason.

Although all the women showed encouraging results, nine proved to be excellent masons; their work and speed were good. They had had an opportunity to work in the individual latrines as well as the complexes where they learnt to plaster, fix doors and lay the floors and roofs. The plan was to enable all the women to work on the construction of complexes after they had learnt to construct individual latrines. Four complexes were to be constructed but unfortunately land problems meant that work on two had to be stopped. Since the remaining two did not provide enough work or space for fifteen women, six had to continue to work in the individual latrines. Towards the end of the training programme a third latrine complex was begun and the six women were placed there. It was agreed that the training period for these women would be extended by one month.

From the end of the planned on-the-job training period, all women were paid a stipend by Sulabh International; the nine fully trained women were paid Rs40 per day (this being the rate of a mason) and the six who remained under training were paid Rs20 per day until their training ended. After that they were to receive the same rate as the others if they proved satisfactory.

The plan was that fortnightly meetings should continue to discuss the formation of a formal group; to review the work and working problems on site; to discuss the health problems of the women and to look at informal education. It was important for the women to share each other's views, learn from each other and gain experience. Many issues which could not be solved individually, could be solved collectively. It was expected that once they had proved their credibility as efficient masons, they would be in a position to find work on the open market. Future work possibilities were discussed with the women at length during meetings, with government officials and Sulabh personnel.

Life for the women after training was not smooth. Three women moved out of their home town, leaving their families behind. They managed to get work in this male-dominated sector on an *ad hoc* basis, but this was not because of their skills but because of my pressure on the employer. After three months, these brave women had to return back to their homes.

Having initially found work for the women, I moved out of the project. This was a testing time. I had initiated the whole programme, and the women relied a great deal on me. Suddenly the group was shaken; meetings did not take place regularly and the work was not up to standard. Sulabh's construction work then stopped because of paucity of funds due to bureaucratic difficulties. The trained women could neither work as labourers as they had done prior to the training, nor could they get masons' work. There were exceptions; two women did manage to get masons' work on the open market. During this period an effort to form an official women's collective was made and finally the collective was registered.

Eventually, the project managed to secure a contract from the local municipality; the women now construct latrines in the urban slums.

The women have been trained; now it is time to discover how women will be treated in a man's domain.

Renu Wadehra currently works as a freelance consultant advising on women in development issues, particularly those relating to rural water and sanitation. She has worked with tribals in coastal Andhra Pradesh and also in the urban slums improvement programmes in Kanpur. She is an active member of Women and Environment Group of IUCN, Geneva, and the founder of SHACTI, a grassroots NGO in the Kumaon hills of north India working with women for environmental conservation.

PASTORALIST WOMEN'S WORKSHOP

CANDIDA MARCH

In May 1989 Oxfam hosted a three-day workshop for pastoralist women from Turkana, Samburu, Massailand and Somalia. There was a mix of women; young and old, Kenyan and non-Kenyan, rural and urban.

Most of the pastoralist women were illiterate and spoke their indigenous language; few had travelled outside their own area before and rarely or never alone. Songs, pictures, case studies, role plays, traditional artefacts, video, and discussion around, for example, the meanings of names and proverbs, were all used to explore the position and problems of women in pastoralist society and their role in development.

The purpose was to build an understanding of what development meant to pastoral women; to discover what kinds of projects lead to this development; and to hear women's hopes and worries. It was also intended to look for ways in which women could work constructively together to develop confidence, solidarity and faith in women's own worth and ability. The participants visited a project where women masons, plumbers and brickmakers building a meeting centre showed how much women working together could achieve. The workshop also helped to break down the isolation of the women and allowed them to share experiences and learn from each other.

The following exercise illustrates one of the methods used: proverbs were shared to begin exploring the traditions, myths and attitudes which hindered development. The proverbs and then their analysis came from the women at the workshop.

The women went into groups, according to which pastoral society they came from, to find examples of proverbs about women. One group was made up of non-pastoralist women including a European. Some proverbs which encouraged women are:

Woman is the home.

Children are their mother.

When you are a girl, help your mother to build a good house, so that the sun will not scorch her, since she gave birth to you.

Behind every successful man is a good woman.

You can never achieve like the man who has a better wife than you.

A man is only as good as his wife.

The hand that rocks the cradle rules the world.

Women hold up half the sky.

You have struck a rock.

If I leave, you will really look for me (telephones will ring).

Turkana songs praising women, their background and origin, were also shared.

There were other sayings which the women also thought encouraged women but on further discussion it was seen that instead they simply kept women in their place. It was hard to find proverbs that really encouraged women as people in their own right rather than just encouraging them to bear their burdens.

If a woman wants anything at home she must do it herself.

An elephant never fails to carry its tusks.

Have patience for the sake of your children, who may change the situation.

You can't leave troubles behind because of your children.

In a home where there are sons, troubles will only last a short while.

Don't take shit with one hand, seize it with both hands (you agreed to be married, see it through).

A lazy woman gains nothing.

If you will not be advised, your shoe will break.

Finally, it was easy to find proverbs that oppressed women:

The body that holds milk cannot hold intelligence.

The neck can't grow past the head (women are the neck, men are the head).

A woman without a husband can't think for herself.

You are so stupid you can even be misled by a woman.

Women will say nothing of meaning at a baraza.

A woman's work is to be pretty, not to think about serious matters.

A woman should stay by the store and produce children.

A woman is like the shaft of a spear.

Women can't make decisions in the home.

A woman can't build a home without a man.

A woman can't get satisfied with what she has to beg from her husband.

A woman doesn't know how to solve a problem, but only how to cut her throat.

If you praise a woman, she becomes useless.

If your wife dies, don't cry, it's only the house fallen down (you can easily marry again).

If you are 'proud' your husband will not lie with you again (men don't want educated women; 'educated women are prostitutes' but also, until recently, boys who were educated were seen as having been thrown away).

You are frightened like a woman.

You left but you came back (women have nowhere to run to).

A woman's work is never done.

A woman owns no wealth.

A good child is praise to the father, a bad child shames the mother.

Discussion: How do these sayings affect women?

'They cause us not to believe in our own abilities, and prevent us from making progress. We kill ourselves with work, it breaks our backs, yet it is as though we have done nothing, we get no benefit ourselves from our work. We have nowhere to go, and lose hope.'

And to the question of who perpetuated these myths, the women answered — both men and women; men to maintain their position and women because of fear:

'Because of fear we don't ask ourselves questions, challenge our situation or defend ourselves. We fear that if we challenge these myths we will get worse problems; if we challenge and are chased away, another woman won't refuse to take our place. We do on despising ourselves and have no time to sit together and discuss these problems. We also perpetuate these myths because of conflict between women. Men don't accept things from women, and we don't challenge this.'

The women realised that they shared things in common:

'We are kept down in all our cultures, for example we cannot own homes or animals. We are taken as nothing, kept at home and not allowed to speak in public. Even the son we suffered for will grow up to look down on us; our problems will continue as our sons follow the examples of their fathers We thought that it was only Turkana women who were beaten, but we see it is true everywhere. What has kept us back was staying isolated — now we have a chance to meet together and speak out.'

'We need to see what we, as women, can do to change this situation — but slowly, slowly we will fill the gap... We can't go back from this seminar and start accusing — we will be beaten.'

At the end of the workshop the women were asked how they would use what they had learnt and what would happen:

'We have seen how we are chained. But the chains are of steel, they have existed in our culture for so many years, so these three days are not enough to cut them. We must work for change slowly; if we try to change quickly, we will be beaten and what

development we have so far achieved will also be taken away.'
'We need to deal with our fear, and start with what is in our
power to change. We could start by educating our children to cut
the chains.'

Since all felt that they needed more time it was agreed to arrange
more workshops; each should be five or six days long, in pastoral
areas and when the children were home from school. Workshops
were also needed for the other women at home so that they could
keep up.

A second workshop, six days long, was held in December 1989,
bringing most of the women together again. In one session the
women discussed their involvement in development:

'We can see that women are beginning to come together in
groups to determine their own development. Those of us who
are beginning to develop understanding can help to light the fire
of development for other women, but we must be careful that we
don't cause too many problems. Together, women have strength.'

'Women have great spirit for development — far more than men
do. Development helps the community, men included, but it is a
burden which is placed on women.'

The women separated into groups to discuss the activities that they
were involved in which helped 'make the tree of development
grow'. Their answers included: agriculture; buying, selling and
looking after animals, including veterinary care; making, buying
and selling beads, hides, skins, food and utensils; setting up stores;
health and adult education; skills training e.g. technicians,
ploughing with draught animals.

The Samburu gave an example of a development project in their
area:

'In Latakwen, men and women joined together in a development
project. Each provided two goats and 200sh; the money was used
to buy skins and the goats were exchanged for food for sale in
the store. The men said they would do the work, and they would
meet with the women every Friday to discuss the business and
share the profits. Each Friday they put the women off with the
excuse that there was too much work at home... all the food and
skins were sold and the men had the money in their hands but

the women saw none of the money. On top of this the men had failed to pay the rent of 100sh per month for the weighing scales, and the owner finally came to the women after 6 months and forced them to have a *harambee* to pay the rent. The women did not follow this matter up with the men, but they themselves met again and this time kept the men right away from their group. They are now carrying on, but they have learnt the importance of being together as a group of women: from working together they have been able to push up the price of skins so that it is fair — and everyone has benefited from this. As a group they also visit and help each other — they have saved lives; and have helped each other to pay school fees for children.'

From the discussions held over several days the participants concluded:

'We see that all women are doing important work to help the tree of development to grow.'

This report was compiled by Candida March from reports by the facilitators: Rose Akobwai, Rosemary Benzina, Rhoda Loyor, Nicky May, Rhoda Mohamoud and Adelina Ndeto Mwau.

5

GENDER DEBATES

Introduction
Candida March

An individual's reactions to gender issues are rooted in experiences of, and attitudes towards, power, politics, culture and everyday social interaction. Concepts of gender roles, desirable behaviours and appropriate expectations are learnt from a very early age so that gender becomes an integral part of a person's identity and gender roles are seen to lie at the centre of people's cultural and religious heritage.

In consequence, many discussions around the issues of gender are highly contentious and all work in this field needs to be particularly sensitive, both in building awareness of the problems and in proposing strategies for confronting them. The extent to which gender inequalities should be challenged is a recurrent theme throughout the book (see, for example, April Brett's and Caroline Moser's articles). Approaches to working with gender issues vary widely.

Oxfam, like most development agencies, has only relatively recently recognised that the needs of women can be separate from those of men, and that they may require different development strategies. The views of Oxfam's workers vary from those who do not accept that women are a separate or priority concern, and are unaware of the gender implications of their work, to those with a determination to support the improvements of women's lives and status as a priority. For example, one country programme has a commitment:

'..to ensure that the interests of women are considered explicitly in each and every development programme. All projects and organisations we support must demonstrate their understanding of, and show commitment to, this issue before funding is approved.'

We end this book with some articles written by Oxfam staff members, giving a glimpse of some of the issues that are debated in our offices around the world. All the authors are working in the field, in Africa, Latin America or India (except Liz Gascoigne, who has recently returned to the UK from the Yemen).

The first four articles look at some of the basic beliefs and 'myths' that underpin approaches to development work in gender; tradition, the 'system', the 'enemy', the 'household unit', and 'women as property'. Adelina Ndeto Mwau looks at African women's existing 'over-integrated' role in development, and poses the question: 'is it enough to integrate women into an already unequal and unjust economic system?' This same question is at the heart of the analysis by Development Alternatives with Women for a New Era (DAWN), a network of Third World Women. In the challenging and powerful postscript to this book, Peggy Antrobus, a member of DAWN, stresses that women's contribution has been central to traditional development but in a way that has been deeply exploitative of their time, labour and sexuality. She outlines DAWN's alternative approach, the potential for change and a vision for the future.

The other articles consider in more detail the role of non-governmental organisations (NGOs) in raising gender issues, and discuss the many dilemmas arising from development workers' positions within or outside the system of gender roles. All explore ways in which the potential dangers of imposing values from the outside can be minimised. The articles echo to varying degrees Mona Mehta's argument that the aim of outside interventions is not to 'tamper' with existing culture, but by constant dialogue and questioning create a new awareness, so that the people concerned can make their own choices for action.

Mona Mehta asks the fundamental question, also posed by April Brett in the Introductory section: 'why is it that challenging gender inequalities is taboo, while challenging inequalities in terms of wealth and class is accepted?' She explores the reasons why gender inequalities have been excluded from a class analysis of society. She argues that accepting the taboo would mean that Oxfam should only attempt to make life easier for women in their accustomed tasks. But this 'sticking plaster' approach has been given up by Oxfam in other areas of development work, because it was seen not to offer real long-term help; the real need was for empowerment.

In exploring outside intervention, Barry Underwood and Abdou Sarr touch on the nature and role of feminists. Both recognise that women from different backgrounds have different perceptions of gender issues. Abdou Sarr calls for a questioning feminism, which discusses issues with both men and women in order to arrive at a resolution which is acceptable to all. Barry Underwood makes the point that 'the irrelevance of many aspects of the feminist movement in the West to women in the developing countries is often commented on'. The view that all feminist analysis stems from Western feminism is an argument frequently put forward. The indigenous group Women in Nigeria (WIN) have an answer:

> 'It needs to be stressed that there were indigenous "feminisms" prior to our contact with Europe, just as there were indigenous modes of rebellion and resistance in the mythified African past. Therefore "feminism" or the fight for women's rights and interests is not the result of "contamination" by the West or a simple imitation... One of the most recurrent charges made to and about Third World women is that of being blind copy-cats of Western European feminists. Many Third World feminists, in awareness of [these] "divide-and-rule" tactics... have replied perceptively that the accusers' play is consciously conceived and maintained to confuse women, to bind them to their respective men and male systems and to prevent a dangerous comparing of notes and a potentially dangerous unity. The truth is that there has always been, in every culture, indigenous forms of feminism... as in Nigeria.' (Mohammed and Madunagu, 1984.)

Peggy Antrobus, in her call for 'an analysis which is feminist in orientation', quotes DAWN as recognising that feminism has to be responsive to the different needs and concerns of women, as defined by them for themselves.

Abdou Sarr and Barry Underwood go on to look at the various groups that NGOs might support. The problem of finding appropriate ways of working with the 'poorest of the poor' is particularly acute when working with women. It is difficult for the poorest women to organise, because of either cultural or economic constraints or lack of free time (see Betty Wamalwa's and Linda Mayoux's articles in Section Four and Eugenia Piza Lopez's article in Section Two). Liz Gascoigne explores some of these problems, in the context of work in the Yemen. As she explains, 'the bureaucratic and social aspects... encourage foreign agencies to co-operate with the more mainstream groups which are accessible, articulate and well-connected'. She then goes on to consider the very difficult ethical problems faced by NGOs working with gender issues in conservative, patriarchal societies. She believes that working with women, at whatever level, raises the possibility of a change in the role of women in the society, yet this is rarely explained to project partners; agencies seldom even acknowledge this moral dilemma. She argues that it is incumbent on agencies to open the debate, particularly on the extent to which it is appropriate to attempt to re-shape the social order.

In all societies, a project partner's degree of gender awareness obviously shapes the role of the NGO. Deborah Eade suggests some types of support that can be given to groups with different attitudes to gender. She concludes by stressing that NGOs should encourage and build on existing levels of concern and analysis, but they cannot determine where the space for social change is going to emerge or what form it will take.

Finally, as Barry Underwood concludes, 'the gender issue is not a component of development... it is, or should be, an integral part of the whole development process'. All projects should be considered with a gender perspective, though the problems encountered in working in this field should not be underestimated. Women are often 'hidden' members of society; barriers of language, culture and religion, and women's heavy workloads and lack of free time may make direct contact with women impossible. In certain situations, women may be so unused to articulating their needs that they find it very difficult to get together and work on their problems. Men often find it hard to listen to what women are saying.

However, the challenge is there. The challenge to help women take an equal part in the struggle against injustice and poverty; to improve women's position in every area of life and enable them to make meaningful choices and changes in their lives; to link up with women who are organised, and undergoing radical transformation; to seek out and work with those who are not; to network with women across the country and the continent; to provide support for development staff involved in this work; and to find ways of improving their knowledge and understanding through different forms of training and information exchange. The challenge must be taken up by men and women; the need and responsibility for change lies with us all and, quoting Peggy Antrobus, 'our work is just beginning'.

References

Mohammed, A. and Madunagu, B. (1987), 'WIN: a militant approach to the mobilisation of women', *Review of African Political Economy*, 37.

'INTEGRATING WOMEN IN DEVELOPMENT' IS A MYTH

ADELINA NDETO MWAU

In examining women's role in development we must realise, and appreciate, that women are already over integrated, and ask why their roles are not recognised.

Women perform half of the world's work (most women in Africa work approximately 17 hours a day) and yet women earn only one-tenth of the world's income. Women's share of labour in Africa is:

Domestic work	95%
Processing and storing	85%
Weeding	70%
Harvesting	60%
Caring for livestock	50%
Planting	50%

Let us look at the constraints that women face in participating in development. In Ghana women grow half of the food, one-third of cash crops like cocoa, rice, sugar and cotton, and manage two-fifths of coffee; yet 70 per cent of agricultural trainers assigned to work with women train them only in nutrition, food preparation and storage.

In Kenya agricultural workers visited men growing cash crops five times more often than they did women growing the same crop. Ten times more female than male farmers in Kenya have never spoken to an agricultural worker, yet it should be noted that in Kenya 38 per cent of the farms run by women manage to harvest the same yields as men. The facts show that women are farmers in Africa; the planners, policies and extension services treat women as invisible farmers.

The *Report on the State of the World's Women 1985* shows that women do almost all the domestic work, as well as productive work outside the home, which means most women work a 'double day'. Women are one-third of the world's official labour force; they are the lowest paid and are more vulnerable to unemployment than men. Although there are some signs that the wage gap is closing slightly, women earn less than three-quarters of the wage of men doing similar work. Women are known to provide more health services than all other health services put together, and are involved in the new global shift in prevention of diseases.

Women continue to outnumber men among the world's illiterates by three to two. The education gap between girls and boys was closing until the economic crisis and structural adjustment programmes forced cuts in government spending in many countries. While 90 per cent of countries now have organisations promoting the advancement of women, women, because of their lack of confidence and their greater workload, are still not represented in the decision-making bodies of their countries.

The results point, again and again, to the major underlying cause of women's inequality. Woman's domestic role as a wife and mother — which is vital to the well-being of the whole society and consumes around half of her time and her energy — is unpaid and undervalued.

The questions that need to be addressed to demystify the myth of the need to integrate women into development are:

What is the relationship between gender subordination and economic policy formulation?

Who formulates the policies?

How much more should women be integrated into development while the emphasis is focused on women's traditional roles and their productive activities in their societies are ignored?

Is it enough to integrate women into an already unequal and unjust economic system?

Adelina Ndeto Mwau has been a gender project officer in the Oxfam office in Nairobi for two years. Before this she worked for development education in Kenya with the Catholic Church.

GENDER, DEVELOPMENT AND CULTURE

MONA MEHTA

Why is it that challenging gender inequalities is seen as tampering with traditions of culture, and thus taboo, while challenging inequalities in terms of wealth and class is not?

What if we accept the taboo? If we accept that challenging gender inequalities is taboo then we can only support projects and programmes aimed at making life easier for women and helping them in their given tasks. Would this approach be acceptable? If we look at Oxfam's history it can be seen that Oxfam gave up this 'sticking plaster' approach to its work many years ago, as it became obvious that it was not providing real, long-term help to the poor. Oxfam now aims to support projects which identify and remove the root causes of poverty and exploitation.

In 1961 we accepted the challenge of the United Nations Freedom From Hunger Campaign: 'Give a man a fish and you feed him for a day. Teach him to fish and you feed him for a lifetime.' Now even this is not enough. The challenge to Oxfam is not just to teach a person to fish but to help him or her get access to the water to fish in.

Our approach to gender development has to be in harmony with Oxfam's overall aims and ways of working. Thus, to take the 'easier life' approach to gender development would be contrary to the rest of our work and quite unacceptable.

If we claim that the taboo is unacceptable, then we have to deal with the concern that challenging gender inequalities is 'tampering', while challenging other inequalities of class is not.

I would like first to draw attention to the fact that the existence of gender inequalities is accepted without argument. I have never found, in meetings at the organisation level or village level or in individual discussions, denial by men or women that there are gender inequalities. Thus, the reluctance to challenge this accepted fact of gender inequality is very puzzling. I understand it as arising from two deeply embedded concepts in society: the concept of a 'household unit' in class analysis, and the concept of 'woman as property' — man's or family's.

The first, the concept of a 'household unit', exists in most class analysis. Exploitation and inequalities are seen as inter-unit and not intra-unit, i.e. between households — rich and poor, powerful and powerless. This leads to the concept of a unit as indivisible and sacrosanct. The challenging of gender inequalities is an intra-unit question. It would be seen as potentially dividing the sacrosanct and necessary unit, leading to a collapse of the whole class model. This would make it an unacceptable proposition, and experience shows that most left-wing movements do not accept the idea of challenging gender inequalities, which is seen to be divisive and ultimately a weakening of the class struggle.

The second concept of 'women as property' was, and still is, widely prevalent in many cultures. (The example of the selling of wives in the market place can be found in the 18th century history of England too!) In India, many tribal societies follow a system of 'bride price', where the bride's parents are paid a sum of money and then the girl's work and wages become the property of the husband. Hindu society, too, treats women as goods which are transacted, through the dowry system. Once this concept is accepted in a society, and the woman is seen as property, any attempts to challenge ensuing inequalities are treated as unwarranted interference in matters of 'property'. Certainly none would wish to or have a right to interfere in a man's treatment of his land — it is his property and so he has a right to do what he wishes with it.

This attitude of non-interference is obvious when there are quarrels in the village. If it is between two men, be they brothers even, others will intervene and set up a system to settle it amicably. However, if it is between a man and his wife, it will be considered a personal matter and any interference would be termed unwarranted! Similarly, divorces will come to the community leadership; but whereas in other disputes both parties are present and listened to, in divorce the woman rarely appears; at best, some other men represent her and settlements are made by the men amongst themselves.

The 'easier life' approach to working with women is acceptable to most people concerned, as it does not challenge society's structures and power relations. It is true for all development issues that the challenge of root causes means conflict; and very few, even among the poor, are ready for it. In the case of challenging gender inequalities we are faced with a two-fold problem. Our present partners — mostly men — find it difficult to take this issue up, as it implicates them, too, as men and thus they find it very threatening. The women, without adequate awareness, are not ready for the challenge and ensuing conflict. However, just as in all development issues we identify the root causes of a problem and support their removal, in this, too, we cannot close our eyes to the truth.

Certainly, in the case of the landless poor demanding their right to land, there will be a challenge to the existing culture of domination. Similarly, if women demand a fairer system of marriage settlement, there will have to be a change in the existing culture. It can be seen as 'tampering', in either case, if support is given thoughtlessly, leading to needless conflict which the people are not prepared for.

Tampering can be defined as frivolous, thoughtless and disrespectful interference. Any useful intervention from outside needs adequate knowledge and understanding of the different values and norms of the particular culture. It has to involve a respectful questioning of the existing inequalities in the society. Even then, any outside intervention runs a high risk of tampering through inadequate knowledge and imposition of values.

The way to minimise this is by constant dialogue and exchange of ideas through questioning, which will lead to a new awareness and will bring the people concerned to a position where they can make their own choice of action. For example, a hilly tract of land with poor farming could be improved by terracing — a good idea. But if an outsider went in and carried out the programme, it would be an imposition leading to unknown consequences for the beneficiaries. However, if a dialogue were set up and the idea of terracing introduced, the people concerned might take it up on their own, or adapt it to their own methods, leading to good development.

Women, just as much as poor men, have the right to new ideas and awareness. They can then, through their own awareness, choose to challenge the inequalities if they wish to do so. Oxfam, on its part, has the right and the duty to help poor women to reach this awareness and exercise their choice.

It is high time we buried this bogey of 'tampering with culture', and took up the long and difficult task of gender development, which affects half our partners who, till now, have remained silent spectators.

STRATEGY FOR THE LIBERATION OF AFRICAN WOMEN: THE VIEW OF A FEMINIST MAN

ABDOU SARR

Men have the power

It is indisputable that, historically, tradition, religion and the law have given power to men. Therefore the inequality with which we now live is approved by tradition, by religion and also by the law. This has created a sort of mental oppression. A woman may be unable to consider herself as oppressed, because she believes that tradition is the source of her responsibilities and problems. Therefore she is not in conflict with men and does not consider men as her enemy. In the same way, men do not consider women as particularly oppressed because tradition, laws and religion have made the men powerful individuals. We, who want to change the situation, are outside this system and are therefore presented with a delicate problem. This is the case whether we are feminists, governments or NGOs like Oxfam.

If we want to change the existing situation, which is accepted by both men and women, we have to work to raise the level of people's consciousness. We are in the throes of a struggle, almost a revolution: a revolution entails the reversal of an established order, and the current situation is an order, an equilibrium. A revolution must be waged against an enemy whose behaviour we must try to change. If we do not carry on the struggle together with men we risk achieving no victories, or only very short-lived ones, and ultimately we will have no effect. That is why I want to insist that a very hard-line, purist feminism will not resolve the problem.

The need for change

What will resolve the problem is a type of feminism which is well thought out, which is not narrow, which poses problems, which asks questions, and which discusses issues with both men and women to arrive at a resolution which is acceptable to all. It is a revolution which must be carried out subtly. Without men, without these 'enemies', success is impossible since the weapons available to women are very light in comparison to those which are available to men. This is not to say that the struggle is impossible but that it must be carried out in an intelligent manner. This leads me to pose several questions which concern us all: What kinds of projects should be undertaken for women? What strategy should be adopted in women's projects? What are the benefits and for whom?

We must reflect on these questions in order to try to understand the route of the 'revolution' in which we are involved.

What projects for women?

Women have always been engaged in a number of activities which can be covered by projects: activities in agriculture, at the household level, income generating activities, productive activities, those concerning children's education, as well as activities concerning the well-being of the family. Nevertheless, women are currently carrying out these tasks under extremely difficult conditions which include lack of time, of education, of organisation, of physical strength, etc. The resulting image is of women working relentlessly without ever achieving concrete results because they are always very poor, suffering ill-health and constantly tired. Despite all her activities, despite all that she does, the woman still remains the poorest person in the community. She deserves a 'revolution' to solve her problems.

Nevertheless, many projects for women have failed. Sometimes this is because the activities that have been undertaken have exceeded the technical knowledge of the women and sometimes because the social organisation which should have underpinned these projects was not sufficiently taken into account when the projects were planned. Unfortunately, the activities which preoccupy women often fall outside the categories which traditionally interest NGOs.

NGOs fund projects in the fields of health, agriculture, training, etc. When women's activities fall outside these categories NGOs do not directly support such activities. One can cite dozens of projects which NGOs have rejected in favour of activities which do not interest women (or which do not interest them enough); or where women's projects have not been a priority in comparison to those wanted by men.

Which women to support?

What we have seen since the upsurge of feminism is that all the rare initiatives which have taken place in the rural field have been directed towards women who are already organised; in other words, towards the groups of women we already know. We have ignored many women who are very important in this struggle; for example, young women, peasants and urban women. Young women have not been sufficiently well organised, or have had short-lived organisations which, therefore, cannot be taken into account. Nevertheless, it is wrong to talk of liberation without including young girls, who are the women of tomorrow. The liberation of women is a problem of awareness, so if one does not intervene on behalf of the young, one will always perpetuate the current situation. There is a lack of methodology in the conscientisation of these girls. This gap has never interested NGOs nor even feminists. Oxfam should think about methods of intervention in the education of young women.

Urban women have also been forgotten. They are not as organised as those in the rural situation, and we currently have no method for reaching them. These women, who still maintain links with their villages, could be spokeswomen for them. The rapidly changing urban environment is one which could most easily sustain liberating changes for women.

Urban feminists have also been neglected. I believe that they have a potential which we have not exploited. Thanks to their position, their knowledge and their studies, they can bring women's plight to the attention of men who have the power of the law. But I maintain that we in NGOs are not trying to support these women, to help them to fight to change things. We have a very narrow point of view, and we risk losing a crucial element if we do not integrate these women into the struggle.

What strategy?

We must consider our strategy. I believe that the struggle for women's liberation is a struggle at the level of consciousness; the strategy must take that as its starting point. I would like to suggest a number of important points. The first is the integration of men into women's projects. They should not be integrated so that they become actors, technicians or even beneficiaries, but one must integrate them in order to have their approval and support at the outset. The problem of women should be perceived in the context of the community and one must never marginalise women's activities. All projects which are conceived without men risk being marginalised and not having the approval of men.

Serve women, not ourselves

Secondly, the projects should be projects for women and not projects for donor organisations. We often make projects for ourselves. We pose questions about women and the women respond in the way that we want them to. Then it becomes a project which belongs to an NGO instead of to the women. It is normal for the women not to communicate their aspirations in the beginning. The NGO can arrive with ideas or hypotheses, but on a short visit may not perceive what the women are feeling. So case studies, and days spent in villages, are essential before a project can be funded. One also needs a woman in the team with whom the women can discuss issues.

Thirdly, it is important that women do not do all the work on the projects, or do work which does not benefit them. Take, for example, the case of Federation des ONG au Senegal (FONGS), a NGO uniting men and women for the introduction of a large programme of credit and savings. At the time of the final meeting — at which we had to take decisions — FONGS asked the women to contribute 2,500 francs, while it asked the men for 5,000 francs. When the men explained that the sum would be 2,500 for the women because they were poor, the women accepted it. The problem was that this money serves as a bank guarantee, which allows FONGS to have access to inputs of seeds and pesticides. The women, who have no land, have no need of inputs. Women contributed so that men could have new equipment. The women were exploited; they had stretched their resources to make their contributions, but the money went to finance inputs of no interest to them.

Follow women's existing knowledge

We must also take into account the strategies developed by women. Women have always been very ingenious in, for example, the area of credit and savings or organisation. However, usually the NGOs arrive and propose a modern kind of management, which kills the systems which have been developed, perhaps over centuries or at least over decades, and which have been proved in their particular community. The NGOs then create another system which is not appropriate for the society. One can cite as an example the setting up of a cereal bank at Bamachellan. The religion of the people (Muslim) forbade charging interest, yet the bank needed to make a profit on the scheme. The peasants found a solution. They proposed a system which worked like this: in June the bank lent an individual a sack of millet worth, at the time, 8,000 francs. At harvest time the individual paid back the 8,000. Since the grain was cheaper at harvest, the bank could afford to buy more grain and thus make a profit. I believe that such systems, developed by individuals, are very useful. They allow us to listen to people and see what they suggest. On the other hand, as NGOs, we cannot be passive. There are things which we must suggest, because not everything that happens in the rural situation is ideal. We must consider this whether we are foreigners or nationals. To listen only to the peasant and only to do what he or she advises is a very easy attitude, and one that we must suppress, because it does not always work.

Who benefits?

The last question which we should look at is 'who are the beneficiaries?' Projects can appear to have many benefits, in monetary terms, in terms of health, and in terms of the alleviation of women's workloads. One must avoid the 'mirage' effect, so that a project does not disappoint women. For example, the first generation of projects on sewing and embroidery have cost a lot in terms of women's time and have not actually achieved anything in terms of profit for these women. We must, therefore, distance ourselves from this kind of project, which only overburdens women and which discourages women from risking any attempt to gain liberation. We must be cautious about the notion of community development, which has been relied on a good deal theoretically. We have seen, for example, projects where NGOs have bought animals for 'the community', but in fact the men have looked after them and benefited, in keeping with their traditional role. One can also cite communal gardens where everyone works together. We must think a lot about such projects, because they are introducing systems which are not traditional systems. Therefore, if we want people really to benefit, we must support the system which is traditional and which has given results.

The last thing that I want to say is that in the hierarchy of benefits, the first benefit should be the alleviation of work. For example, Senegalese women spend 45 per cent of their time pounding and grinding millet. The first thing that an NGO must think of, therefore, is to try and help women in this area. If one does not do so, a woman will not be sufficiently strong or have enough time to reflect on her situation and carry on the struggle of liberation.

(Translated by Anne Penny, GADU.)

Abdou Sarr is Oxfam's Deputy Regional Representative in Senegal. He has a Diplome de L'Ecôle Nationale d'Economie de Dakar.

GENDER IN DEVELOPMENT AND FEMINISM: RELATED BUT SEPARATE ISSUES

BARRY UNDERWOOD

Both Mona Mehta's article 'Gender, development and culture' and Abdou Sarr's 'Strategy for the liberation of African women' seem to agree on the need to change society, but here the similarity ends. Mona Mehta proceeds to analyse the conflict that must ensue and states that one must be prepared for this right down to the level of the family. Abdou Sarr, in effect, makes a plea for avoiding conflict at this level. I find the former argument more consistent and convincing.

The answer or the problem?

I would like to challenge Abdou Sarr's assumption that 'we are outside the system' of oppression of women. Where gender is concerned, we are all, both men and women, part of the problem. It is our attitudes that keep the system going. There are countless examples whereby the 'system' of law, religion or tradition has been changed because of a change in perception and attitudes. It is our attachment to traditional attitudes that prevents changes from taking place more frequently or faster.

As a survey of gender attitudes among Oxfam staff in the Indian sub-continent showed, we all, men and women of all cultural backgrounds, subtly and not so subtly, hold on to traditional attitudes that keep women oppressed.

Who is the enemy?

In a class analysis of society there has to be an enemy, and in the gender situation Abdou Sarr defines this 'enemy' as 'men'. But Mona Mehta has clearly shown that class analysis does not recognise the problem of intra-class gender inequality, particularly among the downtrodden.

In gender inequality there can be no traditional 'enemy' in the Marxist sense of that word. If there is an enemy at all, it is the enemy within each one of us, the attitudes that perpetuate an unjust system by refusing to challenge it fully. If we encourage women to see men as enemies, then we, and they, are surely headed for conflict of the most unproductive kind.

A gender compartment?

If we carry this idea of the 'enemy' within each one of us further, then it is clear we cannot have a separate development compartment labelled 'gender'. Abdou Sarr seems to be saying this when he says men should be 'integrated' into women's projects. But why should men be integrated in order for the projects to have men's 'approval'? Surely this is a reinforcement of the idea of men having power over women?

Men do need to be integrated into women's projects — but for countless years why have we not been saying that women ought to be integrated into men's projects? The question is not one of seeking approval from either men or women. It is a question of believing in the essential equality of women and men, and we therefore need to ensure that all projects, whether community, men's or women's, are examined from the gender point of view. We should not think of the 'kinds of projects to be undertaken for women', or 'the strategy to be adopted in women's projects' — this is a compartmentalised view of the gender problem. Inappropriate projects and strategies are inappropriate, whether for men, women or the community.

We need to develop our gender perspective so that it is an integral part of all our development work and not a separate compartment on the development 'train'.

The myth of sisterhood

There is a fairly widespread belief that there is a unity among women, a caring for each other. In the feminist movement this belief often holds true. Many people carry this concept through to the development field, believing that 'sisters' will carry their concern for each other through to a caring for poor women. Indeed, it is quite likely that women sensitive to their own plight will also be sensitive to the plight of other classes of women, but it is not necessarily so. The irrelevance of many aspects of the feminist movement in the West to women in developing countries is often commented on. Similarly, there are obvious differences of perception between urban women and rural women in developing countries. Class is, or can be, a barrier between women.

As I have argued, the ideals and aims of the women's movement are to be carried into all aspects of our development work; but class is inherent in the women's movement, as in most things, and so we should be careful to distinguish between the aims of the movement and the movement itself. Class is an important part of our development analysis, and we should not discard it when it comes to development of women.

Who are our funds for?

It is tempting to succumb, as many do, to the concept of 'sisterhood' and say that class does not matter when it comes to gender issues. We hear arguments in favour of support for urban feminists. Urban feminists can be useful, because of their sensitivity to gender issues, in development work for the poor and it is primarily for the relief of the poor from poverty and oppression that our funds are given. Urban feminists can be linked with groups of the poor and be used as consultants and resource people, and can help to disseminate to a wider audience an understanding of gender issues among the poor; but generally, unless they are poor urban feminists, our funds should not be used for their support. Withholding financial support from such groups does not mean we disapprove of them, or that we ignore them. On the contrary, it simply means that we are clear in our priorities.

Tradition — another sacred cow

Just as Mona Mehta correctly pointed out that we shy away from intervening at the family unit level in development, as this is considered a sacrosanct unit, so many people see all outside interventions as inappropriate and say that we should support 'traditional' roles and systems.

There is a certain romantic view of tradition that many adhere to. Carried to its extreme, this view supports the idea of preserving the ethnic purity of groups and cultures, and of encouraging only those technologies and projects that are 'appropriate' to that culture. No doubt there is much that is good about tradition and continuity. But there is also a lot that is wrong with it. As Abdou Sarr says in the opening line of his paper, tradition, along with religion and law, is what has given power to men. And it is usually tradition which keeps women oppressed. We should therefore be careful in falling back on traditional projects and approaches in our work.

But what, anyway, do we mean by the terms 'traditional' and 'appropriate'? In the case of the first generation of women's projects such as sewing and embroidery, Abdou Sarr seems to be saying that introduction of such projects are alien and not traditional. Yet they can equally be seen as very traditional in that they reinforce the idea of women being gentle creatures whose place is in the home only. Both points of view are partially correct, but neither of the analyses is fully correct.

The last word

To sum up then, I believe there is a struggle, and an enemy — but it is within each one of us. The gender issue is not a component of development, like agriculture or income generation; it is, or should be, an integral part of the whole development process. We are not apart from the system of oppression of women — we are a part of the system. In development we should not be primarily concerned with the feminist movement, our priority should be the issues of poor women.

Barry Underwood lives in India where he has worked for the past 14 years, firstly at Sarvodaya Planning and Training Centre in Surat district of Gujarat, then as the convener and guide of the Gram Vikas Mandali Association Trust (GVMAT) tribal organisation in Dangs District, and lastly as Oxfam's representative in West India since 1983.

FINDING WAYS OF WORKING WITH WOMEN IN PATRIARCHAL SOCIETIES

LIZ GASCOIGNE

It is a declared aim of Oxfam that women should be fully involved in all aspects of the development process. The extent to which this ideal is, and can be, attained is determined partly by the gender awareness of the development personnel, and partly by the existing social order in a particular country. In countries whose traditions are patriarchal and where change is strongly resisted, involving women in development may be extremely difficult. The development approach has to be shaped in such a way that it is compatible with the existing culture and social order. In such societies, Oxfam faces many problems in taking a gender perspective and must accept that social change can only be a long-term process.

*Yemen: a case study of cultural and bureaucratic constraints

Yemen Arab Republic is an example of a strongly patriarchal and conservative society. Men are accorded responsibility for women as part of the traditional set of social norms and an Islamic way of life. The practical manifestation of this is that the majority of women are protected and their social mobility restricted as far as possible, in order to preserve the honour of the family. Women have an extensive reproductive role that includes all activities which contribute to the reproduction of the next generation, such as subsistence food cultivation and making the family's clothes and other household items. They also play an important productive role in those activities, usually agricultural, which contribute to the household's income; but their involvement in the social and political domains is extremely limited.

The different roles of women can be categorised according to their levels of social mobility. The activities which constitute their

* This article was written before the unification of Yemen in 1990.

reproductive and productive roles fall into the private sphere and take place within the home and compound of the extended family, and other areas which women frequent while carrying out their household and agricultural duties. The activities which would be associated with a social or a political role would necessitate women's greater involvement in the public sphere of the 'outside world'; for example, would require visits to the market, to government centres and other institutions and services of conurbations, and involve the use of public transport.

In order for women to participate more fully in development activities, their increased involvement in the public sphere is a prerequisite. But there are great problems for women in terms of their access to the public sphere. There are two contradictory trends concerning women's seclusion and social mobility. Most notably in the three main cities, there is a growing acceptance of girls attending school, and women's employment is very gradually becoming a recognised option — and for poorer families it is an economic necessity. While this trend can be found to a lesser extent in rural areas, there is a counter trend developing from the new opportunities arising from urban and overseas earnings. Higher status or richer rural families may choose to increase women's seclusion through new agricultural practices, for example by hiring labour, sharecropping, or selling land; and by the purchase of fuel for cooking, water, household items and food. Rural women react to this with mixed feelings — on the one hand they are gaining a more relaxed and secure lifestyle in the private sphere but on the other it restricts their level of social interchange and mobility. Ironically the 'modern' lifestyle to which many rural women aspire is one in which they are less active in their productive role and spend their time in domestic and leisurely pursuits.

Yemen has some of the worst social and health indicators in the world, with over 90 per cent of women illiterate (as compared with about 60 per cent of men), an infant mortality rate of 159 per thousand, and 70 per cent of the population having no access to potable water. Given the high correlation between improved family health and women's literacy, Oxfam has concentrated upon these two aspects of development work. Despite the relative acceptability of projects in these two areas, it has still been necessary to take a fairly cautious approach to ensure that credibility with project partners, the community, local leaders and government officials is built up. It is always extremely difficult to recruit women who have any degree of social mobility, but some of the rural health projects supported by Oxfam have shown that it is possible to convince communities of the acceptability of training female health workers on residential courses away from the village.

The Yemeni Government has a top-down approach to development, and all co-operation involving a foreign agency has to be officially approved. In addition to cultural constraints, the nature of Yemeni officialdom effectively deters women from playing an active role in planning and implementing development projects. Although a few women do now hold more influential ministerial positions, the bulk of the bureaucratic procedures associated with development work have to be carried out by men. Thus women rely upon men's goodwill in facilitating development activities which benefit women. An important role for Oxfam is to assist women in negotiating with officialdom to try to ensure that national programmes are adapted to reflect their demands.

Yemeni official development plans include women in a socially acceptable way by mainly proposing activities linked to their domestic role. Women's so-called 'involvement' in national sector plans usually relegates them to a passive situation of being 'trained' or 'employed', where they are not adequately consulted on essential decisions. However, Oxfam does co-operate with projects where women are at the very best only 'included', on the premise that supporting women entering the public sphere both increases the pool of more active and aware women and makes the community more accustomed to the notion of women having a respectable public life. As might be expected, this pool of women will tend to have limited aspirations about their role in Yemen's development because they share the values of a patriarchal society. Nevertheless, it is important that, at the very least, women are brought together; there then exists the possibility of interaction with women who have a more progressive vision of women's position in Yemen. Even where Oxfam is able to identify a Yemeni woman project partner with potentially good ideas, her effectiveness will depend on the extent to which she is able to generate a broad basis of support and understanding amongst other women.

In Yemen, Oxfam aims to work with groups which are marginalised in the development process — that is, the poorest, most disadvantaged and inaccessible groups. However, the bureaucratic and social aspects of the working context encourage foreign agencies to co-operate with the more mainstream groups which are accessible, articulate and well-connected. While not suggesting that the latter should be totally ruled out as suitable partners, their need in comparison with the marginalised groups is not as great. In both groups, women are systematically excluded from the political and economic sphere which determines their lives, and Oxfam has to concentrate upon finding ways of encouraging women to take a greater role in this sphere. Given the additional constraints upon women from marginalised groups, working with them is expected to be a much slower process.

The question of how Oxfam takes a less stereotyped approach to women's involvement in development brings us back to a recurrent concern in the Yemen programme: how to approach working with female or male grassroots groups in initiatives which do not clearly fall into national sector plans. Foreign agencies are likely initially to find it difficult to contact women from marginalised groups or areas (especially if they are remote) except through official channels. Subsequently there can be problems in arranging official approval for co-operation, particularly if the initiative does not fall into the traditional range of women's projects. There must also be a suitable male representative of the women who is prepared to follow through the administrative procedures, the women being unhappy to spend hours or even days going from one (male) government department to another.

To date, Oxfam has taken a relatively cautious approach in order to build up a basis of confidence with project partners. This has usually involved negotiating with men so that they will allow women to participate. The intention is to demonstrate that women can usefully and honourably be involved; and the hope is that this will in turn facilitate more women to participate.

In Yemen the Oxfam programme needs to have a coherent approach in which the social and institutional constraints upon women's real involvement in development projects are recognised and overcome, as far as this is reasonable. All projects, whether or not they are specifically targeted at women, must be assessed and implemented with full regard for their direct and indirect impact on women. Oxfam's work needs to be based upon a comprehensive understanding of the reality of Yemeni women's lives and the various opportunities that they have for improving their position.

Some implications

This article has taken the Yemen as a case study of a conservative, patriarchal society. Other societies in which Oxfam works, including Sudan, Somalia and Afghanistan, operate in a similar way and the following comments hold for all such societies.

In these societies, due to a combination of cultural and bureaucratic constraints, Oxfam can only expect to proceed cautiously and to work towards a very limited form of social change. Initially, ensuring that women are 'included' is a small step forward. Simply bringing more females into the public sphere (be it by attending classes, training or participating in some form of project activity) in itself signifies an immense social change: it is increasing the acceptability of a new concept that women leaving the private sphere of the extended family can retain family honour. However, it may take another generation or two before there is any more fundamental change in women's position.

The process of social change in a community cannot be easily contained, once the momentum is under way. Girls and women who have glimpsed life in the public sphere often begin to realise how constricted their activities are, how limited is their role in actual decision making and how prescribed their thinking has been. For those who try to become more active, most will meet with resistance and even ridicule from their families; particularly from male relatives but also from conservative female relatives who adhere to social norms. Ultimately, women who attempt to change their lives will probably be frustrated, but that may strengthen their resolve that life for their daughters will be different. A few women will be permitted to pursue a training or occupation outside the normal range; but usually only until they can be persuaded to marry. From then on, their commitment will be to their husband and children. By and large it is still only women who manage to remain single who have any prospect of playing an active role in the public sphere. These women, of course, encounter other limitations from never having married. There are also a few exceptional women who reach positions of prominence by virtue of their husband's connections.

We can make a simple distinction between development agencies whose work with women aims at the provision of basic needs, for example, a primary health care system; and those agencies whose work with women has a more strategic aim, for example, conscientisation through projects which aim at the empowerment of women. In the context of a conservative, patriarchal society, a basic needs project for women is far more likely to be accepted by community leaders and government alike; whereas a women's project with a strategic aim would probably be rejected outright. However, even basic needs projects, because they involve females entering the public sphere, may help to bring about a level of change in the long term which accords with a more strategic aim. Of course, agencies are not the only influence; there is a dynamic of change in all societies in response to changing environmental, political and economic conditions as well as contact with neighbouring regions. But agencies are faced with a moral dilemma, which is rarely acknowledged, let alone discussed.

The question that aid agencies working in conservative societies have to face is to what extent should the long-term implications of the involvement of women in development work be addressed as an issue? Should the underlying strategic aim of fundamental social change be disclosed? Should agencies encourage communities to strive for development when the exercise will ultimately lead to a substantial shift in social values? Should agencies assess their role in terms of the degree of cultural interference or social disintegration that is being foisted on communities?

When considering the role of women in development it is important that cultural and ethical concerns are not neglected. Yet agencies do not state their underlying strategic aims when discussing prospective projects with community leaders, government officials and the women concerned; although it is quite common for these long-term aims to be stated in written and verbal reports to the head office. Perhaps the fact that the 'plot' is not usually fully revealed to local participants is because it all seems such a natural sequence of events, and because at the outset it seems too premature. But no doubt another reason is that the agency realises that the project would then become unacceptable to the local leaders and community. Certainly, the agency is not being deliberately deceptive; it just seems to be one of the practices which is accepted under the 'greater good' of targeting women and children.

But people in conservative societies are not so naive that they do not realise what is at stake. The development project under discussion may sound a great idea to the community but in practice it is very often difficult to get families to offer their girls and women as candidates for the training course. This reflects an unease about respectable women embarking upon any activity which brings them into the public sphere. It will probably be the poorer and lower status families who allow their females to participate because any payments involved will be very useful to the family. The fact that candidates are not from a cross-section of the community can in turn create problems with the project's acceptability and credibility later on. In a society where women are protected and secluded, families recognise that training their girls and women is the thin end of the wedge — at worst, if they are literate they may be suspected of writing love letters and if they are mobile, of adultery.

The intention of this article is not to suggest that agencies take a reactionary stance when working in strongly patriarchal, conservative societies, but rather to outline some of the issues that have to be faced at the outset. An element of subversiveness currently exists when international agencies work in such societies. It is therefore incumbent on agencies, and especially those with a strategic needs approach, to open the debate on the implications of working with women, in particular the extent to which it is appropriate to attempt to reshape the social order. Societies themselves have to accept that development and social change are inextricably linked. It is the role of development workers to ensure that communities and officials are aware of the full implications of the development process. It is not acceptable for the agencies to be aware of them and yet not disclose them.

Liz Gascoigne is a social scientist who has specialised in rural development. From early 1981 she worked with a remote rural health project in Yemen Arab Republic as a social researcher. In 1983 she was responsible for setting up an office in the capital, Sana'a, when she became Oxfam's Country Representative. Since the end of 1986 Liz has worked as the Sudan Desk Officer based in Oxfam House, Oxford.

HOW FAR SHOULD WE PUSH?

DEBORAH EADE

We do not see our relationship with projects to be one of using financial power to 'push' anything, even were we clear about what Oxfam wanted to push.

Firstly, unless the local counterparts are convinced of the validity, importance and priority of concerning themselves with gender analysis in a self-critical way, then no amount of 'pushing' will give rise to authentic — let alone effective — responses. Rather, one ends up with a plethora of so-called women's projects. These, far from developing an autonomous space for women to use for organisational purposes, are little more than appeasements to 'agency obsessions' and/or fund-raising devices on the one hand; and a means of capitalising on agency money to expand their affiliated membership on the other.

Secondly, the relationship with Oxfam, however rich, forms only a small component of the wide range of stimuli, influences and pressures experienced by our project partners and we would be arrogant to assume that our role is (or should be) the determining factor.

Thirdly, in the specific case of gender, it is not clear what Oxfam would be 'pushing' in any case: ideological convictions? Formal agendas for staff and projects? Standard reporting and data collection methodologies? Or how: by withdrawing funding if projects fail to come up to our idea of what their standards ought to be, and which Oxfam itself certainly does not meet? Obviously not. But the questions themselves do serve to underline that the 'pushing' has to come from the inside, from local people with the strength and authority to assume the challenge, and not from the outsiders with the analysis and the money. Put succinctly by a Nicaraguan participant in the IV *Encuentro Feminista Latino-americano*, at Taxco, Mexico in 1987, '*las revoluciones no se exportan; las revoluciones nacen de la necesidad de un pueblo*': revolutions are not exportable but grow out of people's needs.

Assuming, then, that we do not see ourselves as having some

Messianic duty to deliver analytical packages to our counterparts, how do we meet our commitment to raise the issues of gender analysis? (Just as important, though not addressed in this article, how do we document our having done so and to what effect?)

Merely raising the issue can meet with quite different kinds of difficulty in different kinds of group:

the group which does not recognise the issue as a political priority and which will argue its case to this effect;

the group which, for whatever reasons, acknowledges the issue, but in such a fashion as to raise more questions than it resolves;

the group which is self-critically concerned to take the issue on board but which, perhaps for lack of methodological tools, is unable to do so satisfactorily;

the group which is clear and enlightened in its analysis but which represents a sector which would not normally be a priority for Oxfam.

With the first group, the most Oxfam can do in a non-funding sense is to appeal to the intellectual and political integrity of its leadership. Oxfam can provide analytical materials which should stimulate self-questioning. It can also ensure that at least women are not worse off as a result of interventions (or failures to intervene) by Oxfam-funded partners. The last will be difficult precisely because it is unlikely that such a group will differentiate its reports by gender.

In the case of the second group, the question may rather be how to avoid being pushed into funding activities which at best are likely to be ineffective — and at worst may actually be demobilising. In my experience, a rabbit-keeping project, for example, which does not have more profound organisational perspectives from the outset, is unlikely to acquire them *en route*, as the *companeras* become absorbed in the everyday problems of its administration. In other words, if there is no capacity to learn from failure, or to build meaningfully on success, we are best keeping our distance. The same is, of course, true for men-exclusive projects.

With the third type of group, it is worth engaging in dialogue (in which we would include provision of materials, project exchange visits and, where appropriate, the services of a consultant) precisely on the grounds that the process of arriving may well be as significant as the final point of destination. Rather than 'pushing', we should be offering encouragement. We should separate the issue of support in a general sense from funding as such, so that counterparts are not made to feel that our money is conditional on their following a course of action determined both in direction and speed by outside interests. Needless to say, this process is one from which Oxfam stands to learn rather than to instruct.

Finally, and of a slightly different order, the fourth group presents more of a challenge to Oxfam's overall policies, and the way in which these are interpreted in each regional office, than to the local counterpart in question. The two following examples from Mexico and Central America involve the Ford Foundation.

The first, located in Mexico, but with far-reaching consequences, involved the five-year-long struggle to establish an Inter-disciplinary Women's Studies Department in the *Colegio de México*. This was to serve as a methodological resource and data bank for academics and non-governmental organisations. At the same time it was a validation of the academic worthiness of the project. The Ford Foundation did not 'push', other than to lend its voice to the arguments put forward by the women academics involved and, of course, to indicate that it would be prepared to finance the venture. Without this intervention, however, the struggle to win similar recognition elsewhere would certainly have been delayed. At the same time, the space itself can be used to serve interests not narrowly defined by the explicit terms of the project.

The second example is in Nicaragua, where Ford Foundation funding provided the guarantee that the research programme on rural women (and 60 per cent of rural families are headed by females) being conducted by The Ministry of Agrarian Reform (MIDINRA) was not cut for lack of resources. This research programme both provided essential data for any group seriously interested in working with the rural poor in Nicaragua, and is crucial in setting out the background against which agrarian policy has to be defined.

Given that there are conflicts of interest between men and women, it is important to find ways of funding which neither side-step nor exacerbate them in an untimely fashion. The struggles are essentially to be conducted by — and between — our counterparts. Ultimately, these struggles need to be taken on, in as far as they are able or willing to do so, by women themselves. Learning how to do this is an essential part of the women's own process of political organisation, and we would not be doing them a favour as a foreign funding agency by doing battle on their behalf.

If we start from the assumption that the personal is political, this opens up a Pandora's box of issues relating especially to fertility control but also to other culturally sanctioned practices and attitudes. Examples among Central American Indians include the idea that women are the repository of cultural values, and so it is good that they do not know how to speak Spanish (needless to say, the Indian women in question are not speaking for themselves on this point); and that contraception is another expression of the plot to exterminate them. In other, non-war, situations in Mexico, opposition by males to the use of contraception has been found to be rooted in fundamentally different attitudes to issues such as sexuality, multiple pregnancy, large families and virility. In such cases, it is probably even more important not to be seen to be 'pushing' a particular line. More subtle approaches can include suggesting ways in which women health workers can be introduced into, or trained by, Oxfam-funded projects, and looking for ways to enable women to meet beyond their immediate community, however indirect this might be.

Finally, Oxfam needs to realise that female and male staff have different types of opportunity presented to them in terms of relating to projects. Female project staff provoke a different set of questions when visiting a group of women peasants than do male colleagues. The choice of whether and how to answer them is a different matter.

In sum, we reject the idea of 'pushing' as an approach to relating to project holders. Encouragement of, and building on, existing interest would form part of our normal dealings anyway; and it seems important to try to raise the level both of concern and of analysis wherever possible. Here, we are hampered by the lack of methodological principles and fall back, to a large extent, on subjective perceptions and personal enthusiasm (or lack thereof). Fundamentally, we believe that the struggle — both for the recognition of the issue and for the will to act on the analytical challenge in a self-critical way — has to be defined and conducted by our local partners. We can assist in terms of providing all kinds of support (documentary, analytical, experiential, material and moral) and in attempting to find and then operate an autonomous space, within movements, for social change. But we cannot pre-determine where that space is going to emerge or what form it will take.

(This paper was delivered at a seminar on gender and development for staff from Latin America and the Caribbean, held in 1987.)

Deborah Eade has, since 1984, been the Oxfam Deputy Regional Representative for the Central America and Mexico Office. Prior to that, she worked in the Mexico office of the Ford Foundation and studied at the London Institute of Education, specialising in women and co-education.

POSTSCRIPT

WOMEN IN DEVELOPMENT

Peggy Antrobus

We must recognise the links not only between the fate of Third World women and the politics pursued by the developed countries, but also between the fate of these women and the kind of world the generation of the 21st century of all countries will inherit. We share one planet, and our futures are inextricably linked through the economic and ecological systems which unite us; systems which make it impossible for the majority of the world's people to live with human dignity, force them out of their countries, or into methods and means of survival which ultimately threaten the social, economic and ecological environment of those who perpetuate injustice. There is after all a connection between poverty and injustice, and debt, drugs, militarism, food insufficiency, population pressure and environmental degradation.

Women, although the poorest and most powerless, may hold the key to our 'Common Future'. Poor Third World women are the people who do more than two-thirds of the work in their countries; they are the people who are responsible for meeting the basic needs of most of the people in this world; and they have borne the brunt of the burden of current structural adjustment policies. Their central role in human survival places them at the centre of the balance between sustainable development and ecological disaster. They command our attention not simply out of a sense of justice (the goal of Equality) or expediency (the goal of Development) but because, unless their values, views and visions serve as a central focus for our policy-making, we cannot achieve the ultimate goal of Peace.

Women in development: an alternative analysis

But if the analysis of women's role in development is to help us to achieve this goal of peace — a more just and humane world — we need an alternative analysis, an analysis which is different from the one which has guided our policies in the past. For after more than a decade of an international programme on behalf of women, the situation of women world-wide remains an indictment of our policies and programmes. Despite the concerted efforts of governments and non-governmental organisations (NGOs) within the framework of the UN Decade for Women (1975-85), the majority of the world's women, in the countries of the North as well as in those of the South, were actually worse off in 1985 than they were at the beginning of the Decade. For women in the Third World the situation is even worse in 1989! How did this happen?

Instead of pursuing the logic of a structural analysis which linked women's issues to the call for a New International Economic Order (NIEO), women accepted an agenda which abandoned both the structural analysis and the attention to women's strategic interests — i.e. those derived from an analysis of the power relationships between women and men, and women and the state. While the focus on meeting practical needs in the areas of employment, education, health and nutrition was important, we failed to recognise that even these practical gains are easily reversed if women lack the power to protect them when resources are scarce. This is exactly what has happened in the context of the structural adjustment policies pursued by most of our governments in their efforts to deal with the problems of debt, chronic balance of payment imbalance, and budget deficits.

But what is this flawed Women in Development (WID) analysis? The Decade's goal of 'integrating women in development' was based on the assumption that women were 'outside' the process of development and needed to be 'integrated' into the mainstream; and that, if policy makers and planners could be made aware of the important role of women in development, more resources would be made available to them. Women would receive more of the benefits of development — e.g. access to the resources and services required to build their capacity to contribute more fully and effectively to development efforts. A number of strategies aimed to document and quantify women's work, making it visible to planners. This was the 'expediency' approach!

However, the research generated by the Decade showed that women were not 'outside' development. Indeed, to many activists and practitioners alike, it was becoming increasingly clear that women's contribution was central to 'development', the very base on which development was constructed, but in a way that was deeply exploitative of their time, labour, both paid (in the workplace) and unpaid (in the household), and their sexuality. This has been clearly illuminated by the policies of structural adjustment. I would argue that, far from failing to take women into account, these policies are actually grounded in a set of assumptions which assign certain roles and characteristics to women. Indeed, it is clear to me that both components of the structural adjustment policies — those aimed at reducing consumption (the austerity measures reflected in the cuts in government expenditures in social services) as well as those aimed at increasing export-oriented production (the emphasis on the promotion of Free Trade Zones) — are dependent on assumptions about the roles into which most women have been socialised. These roles are mediated by class, race, ethnicity and the level of development of the society. For this reason some people now prefer to speak of 'gender' roles rather than 'women's' roles, to give specificity to the analysis and reveal the differences between women of different social groups.

Moreover, it is because of the central importance of these roles in reproduction, in meeting the basic needs of the poorest sectors of the society, that policies which place them in jeopardy have negative consequences for the whole society, and ultimately for production itself. Production is not only dependent on the availability of capital, technology and markets but also on the physical, psychological and intellectual capacity of the labour force. All of these qualities are determined in the social sector, the sector in which women are key actors, not passive recipients of welfare services. Unfortunately, this critical link between women's productive and reproductive roles is one which is typically overlooked in conventional, growth-oriented models of development.

A gender analysis of these policies calls into question the fundamental assumption of the WID approach. The recognition of women's work has been used to justify cutting resources to them. What is the alternative approach — what I would term the wisdom approach — the alternative analysis of the issues of women, and of development?

Elements of an alternative analysis

The following elements are suggested:

The analysis should recognise the differences between approaches or paradigms which aim at maintaining the *status quo* and those 'alternative' paradigms which seek to promote social change, while recognising the limitations of an 'alternative' paradigm which remains focused on an economistic, materialist, and positivist approach to the social sciences. I would argue that lack of explicitness about theoretical frameworks and paradigms has been a major contributor to the blurring of our analysis of development.

The analysis should be one which attempts to relate experience at the micro level of the sector, community, project, or household, to the macro-economic level. A gender analysis of structural adjustment policies illustrates the ways in which macro-economic policies affect women's experiences at the level of the poorest household. Unless this experience is used to inform macro-economic policies, and vice versa (i.e. unless people at the micro level can analyse and understand their situation within a structural analysis) no meaningful change can be effected.

We need an analysis which is holistic i.e. one which seeks to integrate social, cultural and political dimensions into economic analysis. This has been borne out by the futility of focusing on economic production at the expense of the social sector (reproduction).

We need an analysis which recognises the political nature of the processes of development, and that the concepts and causes of 'development' and 'underdevelopment' reflect imbalances of power within and between nations rather than the presence or absence of resources.

Finally, we need an analysis which is feminist in orientation. We need to reject the separation of private and public domains; of the household from the economy; of personal and political realities; of the realms of feeling and intuition from that of rationality; above all we need to reject an analysis which lies within the monetised sector of the economy.

This analysis emerged from Third World women at the end of the UN Decade for Women. This expanding network of women are proposing Development Alternatives with Women for a New Era (DAWN), and we have established a programme of on-going research, training, communications, publications and advocacy extending from the grassroots to policy making at the international level.

We recognise that: 'Feminism cannot be monolithic in its issues, goals, and strategies, since it constitutes the political expression of the concerns and interests of women from different regions, classes, nationalities, and ethnic backgrounds.' And, therefore, would have to be: 'responsive to the different needs and concerns of different women, and defined by them for themselves'. (Sen and Grown, 1987.)

However, we see this diversity, built on a common opposition to gender oppression and hierarchy, as a first step in articulating and acting upon a political agenda which would include challenging all those structures, systems and relationships which perpetuate and reinforce the subordination of women, everywhere.

Most of all, we see feminism as a transformational politics, with the capacity to transform not only individual lives but all the structures of oppression and domination which shape women's lives, including racism, class and nationality. The concept of feminism itself has been transformed. We argue that there is no issue — from the international debt to military budgets, from the famines in Africa to the industrial disaster at Bhopal — which could not be illuminated by a feminist perspective. Our concern is not just for women, but for our world. Our vision is of:

'A world where inequality based on class, gender and race, is absent from every country and from the relationships among countries. Where basic needs become basic rights and where poverty and all forms of violence are eliminated. Where women's reproductive role will be defined ... and where the massive resources now used in the production of means of destruction will be diverted to areas where they will help to relieve oppression, both inside and outside the home.' (Sen and Grown, 1987.)

Our work is just beginning. We link the past history of development policies to the strategies of the current systemic crises — in the production and distribution of food, water and fuel availability, international debt, militarism — and a growing conservatism opposing women's changing roles. As we approach the 21st century, we hope that the perspectives of poor Third World women will be taken seriously in decision-making processes, from our households, communities, and workplaces to national, regional, and international levels of policy making.

Finally, allow me to observe that, apart from the analysis, what we, the members of the DAWN network, have to say is not so different from many of the statements of those Europeans who have given leadership in the efforts to raise a sustainable and human world by alerting an unconcerned northern elite to the 'Limits to Growth'; to those who call attention to 'Our Common Future'(Brundtland); and to the interdependence of North and South (Brandt).

In 1982, at a time when the North-South dialogue had all but ceased, that visionary Italian of the Club of Rome, Aurelio Peccei, wrote in his foreword to the book *Making it Happen*:

> 'At the root of the problem seems to be an incapacity or unwillingness to change our world outlook, our mentality and attitudes. At the very moment when fundamental change and innovation have become indispensable, we seem frozen in our ways of being and modes of doing.'

The founder of the DAWN network, the Indian economist Devaki Jain, had an answer for this when she addressed the Organisation for Economic Cooperation and Development (OECD) in Paris in 1983:

> 'The more I dissect and analyse and derive and pursue, the more I see hurdles ahead of any attempt to regenerate a just and peaceful society. The tunnel does not find an end through reason alone. But I believe — it is my real belief — that with faith in the ability of humans to change their destiny through their own will and collective determination, I see the potential of a united women's movement being a force in the world which can heal the divisions and thaw the confrontation and perhaps even the order — the economic and social order.' (Jain, 1983.)

This article is adapted from a paper presented at XVth Annual General Assembly of Development Non-Governmental Organisations (NGOs) in Brussels, April 18-21, 1989.

References

Richardson, J. M. Jr (ed.) (1982), *Making It Happen: A Positive Guide to the Future*, Washington: The US Association for the Club of Rome.

Sen, G. and Grown, C. (1987), *Development, Crisis and Alternative Visions: Third World Women's Perspectives*, New York: Monthly Review Press.

Peggy Antrobus was born in Grenada and trained in economics, social work and non-formal education in universities in Britain and the US. She set up Jamaica's Women's Bureau, established the Women and Development Unit within the University of the West Indies and has been a member of DAWN.

INDEX